"Theological and devotional, expositional and inspirational: these are four words that well capture this excellent work on the doctrine of penal substitution. Thank you, Mark and Michael, for this gift to the church of the Lord Jesus. Read it and be instructed. Read it and be blessed."

—**Daniel L. Akin,** president, Southeastern Baptist Theological Seminary

"Dever and Lawrence remind us that at the heart of Christianity is Christ, and the heart of Christ's ministry is the cross, and the heart of the cross is penal substitution. The OT anticipates the substitutionary sacrifice of Christ, the Gospels relate the story of his sacrifice, and the Epistles explicate what Christ has accomplished for his people. What a joy to have the truth of Christ's work for us set forth in sermons, for we see clearly that Christ's atoning work is no abstraction. Dever and Lawrence in these well-crafted sermons both instruct us in God's Word and apply it powerfully to the lives of believers and unbelievers."

—**Thomas R. Schreiner,** James Buchanan Harrison Professor of New Testament Interpretation, Southern Baptist Theological Seminary

"We need a clarion call to bring us back to the hard-won doctrines that the Reformers died to establish. Dever and Lawrence have masterfully traced the thread of one of the most significant of these truths through the Old and New Testaments. They argue that the sacrificial atonement is not merely an image, theory, or perspective; it is the very foundation of how God brought about salvation. To comprehend the gospel fully, we must understand this work of Christ. *It is Well* should be required reading for every pastor and will deepen any Christian's awareness of Christ's work on the cross. I encourage you to read and reread this book and cling tightly to what it says."

—**Dennis Newkirk,** Senior Pastor, Henderson Hills Baptist Church, Edmond, Oklahoma

"Dever and Lawrence remind you of the supreme splendor of the cross. With homiletical wisdom, exegetical skill, and pastoral zeal, they draw your mind's attention and heart's affection to the majesty of Christ in the atonement. In the process, you will not only be exposed to exemplary sermons on this extremely important doctrine, but you will also be overwhelmed by the breathtaking glory of the one who has satisfied the wrath of God by substituting himself in our place. All praise be to God for this indescribably wonderful reality and all thanks be to him for this immensely helpful book."

—**David Platt,** Senior Pastor, The Church at Brook Hills, Birmingham, Alabama

"Dever and Lawrence take a topic that is intimidating to many—substitutionary atonement—and make it practical to both the scholar and the common man. Rich in exposition and application, they point us to God's sacrifice for us in Jesus, and why, because of it, we can never be the same."

—**Matt Carter,** Lead Pastor, The Austin Stone Community Church, Austin, Texas

"In many churches, the cross is sung more forcefully than it is preached. Some of the most moving and memory-shaping hymns and songs of the faith are also the bloodiest, those that remind us that we were purchased with blood. Sadly, for many, the power of the atonement seems simply to be lyrics, left unconsidered for most of life. This book, by faithful preachers Mark Dever and Michael Lawrence, calls us to preach and teach and pray the curse-absorbing substitutionary atonement as emphatically as we sing it. As you see the glory of Christ crucified in these sermons, you will want to sing, and to preach, and to praise the Messiah who stood in our place on Skull Hill."

—**Russell D. Moore,** Dean, Southern Baptist Theological Seminary

"In a day when questions about retributive justice and penal substitution are being raised within evangelicalism, Dever and Lawrence serve us well by leading us to meditate upon the texts of the Old and New Testaments, which have shaped the church's understanding of the atonement. They remind us that though the Bible uses various images to help us understand the work of Christ on the cross, penal substitution is the reality upon which all other images of the atonement stand. Yet this book is no mere apologetic; it is a welcome exhortation to make the cross of Christ central to all of life. I pray that the meditations contained herein will be widely read and would move Christ's church once again to know nothing among us except Jesus Christ and him crucified."

—**Juan R. Sanchez Jr.**, Preaching Pastor, High Pointe Baptist Church, Austin, Texas

"This book is brimming with insights into the text as well as with clear and direct application. A refreshing contrast to the great number of low-calorie atonement books on the market."

—**Simon Gathercole**, Lecturer in New Testament Studies, Cambridge University; Editor, *Journal for the Study of the New Testament*

"Like the sound of a trumpet resonating from castle walls, so has the call to worship sounded forth from the local church of Mark Dever and Michael Lawrence and their expositions on the atonement. This work is sure to humble the reader in the reality of the work of Christ on behalf of sinners and liberate the forgiven with the promise that 'it is finished.'"

—**Eric Bancroft**, Senior Pastor, Castleview Baptist Church, Indianapolis, Indiana

"The theological glue that holds the gospel facts together is the substitutionary atonement of Jesus Christ. Yet no concept is more unique and audacious to the Christian faith than that of a crucified Messiah and Savior. Regrettably, for too long this has been the subject of academia more than the church, until now. Through fourteen expositions that cover redemptive history, Dever and Lawrence have provided an extensive, simple, and practical guide to grasping this subject without compromising its complexity. This study is more than *important* to understand; it is *imperative*. Few books have fueled my worship of the Savior like this one. Read it and expect to find yourself on your knees in wonder at the gospel."

—**Rick Holland**, Executive Pastor, Grace Community Church, Sun Valley, California; Director, Resolved Conference

IT Is WELL

IT Is WELL

EXPOSITIONS *on*
SUBSTITUTIONARY ATONEMENT

MARK DEVER *and*
MICHAEL LAWRENCE

WHEATON, ILLINOIS

Cover design: Studio Gearbox
First printing 2010
Printed in the United States of America

Trade paperback ISBN:	978-1-4335-1476-0
PDF ISBN:	978-1-4335-1477-7
Mobipocket ISBN:	978-1-4335-1478-4
ePub ISBN:	978-1-4335-2443-1

Library of Congress Cataloging-in-Publication Data
Dever, Mark.
    It is well : expositions on substitutionary atonement / Mark Dever and Michael Lawrence.
        p. cm.
    Includes index.
    ISBN 978-1-4335-1476-0 (tp)
        1. Atonement—Biblical teaching. I. Lawrence, Michael, 1966- II. Title.
BS680.S2I7 2010
234'.5—dc22
                                      2009036658

Crossway is a publishing ministry of Good News Publishers.

VP		21	20	19	18	17	16	15	14	13	12	11	10
14	13	12	11	10	9	8	7	6	5	4	3	2	1

To J. I. Packer,
Messenger of the cross
(1 Cor. 1:18)

CONTENTS

PREFACE

My conversion occurred as a very abrupt and sudden change in my life. I can recall the moment when the Lord shook me out of my former self. Sitting in the pew on a Sunday morning next to Rebeccah, we were hearing of the crucifixion from the book of Luke. I had never read or heard the text. The Lord, in his mercy, very clearly showed me the differing fate of the two men crucified next to Jesus, and that the defining difference between them was in their hearts. I was shaken by the intensity and immediacy of the scene at Calvary, the certainty of death, and, through it all, the calm assurance Jesus offered. He would remember the man who asked to be remembered.

Prior to that morning I was not just an unrepentant sinner, but I was in love with my sin. And I was unwilling or unable to understand the significance of the death of Jesus. But shortly after my conversion, I had a dream, about which I told my senior pastor Mark, in which I awoke in a room filled with treasure, treasure that I hadn't earned but that I owned, that I hadn't worked for but that I now possessed.

Praise the Lord! He knew what my hard heart needed! Before that day, my experiences in church had been interesting and mostly academic. But since then I have not read or sung of Christ's crucifixion without being emotionally stirred and freshly affected by his work on the cross for me.

That is the story of Hanz, a good friend of mine and a new Christian. As he talked to me about his story, he said, "I still weep when we sing about Christ's death for us, or when I read about it." Hanz first heard the story of Christ's substitutionary death on the cross during that sermon series on Luke's Gospel. By God's grace, he hasn't been the same since.

Of course, not everybody is like Hanz. Other people may come into the same church hall, the same sanctuary, and not see the cross at all.

From time to time I've been asked, "Where is the cross in your church?" People look around our 1911 meeting house and find no cross there. You won't find it in gold, silver, or wood. You won't find it embroidered on a banner or carved in the paneling. It's nowhere on the pulpit or on the table. Where is it?

It's there. It's there at the heart of our church. It's in the Bible. It's in the sermons. It's in the songs and the prayers. And it's in the hearts of the people—like it is in Hanz's heart.

Today, the cross is hard to find in many evangelical churches. Even as crosses proliferate on screens and Web sites, the cross seems to be fading in public worship. It may be more common in architecture and ornament than in the past, but it seems to be disappearing from our songs and our sermons.

What's going on?

For centuries now, there has been a move to understand Christianity more by the religious experience it provides than by its doctrines. We want to feel God, or at least feel better. We want to feel joy or commitment or sobriety or intimacy with God. We want to see our lives here and now improve. The crucifixion of Christ seems like an important, even necessary, event historically, but not anything that needs to be highlighted today. It may be a moving story, but how will it help my work on Tuesday or my marriage tonight?

Yet the neglect of the cross in our churches is the result of more than our growing fascination with the subjective and with self-improvement. There is also a growing hostility to the whole notion that Christ suffered as a substitute, that God would desire such a thing, or that God is at all wrathful. Theologians and biblical scholars have reread parts of the Bible—or set it aside—in order to fashion a seemingly more humane religion, a religion of improvement rather than rescue. In such a domesticated version of Christianity, there is no place for a bloody cross.

That's why Michael Lawrence and I decided that the sermons that have come to comprise this book needed to be preached.

In our congregation in Washington DC, we normally preach expositional sermons through consecutive sections of Scripture. In this series we did something a little different. Rather than preach straight through a book of the Bible, or even do a topical series on Christ's atonement, we decided to take crucial texts from the Old and New Testaments that shape our understanding of atonement, and preach through them in canonical order. In so doing, we helped ourselves and the congregation see how deeply rooted atonement and substitution are in the story of the Bible. We also saw the beautiful development of this doctrine from its beginnings in Genesis through Isaiah, to the teaching of Christ, to the crucifixion itself, and finally to the Holy Spirit–inspired apostolic teaching about it.

We Christians serve no mute God. God predicts, God acts, and God interprets his actions. Long ago God revealed the connection between sin and death. He taught his people that forgiveness would involve sacrifice, and he planted the concept of substitution from very early in human history. Isaiah the prophet was given unusual clarity about the substitution that we as fallen humans require, and that God would provide. And in the life and ministry of Jesus, all the prophecies came true. God provided a substitute for us.

These sermons explore the same biblical texts dealt with by Steve Jeffery, Michael Ovey, and Andrew Sach in *Pierced for our Transgressions*.[1] These friends have provided the pastor and serious Christian with a wonderful treatment of the heart of our faith. The sermons in this volume are meant as a supplement, a meditation, a path through the Bible to trace one of the deepest truths in God's Word.

In our congregation, Hanz isn't alone in being moved by the cross. Without fail, it seems, the songs and hymns that we sing that remind us of God's wrath and Christ's bearing it for us stir up solemn joy in the congregation, which then climaxes in wonder and awe. You can hear it and see it and feel it.

This is never truer than when we sing the hymn "It Is Well with My Soul." I wish you could hear the church sing the stanza, "My sin, not in part, but the whole, is nailed to the cross, and I bear it no more, praise the Lord, praise the Lord, O my soul." Our voices join in ecstasy, and we stand amazed at our inclusion, stunned and relishing God's costly, gracious mercy toward us in Christ. The truth of the Word, the cross in the Bible, explodes into glorious joy at the foundation and heart of our life together as a church. When we experience that solemn joy, that deep delight, that loud celebration together, whether we're at the Lord's Table or simply rejoicing after confessing our sins in prayer, the cross is seen to be the center of our church.

[1] Steve Jeffery, Michael Ovey, and Andrew Sach, *Pierced for Our Transgressions: Rediscovering the Glory of Penal Substitution* (Wheaton, IL: Crossway, 2007).

Have you wondered about the cross lately? Have you wondered where it is in your own church, or in your own life? It's our prayer that these meditations will help you re-center your life on God's sacrifice for us in Christ and join in the celebration that's going on eternally as the saints in heaven praise God for the Lamb who was slain for us.

—Mark Dever, Washington DC, June 2009

CHAPTER ONE

THE PASSOVER

Exodus 12

Mark Dever

Why did Jesus come to atone for our sins? And how did he do so? What we hope to do in the fourteen expositional messages in this book is simply to show that the doctrine of penal substitution is clearly taught in the Bible. Now, what we mean by "penal substitution" is simply that Jesus stood as a *substitute* for his people, taking the *penalty* that was due to those who actually deserved it. In other words, when Jesus died on the cross and bore the wrath of God, he was standing in our place.

For various reasons this traditional Christian idea has fallen on hard times in many quarters. Secular writers see the idea of Christ's sacrificing himself for sinners as a vestige of primitive religion, one that should have been abandoned, as religion evolved to a more blood-less, humane theology and practice of peace and goodwill to all. After all, the argument runs, human sacrifice was eventually replaced by animal sacrifice, and even that was gradually phased out, too. Indeed human society has now largely evolved out of such superstition al-together. Belief in sacrifice fades with belief in God, which in turn fades into simple belief in ourselves. And that, people think, is the way of truth.

We are used to hearing such unbelief from unbelievers, but in re-cent years even some self-professed Christians have expressed great discomfort with the idea of atonement, and especially with the idea of penal substitution. Often, their discomfort is expressed in language objecting to anyone who would say that "penal substitution" is the only way to talk about the atonement Christ has made. That would be a sound objection, yet I don't know anyone against whom it could justifiably be made. No one I know argues that "penal substitution" is the only way to talk about the atonement of Christ. Of course there are many images that the New Testament uses to talk about what Jesus accomplished on the cross: the language of redemption speaks economically about buying someone out of slavery; there is medical imagery about overcoming diseases, and martial language about victory and warfare as Christ leads us to triumph. But in addition to all these there is also a very clear theme in the New Testament of penal substitution, from Jesus' explanation of his own death as a "ransom for many" to Paul's declaration that Jesus the sinless one "became sin for us." When we speak of Jesus as our substitute, therefore, we are speaking in a deeply biblical way about what Jesus accomplished for us at Calvary. In these studies of several crucial texts of Scripture, we hope to see this and understand it and exult in the richness of God's love to us in Christ.

We begin our studies in the Old Testament book of Exodus. Exodus begins with Moses' birth and calling in the first four chapters, and then, starting in chapter 5, Moses obeys God by confronting the great pharaoh of Egypt and demanding the release of the Israelites. At the same time, he declares God's judgment on the pharaoh's arrogant refusal to obey by announcing divine plagues on Egypt.

In chapter 12 we come to the tenth, the final, the climactic of those plagues, and the surrender of Pharaoh to God's demands. As we look at this chapter, we want to answer four important questions:

1) What is the Passover?
2) What happens when you have no Substitute?
3) What happens when you *do* have a Substitute?
4) Who remembers the Passover?

1) What Is the Passover?

A short answer to this first question is that the Passover, just as its name suggests, is God's *passing over* someone as he judges, a benefit provided through a substitute.

Here is how the book of Exodus records God's instructions to the Israelites about the first Passover:

The LORD said to Moses and Aaron in Egypt, "This month is to be for you the first month, the first month of your year. Tell the whole community of Israel that on the tenth day of this month each man is to take a lamb for his family, one for each household. If any household is too small for a whole lamb, they must share one with their nearest neighbor, having taken into account the number of people there are. You are to determine the amount of lamb needed in accordance with what each person will eat. The animals you choose must be year-old males without defect, and you may take them from the sheep or the goats. Take care of them until the fourteenth day of the month, when all the people of the community of Israel must slaughter them at twilight. Then they are to take some of the blood and put it on the sides and tops of the doorframes of the houses where they eat the lambs. That same night they are to eat the meat roasted over the fire, along with bitter herbs, and bread made without yeast. Do not eat the meat raw or cooked in water, but roast it over the fire—head, legs and inner parts. Do not leave any of it till morning; if some is left till morning, you must burn it. This is how you are to eat it: with your cloak tucked into your belt, your sandals on your feet and your staff in your hand. Eat it in haste; it is the LORD's Passover.

"On that same night I will pass through Egypt and strike down every firstborn—both men and animals—and I will bring judgment on all the gods of Egypt. I am the LORD. The blood will be a sign for you on the houses where you are; and when I see the blood, I will pass over you. No destructive plague will touch you when I strike Egypt.

"This is a day you are to commemorate; for the generations to come you shall celebrate it as a festival to the LORD—a lasting ordinance. For seven days you are to eat bread made without yeast. On the first day remove the yeast from your houses, for whoever eats anything with yeast in it from the first day through the seventh must be cut off from Israel. On the first day hold a sacred assembly, and another one on the seventh day. Do no work at all on these days, except to prepare food for everyone to eat—that is all you may do.

"Celebrate the Feast of Unleavened Bread, because it was on this very day that I brought your divisions out of Egypt. Celebrate this day as a lasting ordinance for the generations to come. In the first month you are to eat bread made without yeast, from the evening of the fourteenth day until the evening of the twenty-first day. For seven days no yeast is to be found in your houses. And whoever eats anything with yeast in it must be cut off from the community of Israel, whether he is an alien or native-born.

Eat nothing made with yeast. Wherever you live, you must eat unleavened bread."

Then Moses summoned all the elders of Israel and said to them, "Go at once and select the animals for your families and slaughter the Passover lamb. Take a bunch of hyssop, dip it into the blood in the basin and put some of the blood on the top and on both sides of the doorframe. Not one of you shall go out the door of his house until morning. When the LORD goes through the land to strike down the Egyptians, he will see the blood on the top and sides of the doorframe and will pass over that doorway, and he will not permit the destroyer to enter your houses and strike you down.

"Obey these instructions as a lasting ordinance for you and your descendants. When you enter the land that the LORD will give you as he promised, observe this ceremony. And when your children ask you, 'What does this ceremony mean to you?' then tell them, 'It is the Passover sacrifice to the LORD, who passed over the houses of the Israelites in Egypt and spared our homes when he struck down the Egyptians.'" Then the people bowed down and worshiped. The Israelites did just what the LORD commanded Moses and Aaron. (12:1–28)

Here the Lord instructs Moses about the Passover and especially about his people's need for a substitute to die in their place. In verse 3 specifically, the Lord instructs Moses to "tell the whole community of Israel that on the tenth day of this month each man is to take a lamb for his family, one for each household." A lamb would be needed, a Passover lamb that would die sacrificially so an Israelite family would be passed over in judgment.

The Israelites were to make a meal of the lamb. It was important that there be enough, verse 4 says, so that everyone could participate, but equally so that there not be too much, so that none would be wasted. Not only so, but the Passover lamb was to be special! Just like other sacrificial animals, this lamb was to be without defect (v. 5).

Now, the fact that the lamb was to be without defect makes you think of what? Peter wrote in 1 Peter 1:18–19:

For you know that it was not with perishable things such as silver or gold that you were redeemed from the empty way of life handed down to you from your forefathers, but with the precious blood of Christ, a lamb without blemish or defect.

Jesus is the one whom John the Baptist called "the Lamb of God" (John 1:29, 36). And John of the Revelation reported seeing in his heavenly revelation "a Lamb, looking as if it had been slain, standing in the center of the throne," (Rev. 5:6). All these images were reflecting the Passover. Moreover, we see in Exodus 12:6 that the lamb was to be sacrificed "at twilight." According to the historian Josephus the Passover lambs would be killed at about 3 PM, the same time that Jesus died (see Luke 43:44–46). Something else about this slain lamb is that its blood seems to be especially significant. According to Leviticus 17:11, blood symbolized two things: the life of the victim *and* the life of those for whom it was substituted. Thus, in verse 7 comes the most important instruction of all: the Israelites were to take some of the slain lamb's blood and put it around the entrance to the house, "on the sides and tops of the doorframes" of the house where they would eat the meal. It is in Exodus 12:12 that the Lord is clearest about why he instructs his people to do this: "On that same night I will pass through Egypt and strike down every firstborn—both men and animals—and I will bring judgment on all the gods of Egypt. I am the LORD." Yahweh, the one true God, the Creator and Judge of all, is executing judgment on all the gods of Egypt! The ones in whom the Egyptians' hopes rested were to be killed, and in such a way that there would be no natural explanation for it. This was to be a clearly divine statement. The Lord would show publicly that the Egyptian gods were utterly powerless to protect them. That, by the way, may be why the animals were included in this fate, because many of the Egyptian gods were represented as various animals. So the Lord was making it crystal clear that even these animals—or more specifically, the gods represented by them—couldn't protect them from the real God.

The Lord continues in verse 13: "The blood will be a sign for you on the houses where you are; and when I see the blood, I will pass over you. No destructive plague will touch you when I strike Egypt." The blood is a sign of salvation for the Israelites, but notice that it was not just the Egyptians who were subject to God's wrath and deserved his punishment. God does not say that the Israelites were exempt from judgment just because they were Israelites, or because they lived better lives than the Egyptians. No, the Israelites themselves were under God's wrath, and so they needed to be protected. If they would be saved, it would not be because God's justice had no claim against them; it would be because when God saw the blood on the doorframes, the blood of the sacrificial substitute, he would in grace pass over that house as he judged. Spread upon the doorframes, the blood of the lamb symbolically covered those within whose own blood rightfully should have been shed in penalty for their sins.

In verses 8 to 11, the Lord specifies still more about this meal, and each detail points us to the salvation that God was giving his people through the death of the Passover lamb. In verse 8 he tells Moses: "That same night they are to eat the meat roasted over the fire, along with bitter herbs, and bread made without yeast." The bitter herbs mentioned here were to recall the bitterness of Israel's slavery (see Ex. 1:14), but their bitterness would be overwhelmed by the sweet taste of the lamb! Look also at the reference there to the bread made without yeast. In 1 Corinthians 5, Paul understands this as an image meaning "without sin," and he calls the church to live up to that purity.

Then, in Exodus 12:9, some very specific instruction is given, which many have wondered about: "Do not eat the meat raw or cooked in water, but roast it over the fire—head, legs and inner parts." Why would the Lord give such instruction? Well, perhaps eating raw meat was prohibited here in contradistinction to some pagan festivals with sacrificial meat eaten raw, including with the blood. God did not want his people to think that he was giving them magical powers of the slain victim somehow; nothing like this was going on with this sacrifice. But even more importantly, he was teaching them about some spiritual realities such as the connection of sin and death, and preparing them for the planned Messiah, who would come, who would be slain as a substitute for them. Thus the Israelites wouldn't have before them on their festal table a stew made of unrecognizable meats, but rather a whole lamb—an uncomfortable reminder that they as a community were dependent on another being slain in their stead.

In verse 11, the Israelites are instructed to eat in a hurry and with trembling, with alarm at all that was going on and perhaps also in anticipation. This was the night of their deliverance, their liberation, their redemption, their salvation! Passover is the oldest of the Jewish festivals. It is their founding festival, their July 4th, and it is fixed as firmly in the Old Testament mind as anything could be. And what is at the very center of that festival? The lamb without defect that is slain as their substitute.

So did God intend the Passover lamb as a preview of Christ? Yes! The apostle Paul could not be clearer than in 1 Corinthians 5:7–8: "Christ, our Passover lamb, has been sacrificed." Christ is the only-begotten Son of God, and the seed of Abraham, and also the Passover lamb.

You and I need deliverance from bondage to sin and from the fatal judgment of God, and that deliverance will come only through the blood of the firstborn lamb without blemish. Just as the Passover lamb was a substitute for sinners, so too is the Lamb of God. You see, all this was done for Israel so that they—and we—would see and know that God's people would be saved by a substitute. That's what God is teaching his people here as he instructs Moses about the Passover.

Do you see what is going on here? Deep in the story of the Bible we see that while the Israelites were just as subject to God's wrath and judgment as the Egyptians, the lamb became a substitute for them, and the application of its blood became the only way of their salvation. While there may be no explicit mention of the lamb bearing the sins of many, that is implicit in the lamb bearing the punishment for the Israelites' sins, and in those who are marked by the lamb's blood being delivered from the penalty they justly deserved. In the death of the Passover lamb, therefore, God was laying down part of the most basic vocabulary by which we were later to understand the death of Jesus, the Lamb of God, the Messiah.

In Exodus 12:14–20, the Lord instructs Moses about the Feast of Unleavened Bread, by which the Israelites were to *remember* the results of the substitute. They are to memorialize forever the deliverance that God is about to perform for them in the exodus.

Now, Christian, what does this remind you of as you're seeing this memorial meal here? Yes, the Last Supper. In fact, remember that Jesus' sacrifice was made during the Passover festival in Jerusalem. That was no mere coincidence; it happened at that time *for a reason*. Just as the Passover meal was to aid the memory, so is the Lord's Supper. In remembering what God *has done* for us, we come to believe in what he has promised he *will do* for us! That's what the Lord is making sure here his people will do.

That is also why, in verse 15, the person who does something as insignificant (we might think) as eating leavened bread during these days is treated so severely—he must be cut off from Israel. Not to keep this festival is to begin to forget the Lord's deliverance of his people, and that is to lead them ultimately to stop worshiping the Lord. To forget what the Lord has done is a kind of blasphemy, a denial of God in his goodness. That's why the punishments for violating the feast were so severe. The Lord was making sure that his people would always remember this night when they were delivered from their bondage immediately by the power of God.

In verse 21, the Bible says that Moses obeyed the Lord in all of this. He instructed the elders of the Israelites about the Passover, and thus instructed them about their need for a substitute. The Lord would only bring death if it was deserved. He is a good and just God. What had the firstborn done to so specially deserve death? Nothing especially. But they stood for the whole. They stood for the strength of the people and for their future hopes. The Israelites did not deserve God's deliverance. That was pure mercy, as was this instruction to them about a substitute. The Lord wanted them to forever remember what he in his grace had done for them; he had provided them a substitute. So he gave them this meal, and then this special week, to act as a reminder to them, to teach successive generations the truth about himself and his kindness to them and to help them reflect upon all this year after year.

Isn't that what the Lord Jesus did for us in giving us baptism and the Lord's Supper? Both ordinances—baptism as the initial rite and the Lord's Supper the repeated rite—remind us of the great deliverance the Lord has wrought for us in saving us from our sins, in delivering us from the penalty we deserve. That's exactly what we see here in Exodus 12. See what the Bible says in verse 24: "Obey these instructions as a lasting ordinance for you and your descendants." We obey these commands of Christ as one way of passing the gospel message down to the generations to come. How would they explain such actions? They're going to have to know the gospel of the Lord Jesus Christ to make sense of all this. So we obey, and we continue to show that the Lamb of God was slain for the sins of all those who would trust in him.

In verses 26 and 27 we see clearly this concern that the truth about God and his great acts be faithfully passed down to the generations to come. The Lord is concerned about the children, even if some of us too often aren't. He builds into the very structure of things reminders that will go on beyond our generation, because he cares about the rising generation and the generation to come. The Israelites were spared because the lamb was sacrificed. That's the story that keeping this meal tells people.

And then, in verses 27 and 28, we see the response of the people to all this. "Then the people bowed down and worshiped." The words *bowed down* and *worshiped* are used in parallel, which tells us that they refer to the same thing. "The Israelites did just what the LORD commanded Moses and Aaron." This is a kind of repentance and faith. They killed the animal, had the meal, marked the doors, and stayed in their houses. This obedience was a placing of their confidence in God's promise that this substitutionary sacrifice would be for their redemption. They were showing that they had faith. They were doing what the Lord had called them to do.

My friend, if you're not a Christian, God is calling you to trust him, to believe that One has been sacrificed to pay your penalty, to bear your burden, to save you from God's judgment for your sins. That's the message that this Passover account has for us. The Lord God made us all in his image and yet we all deserved to be judged, even as God judged the Egyptians. Indeed we all deserve that judgment totally and forever because of our rebellion against him. But God in his great love caused this punishment to fall on Christ. The Son of God voluntarily laid down his life for us if we would trust him and repent of our sins. Jesus Christ is the Passover Lamb sacrificed for all who will be his people. The Lamb without defect became *our* substitutionary sacrifice, if we will repent and believe. As John Stott has said, "The concept of substitution lies at the heart of both sin and salvation. For the essence of sin is man substituting himself for God, while the essence of salvation is God substituting himself for man. . . . My contention is that substitution is not another 'theory' or 'image' to be set alongside the others, but rather the foundation of them all."[1]

So yes, let's speak well of Jesus. Let's admire his exemplary life, and imitate it. But let's also remember that we have *nothing* unless he is our substitute. If Jesus has simply come to teach us how to live, then we all fail. And we all fail eternally. Let us therefore praise him that he has become our substitute, when we were utterly helpless, prostrate before God's just claims.

[1]John Stott, *The Cross of Christ* (Downers Grove, IL: InterVarsity, 1986), 160, 168.

"But," I can hear someone say, "I don't need a substitute. I don't even know if that is *fair*! I can get everything I need from reading my Bible, from my own interior sense of right and wrong, and from reading and watching others." But, oh, my friend, the point of the Christian good news is not so small a thing as to give us what we think we need or want. Do you know how some people get religious because they kind of want to use God to have a little bit more peace in their life? They just need a little moral sense of some forgiveness from God, a little sense of order, a little religious pick-me-up. That's not Christianity. If that's how you've thought of Christianity, that's not really it. There is much better news out there than that. God has come not to provide what you want or what you think you need—a little peace and order in your life, a little hope in a dim and dismal time. No, God has come to meet a much deeper, much more profound need than you may have even known that you have.

I love what Jim Packer wrote years ago about this, contrasting our slighter man-centered gospels with the real God-centered gospel of the Bible:

> Without realizing it, we have during the past century bartered that gospel [the biblical gospel] for a substitute product which, though it looks similar enough in points of detail, is as a whole a decidedly different thing. Hence our troubles; for the substitute product does not answer the ends for which the authentic gospel has in past days proved itself so mighty. The new gospel conspicuously fails to produce deep reverence, deep humility, a spirit of worship, a concern for the church. Why? We would suggest that the reason lies in its own character and content. It fails to make men God-centered in their thoughts and God-fearing in their hearts because this is not primarily what it is trying to do. One way of stating the difference between it and the old gospel is to say that it is too exclusively concerned to be "helpful" to man—to bring peace, comfort, happiness, satisfaction—and too little concerned to glorify God. The old gospel was "helpful" too—more so, indeed, than is the new—but (so to speak) incidentally, for its first concern was always to give glory to God. It was always and essentially a proclamation of Divine sovereignty in mercy and judgment, a summons to bow down and worship the mighty Lord on whom man depends for all good, both in nature and in grace. Its center of reference was unambiguously God. But in the new gospel the center of reference is man. This is just to say that the old gospel was religious in a way that the new gospel is not. Whereas the chief aim of the old was to teach men to worship God, the

concern of the new seems limited to making them feel better. The subject of the old gospel was God and his ways with men; the subject of the new is man and the help God gives him.[2]

Here in Exodus 12 we are introduced to that old gospel, the biblical gospel. God would deliver us—not because of anything we have done or because of anything that we are—but solely because of Christ's substitutionary sacrifice for us.

2) What Happens When You Have No Substitute?

When you have no substitute, very simply, you are not passed over, but rather judged. That is what Exodus 12 teaches in verses 29 to 32:

At midnight the LORD struck down all the firstborn in Egypt, from the first-born of Pharaoh, who sat on the throne, to the firstborn of the prisoner, who was in the dungeon, and the firstborn of all the livestock as well. Pharaoh and all his officials and all the Egyptians got up during the night, and there was loud wailing in Egypt, for there was not a house without someone dead. During the night Pharaoh summoned Moses and Aaron and said, "Up! Leave my people, you and the Israelites! Go, worship the LORD as you have requested. Take your flocks and herds, as you have said, and go. And also bless me."

Do you see what happened here? Judgment fell on the Egyptians while God's people were delivered, not because they were inherently better or because their ethnicity protected them, but because of the substitute slain in their place. The Lord judged Egypt but saw the blood of the slain lamb and therefore *passed over* the sins of his people.

In verse 29 God's judgment of sinners is clear and terrible. From the highest to the lowest in the society, the Lord struck down the firstborn of Egypt, delivering the decisive blow that gained the Israelites their freedom. Some have tried to suggest a natural explanation for this—like bubonic plague—but this does not explain the affliction taking only the firstborn. The final plague was intended to be unambiguously understood as a divine act of judgment. Pharaoh understood; he grieved because of the penalty of God's judgment and sent the Israelites away. You can feel the emotion in verse 31:

[2]J. I. Packer and Mark Dever, *In My Place Condemned He Stood: Celebrating the Glory of the Atonement* (Wheaton, IL: Crossway, 2008), 112–13.

"Up . . . leave . . . go!" Pharaoh feels a deep (and understandable!) sense of urgency to let God's people go.

This judgment on Egypt was a terrible preview of the judgment that is to come on all of us spiritually. God is a good God, and because of that, he will judge us. In fact, God's judgment reminds us of his sovereignty, his goodness, and our need for a savior. How clearly do you see that? Do you see why God's very goodness means that he must judge *you*? If not, pray that God would show you that. To be convicted of your sins would be the best gift you could ever get, because that is the starting point of a new relationship with God, a reconciled relationship with him.

At the time of the exodus, Egypt was the most powerful empire on earth. Yet national strength protects no one from the judgment of God when it comes. Jonathan Edwards once preached in New York City that "death serves all alike; as he deals with the poor, so he deals with the rich: is not awed at the appearance of a proud palace, a numerous attendance, or a majestic countenance; pulls a king out of his throne, and summons him before the judgment seat of God, with as few compliments and as little ceremony as he takes the poor man out of his cottage. Death is as rude with emperors as with beggars, and handles one with as much gentleness as the other."[3]

3) What Happens When You Do Have a Substitute?

The answer is simple: you are not judged but passed over. Look at all the benefits that flow from the substitute:

> The Egyptians urged the people to hurry and leave the country. "For otherwise," they said, "we will all die!" So the people took their dough before the yeast was added, and carried it on their shoulders in kneading troughs wrapped in clothing. The Israelites did as Moses instructed and asked the Egyptians for articles of silver and gold and for clothing. The Lord had made the Egyptians favorably disposed toward the people, and they gave them what they asked for; so they plundered the Egyptians. The Israelites journeyed from Rameses to Succoth. There were about six hundred thousand men on foot, besides women and children. Many other people went up with them, as well as large droves of livestock, both flocks and herds. With the dough they had brought from Egypt, they baked cakes of unleavened bread. The dough was without yeast because they had been

[3] Jonathan Edwards, "The Nakedness of Job," in *The Works of Jonathan Edwards*, 10.406.

driven out of Egypt and did not have time to prepare food for themselves. Now the length of time the Israelite people lived in Egypt was 430 years. At the end of 430 years, to the very day, all the LORD's divisions left Egypt. Because the LORD kept vigil that night to bring them out of Egypt, on this night all the Israelites are to keep vigil to honor the LORD for the generations to come. (vv. 33–42)

God not only passed over those protected by the sign of the substitute, but he also blessed them with a speedy exodus, and even with Egyptian gifts. Verses 37 to 39 give us the historical *account of their deliverance*. This is the exodus. When you see the Bible refer to the exodus, this is it. The Israelites left Egypt completely and directly—no half-measures. And then in verses 40 to 42, we are called to remember this Passover. This very night was the 430th anniversary of the Israelites going down into Egypt. And having used Egypt as his stage to show the world something of his great power, God brings them out.

What was the meaning of it all? God was displaying himself, his character, and his merciful plans. Throughout the rest of the Bible, until Calvary, *this* is the great act of God to save his people—the *exodus*! Oh, my friend, pray that you understand something of the greatness of being delivered from the service of sin and from God's just charges against you. God is sovereign, even over the rise and fall of nations, and Christ is the deliverer he has provided for all who will trust in him.

Brothers and sisters, let us no longer live as those who have not been delivered. Let us marvel at our salvation and thank God for it. As Christians, we celebrate our deliverance by God, not by ourselves. We don't pat ourselves on our religious backs. Rather, we live delighted and a little surprised that God would save us as he has. We rejoice in what *God* has done for us.

4) Who Remembers the Passover?

The answer comes in verses 43 to 51:

The LORD said to Moses and Aaron, "These are the regulations for the Passover: No foreigner is to eat of it. Any slave you have bought may eat of it after you have circumcised him, but a temporary resident and a hired worker may not eat of it. It must be eaten inside one house; take none of the meat outside the house. Do not break any of the bones. The whole community of Israel must celebrate it. An alien living among you who wants to celebrate the Lord's Passover must have all the males in his household circumcised; then he may take part like one born in the land. No uncircumcised male may eat of it. The same law applies to the native-born and to the alien living among you." All the Israelites did just what the Lord had commanded Moses and Aaron. And on that very day the Lord brought the Israelites out of Egypt by their divisions.

Here, the Lord instructs Moses about *how to remind people about the Passover gained by the substitute.* He does this as he instructs Moses on who is to partake of the supper. The Lord seems to have a great concern about this. Thus the meal is held "inside one house." I suppose if it were outside, it would be harder to control and more likely that people who were not members of the covenant community might partake.

The detail there in verse 46—"Do not break any of the bones"—is significant. As we've seen before, God intended the lamb to be presented whole on the table, not only to remind them of the animal that had given its life as their substitute, but also to remind the people that they were part of one community (cf. 1 Cor. 10:17). And, of course, John tells us in John 19:36 that on the cross, quite unusually for one crucified, none of Jesus' bones was broken. The Israelites were not to break up the substitute and take it in smaller units. So, today, the church community as a whole takes the Lord's Supper, not as individuals, or small groups, or families, but as a *church.* Edwards reflected on the community we've been brought into by Christ's sacrifice: "Christ has brought it to pass, that those whom the Father has given him should be brought into the household of God; that he and his Father, and his people, should be as one society, one family; that the church should be as it were admitted into the society of the blessed Trinity."[4]

Notice also in Exodus 12:48 that from the very beginning a way was made to include non-Israelites. There are no social or ethnic restrictions. The word translated "slave" there in verse 44 is a little misleading. It is the word *ebed,* and it simply means a servant, any sort of worker—what we today might call an employee or a hired hand. The point of the meal was to *include* all those who would define themselves as trusting in God and his promises and to *exclude* those who merely happened to be in their physical vicinity at mealtime.

[4]Jonathan Edwards, "The Excellency of Christ," in *Works,* 1.689.

This meal was about more than physical hunger, and therefore God was very particular about who could eat of it and who could not. The people of Israel were not to be merely or even primarily an ethnic community. All who would repent and believe would be included in the benefits won by the substitute. God was building a community to display his character to all creation.

My friend, what do you do to remember God's deliverances? Are you active in remembering or fairly passive? Do you read the Bible and note his goodness there? Do you study the history of his church and see his kindness stretched across the ages? Do you get to know others and search out his mercy in each of their lives? Do you reflect on your own life and record your own experiences and so capture something of his amazing generosity and grace to you? Do you share those experiences with others? Why do we so quickly forget and ignore even God's best gifts to us?

I love Spurgeon's exhortation to elderly saints to talk of God's goodness to them: "Do not die, O ye greyheads—ye who have passed your threescore years and ten—do not pass away from this earth with all those pleasant memories of God's lovingkindness to be buried with you in your coffin; but let your children, and your children's children, know what the everlasting God did for you."[5]

In our congregations we want to be faithful to remember God's great goodness in our lives, and we want to be faithful to tell others of that goodness. In fact, we want to be *marked* by that. Like the nation of Israel, our congregations are called to be both exclusive and inclusive: *exclusive* in the sense that all this is only for those who have known God's love in Christ, but *inclusive* of as many of those as we can be. So we are a community not defined by ethnicity but by repentance and faith—and by gratitude. *We* are the foreigners at the table, you know.

Conclusion

Professor Geza Vermes asked in his book *The Changing Faces of Jesus*, "Why was Jesus executed?" Here is how he answered that question: "Had he not been responsible for the fracas in the Temple of Jerusalem at Passover time when Jewish tradition expected the Messiah

---

[5]Charles H. Spurgeon, "Remembering God's Works," *Metropolitan Tabernacle Pulpit*, vol. 49, 448.

to reveal himself, very likely Jesus would have escaped with his life. Doing the wrong thing in the wrong place and in the wrong season resulted in the tragic death of Jesus on the Roman cross."[6]

The wrong thing? How can we possibly consider Jesus coming and presenting himself as the one who was laying down his life as a ransom for many, and doing so deliberately at the time of Passover, to be "doing the wrong thing"? Professor Vermes may be a good professor of some things, but he is not very good at seeing what God is deliberately doing.

Penal substitution is no new idea. It is as old as the Passover. We agree with these words written by a Christian in the generation after the apostles:

> When our iniquity had come to its full height, and it was clear beyond all mistaking that retribution in the form of punishment and death must be looked for, the hour arrived in which God had determined to make known from then onwards His loving-kindness and His power. How surpassing is the love and tenderness of God! In that hour, instead of hating us and rejecting us and remembering our wickednesses against us, He showed how long-suffering He is. He bore with us, and in pity He took our sins upon Himself and gave His own Son as a ransom for us—the Holy for the wicked, the Sinless for sinners, the Just for the unjust, the Incorrupt for the corrupt, the Immortal for the mortal. For was there, indeed, anything except His righteousness that could have availed to cover our sins? In whom could we, in our lawlessness and ungodliness, have been made holy, but in the Son of God alone? O sweet exchange! O unsearchable working! O benefits unhoped for!—that the wickedness of multitudes should thus be hidden in the One holy, and the holiness of One should sanctify the countless wicked!"[7]

O Lord God, we do stand amazed at your ancient plan of redemption for us—that One holy should be able to hide the sins of multitudes and that One holy should be able to sanctify countless wicked. O Lord, we acknowledge that One holy to be none other than the Lord Jesus Christ, the Lamb of God slain for us. We thank you for your matchless love for us. We remember, and we celebrate. In Jesus' name, Amen.

---

[6]Geza Vermes, *The Changing Faces of Jesus* (New York: Viking, 2001), 280.
[7]"Epistle to Diognetus," in *Early Christian Writings*, rev. ed., ed. Andrew Louth, trans. Maxwell Stamforth (London: Penguin, 1987), 147.

CHAPTER TWO

THE DAY OF ATONEMENT

Leviticus 16

MARK DEVER

What if you were a ruler known as a "good guy," but you didn't take any action against bad guys? What does it mean to say that I oppose murder but then refuse to punish murderers? What does it mean to bear the responsibility to punish? For that matter, does *anyone* bear responsibility to punish? During the reign of one Roman emperor, it was said, "It is indeed bad to live under a prince with whom nothing is permitted, but much worse to live under one by whom everything is allowed."

Christians believe that all such authority is rooted in God himself. So we find King David's last words recorded in 2 Samuel 23: "When one rules over men in righteousness, when he rules in the fear of God, he is like the light of morning at sunrise on a cloudless morning, like the brightness after rain that brings the grass from the earth" (vv. 3–4).

Part of that good authority must be the responsibility to enforce at least the enforceable parts of what you understand to be good. Now, the responsibility to punish evil ultimately belongs to God. He alone is able, ultimately and fully, to fulfill it. But in limited ways it is also shared with parents, judges, public officials, and pastors, with anyone who is entrusted with authority. So what happens when you or I do something bad? If we are children, our parents may punish us for it. If we are adults, then maybe the punishment would come from someone else—our employer or the sheriff's office.

Of course, this is where our atheist friends may sink into their grim confidence that there is truly no one who can right wrongs or reward rights. Where Christians hear echoes of truth in the assumptions we all have of life—assumptions of right and wrong and the rightness of rewarding good and punishing evil—atheists argue that those assumptions are nothing more than reflections of our own groundless hopes and desires. Right and wrong, they would say, are nothing but a social construction, relationships of power. That is how right and wrong are talked about today. "Moral" and "immoral" are mere customs that may or may not be enforced. The cash value of this way of thinking is that we can sin and get away with it. But according to the Bible, what is our situation? And what is God's responsibility in the face of wrongdoing?

It must be great, given who God is. More powerful, more knowledgeable, and more righteous than any other authority, God knows perfectly both who and what merits punishment, as well as what punishment each wrong merits. At the center of this discussion, however, is something much more important than the mere believer-in-God perceives. The Christian understands that at the center of this discussion of right and wrong, punishment and rewards, stands the cross of Jesus Christ and all that flows from it. The Christian's idea of right and wrong, our understanding of reconciliation, of atonement, of forgiveness, of restoration—all this comes from the cross.

What Christ accomplished at Calvary is celebrated in a great profusion of images in the New Testament. He redeemed those in bondage, reconciled the alienated, propitiated God's wrath, and satisfied his justice. On the cross Christ defeated Satan and broke the power of death. One image among this joyous proliferation is under particular attack today—the idea of *penal substitution*; that is, the idea that the penalty we deserved was given to someone else, to another who did not deserve it but who took it voluntarily for us.

Now this very idea, which lies at the heart of the Christian message, is one that has long been denounced by non-Christians. For centuries, Christians have defended their message against those who have attacked it at this very point. About a century or two ago, however, these same objections began to be raised by liberal Christians, and now in the last few years they have even been taken up by some who call themselves evangelical Christians. These objections against the idea of Christ making atonement for us as a substitute must be answered.

However, our task here isn't fundamentally a defensive one. We're not trying to negate these doubts and denials. We want to go around them and behind them and beneath them to the text of the Bible itself. What does the Bible—Old Testament and New—say about the idea of God's pardoning sinners? Of God's punishing of sin? Of God's using a substitute to do that? Is that merely a Western, mechanical, overly legal view of Christ's work on the cross?

Well, of course, today there are questions about the whole idea of retributive justice. Here enters the idea of penal substitution. These days, there is much argument regarding retributive punishment versus restorative punishment, and some argue that all punishment should be restorative. It's thought distasteful by some to have God involved in anything that would be some kind of gross spiritual economics of substitution—one person taking another person's penalty, freeing him from receiving his just deserts. Here's what one prominent evangelical in England wrote just a few years ago:

> The fact is that the cross isn't a form of cosmic child abuse—a vengeful father, punishing his Son for an offence he has not even committed. Understandably, both people inside and outside of the Church have found this twisted version of events morally dubious and a huge barrier to faith. Deeper than that, however, is that such a concept stands in total contradiction to the statement "God is love." If the cross is a personal act of violence perpetrated by God towards humankind but borne by his Son, then it makes a mockery of Jesus' own teaching to love your enemies and to refuse to repay evil with evil.[1]

That was written not by a non-Christian assailing Christianity or by someone who overtly denies the authority of Scripture. It was written by someone who repeatedly and for years has spoken at evangelical Christian conferences and is perhaps the best-known Baptist minister in England.

As we noted earlier, these are not new objections. Faustus Socinus, one of the founders of modern-day Unitarianism, put forward in 1578 the objection that the doctrine of Christ's being substituted for

[1]Steve Chalke and Alan Mann, *The Lost Message of Jesus* (Grand Rapids, MI: Zondervan, 2004), 182–83.

us would put God in violation of the teaching that we are to forgive those who wrong us; a kind of divine hypocrisy would ensue. The Bible, however, disagrees with that. In fact, Paul, in the epistle to the Romans, stated specifically that God has a right to, and in fact *should* and *does*, act differently than we do in this matter. Paul says in Romans 12:19 that we are not to take revenge, and the reason is precisely that we should not expect God *not* to take revenge. Do not take revenge, Paul says, because God most certainly will.

The fact is that penal substitution is not alien to the Bible. Covenantal substitution is deeply embedded in the story of the Bible, and each chapter of this book seeks to prove that this idea of penal substitution is no alien, artificial construct foisted upon the Bible but is woven deeply into the narrative of Israel. In fact, if you deny this, you cannot understand the most basic parts of the Bible. The Bible dissolves into nothing more than a reflection of things you like to think are true. If you want to hear the message of the Bible, you must understand this.

In the last chapter we were considering the idea of something suffering a penalty for someone's benefit and how that was graphically displayed in the Passover lamb being slain for the deliverance of the firstborn of the households of Israel. Now in the wilderness, God makes this principle even clearer by putting another special day—this one not in the spring but in the fall—on the perpetual calendar of Israel. This was a day that would teach them about atonement, Yom Kippur, the Day of Atonement. It is prescribed in the Old Testament book of Leviticus, chapter 16.

Leviticus is a book of laws and sacrifices that God gave the Israelites in the wilderness after they had just been brought out of Egypt. They were on the way to the Promised Land. He gave them the laws because they reflected his holy character, and then he gave them the sacrifices because he knew that they wouldn't keep the laws. Here we want to look at the chief sacrifice of all the sacrifices, the Day of Atonement.

Central to this discussion of God's justice are two issues: (1) the relationship is the challenge, and (2) substitution is the solution.

1) The Relationship Is the Challenge

Moses writes this in Leviticus 16:1–2: "The LORD spoke to Moses after the death of the two sons of Aaron who died when they approached the LORD. The LORD said to Moses, 'Tell your brother Aaron not to come whenever he chooses into the Most Holy Place behind the curtain in front of the atonement cover on the ark, or else he will die, because I appear in the cloud over the atonement cover.'"

We must begin here by knowing that the Lord is holy. That means that he is completely good and right. He is not like us. He is sublimely, perfectly pure. He is in no way morally compromised—ever. His very character defines what it means to be lawful, desirable, and righteous. He is glorious and sinless and unique, and he expresses himself in his holy goodness and grace and wrath.

There is no natural way for us to realize how unlike us God is, so Leviticus 16 begins with this holy God reaching out and communicating to Moses. The Lord reaches out and *speaks* to Moses. The very first words in the chapter are: "The LORD spoke . . ." This, by the way, is the central truth around which we plan our services at Capitol Hill Baptist Church. We believe that the Bible is God's Word to us. This is where our religion begins, with God speaking. We don't come up with our doctrine as religious scientists inductively building up our knowledge, conducting religious experiment after religious experiment, and positing theories. God is not a theory. God is really there, and he has spoken. If we're to understand the Bible, if we're to understand life, we must begin with God and see that he is holy and that he has revealed himself to us. This is exactly why the Scriptures are so important, because you and I will never come naturally to a right understanding of how we are to relate to such a holy God. Our relations with him will not be intuitive, and we cannot assume that the intuitions and hunches that we have, theologically or morally, are correct. We need the Scriptures to instruct us in how we are to relate to God.

Thus, in Leviticus 16 the Lord's instructions to Moses about the Day of Atonement were given. The pressing problem in Leviticus 16:1–2 was apparently a casual entry into God's presence. The Lord wants to be sure that casualness stopped. There is to be no casual entrance into the presence of God.

The presence of God was symbolized here in the wilderness in the presence of the ark of the covenant. It was a box in which there were placed the two tablets on which the Ten Commandments were written, and there were golden cherubim carved on a golden lid. All this was put inside a two-room tent. The smaller room in the tent was called

the Most Holy Place, or the Holy of Holies. That's where the ark of
the covenant was, and that's where God's presence was understood to
specially be. Outside that room was a larger room where the sacrifices
would be made. This was called the Holy Place.

Apparently there had been no regulation at this point about going
into that second and smaller room, the Most Holy Place, and problems
had arisen because of this. The very closeness, the proximity of God
to his people, was a problem because the people were *not* holy and
pure. They were unclean and impure, fallen and sinful. I am making
the aggressive claim that you cannot understand your life without a
concept of sin, and without it you certainly won't understand this
chapter of Leviticus.

You see, in the very beginning of this chapter there is a reference
to something that had happened to Aaron's sons, and it was that
event that provided the occasion for all these rules about sacrifice.
Back in chapter 10, Aaron's sons had offered what the Bible calls
"unauthorized fire before the LORD, contrary to his command." What
does that mean? Well, that's really all we know about it. It was "unauthorized fire," it was "before the LORD," and it was "contrary to
his command." This event is not referred to in any other place, nor
is it defined in any other place. It is simply "unauthorized fire before
the LORD, contrary to his command." Mysterious though it is, that
is a pretty good definition of sin—something contrary to the Lord's
command, doing something that we desire rather than what God has
called us to do.

If you are a non-Christian, I wonder if this is a surprising idea to
you. Does it surprise you that we Christians don't think people are
basically good? We're not the ones who embrace a Hallmark-card
theology that says something like, "Oh, if we just lived like Christmas
every day, then the world would be a great place." We're not the sort
of pitiful optimists that the media presents us as being. No, we Christians are actually the ones who believe that everybody is at root sinful.
We think there is something broken in humans. Augustine said that
we are all "curved in on ourselves." Of course, that's not all there is
to us. We Christians also think that we are all made in the image of
God. But we understand that there is something not right, and that
is why, as Christians, we have limited expectations of each other, of
our government, and indeed of all of society's structures.

Brothers and sisters, this is a good thing to remember as you think about the world around you. Know your Bible's theology. Even as a Christian, you need to have expectations that are somewhat limited. I'm not saying you shouldn't shoot for the stars in some ways. That might be the appropriate thing for some decision you're making, but God has taught us in his Word that we are all turned in on ourselves, that we are sinful and that although God made us in his image and redeemed us in Christ, this world is still under the curse. We are still not home. God is still not finished, and we must be clear about that: we are sinful.

But back to the story. The death of Aaron's sons in Leviticus 10 highlighted the challenge of sinful people living in such close proximity to a holy God. Something would have to be done, some atonement made, or the result would be death. The connection between sin and death is strong in Scripture. Romans 5 teaches that the universality of death is related to the universality of sin. Indeed the universality of death *proves* the universality of sin, Paul says. From the garden of Eden on, the result of sin has been death. In short, if the sinful people of Israel were to be spared from death, then they would need guidance on how they should approach the Most Holy Place.

The death of Aaron's sons was the last big event that happened in the book of Leviticus, and it seems to have set off this long series of God's teaching about holiness. The incident takes place at the beginning of chapter 10, and then there is the phrase "The LORD said" repeated over and over again through the rest of chapters 10 to 15 (10:8; 11:1; 12:1; 13:1; 14:1; 15:1). The spectacular death of Aaron's sons provided the occasion for God to teach his people for six chapters about holiness, purity, and the causes of impurity and uncleanness. But, after all of these rules about how the people should avoid sin (in chapters 10 through 15), the question still remains, what are the people to do with the sins they have already committed and those they will commit? That's where chapter 16 comes in.

In Leviticus 16, God tells his people, essentially, that he would not leave them in their sin. Though he could have left us all separated from him and liable to his judgment, for some reason he has not left the story there. And on that promise hang all our hopes.

Let's look then at the provision our holy God made for his sinful people. Twice in verse 2 is mentioned something called "the atonement cover." The word used there was poorly translated in some earlier translations as "mercy seat." The word *mercy* is okay (*atonement* is better), but it was no kind of seat whatsoever. It was a cover, a lid. And it was on that cover, with the carvings of the cherubim on it and the tablets of the Ten Commandments inside, that atonement would be made for the sins of the people. It's amazing when you think about it that God's meeting place with man, the place where atonement would be made, was in the very symbol of his holiness and righteousness. This room, separated physically and by rules—with the ark of the covenant, the bowing cherubim, the law written by God's own hand—is where not only God's righteousness and holiness but also his mercy would be shown most clearly.

What an amazing message this is! But the question is, *Are you aware that an atonement needs to be made for you?* Many people don't think about that as they live their days and as they make their decisions. But, friends, if you're not aware of that, or if you would challenge that idea and say, "I'm not that bad," then you just need to have an honest conversation with your spouse, with your parents, with your children. None of us lives exactly as we should. We are all sinners, guilty before God and liable to his judgment. And the solution for that is not in our own moral improvement or in doing good. No, our only hope is for God himself to provide a way for us to escape the penalty of death that is due to us because we have sinned.

2) Substitution Is the Solution

The solution to this problem—for Israel and for us—is substitution. That is the message of Leviticus 16 and indeed of the whole Bible. In his amazing love and grace, God found a way to release his people from their guilt. As we look at this amazing provision, I want to call to your attention seven different aspects of the Day of Atonement, all of which point to the necessity of substitution.

First, consider the humble garments that Aaron wears. Verse 4 says, "He is to put on the sacred linen tunic, with linen undergarments next to his body; he is to tie the linen sash around him and put on the linen turban. These are sacred garments; so he must bathe himself with water before he puts them on." Then again, in verse 23, Aaron is to go into the Tent of Meeting and take off the linen garments that he put on before he entered the Most Holy Place and he is to leave them there. Many religions will talk about certain special clothes that one must put on for certain things—Mormons and Masons are two examples. Here in the Old Testament, too, the priests had special clothes that they wore, and the high priest Aaron's clothes were even more ornate and elaborate. But here, on this day, the High Day of the year, Aaron puts on not his high priest's garb, nor even the garb of a regular priest, but rather the most plain and humble clothing imaginable. He puts on a garment of simple white linen, symbolizing that he has nothing to bring. He speaks to God with no status, no emblem of office, no authority. It is a striking image: when Aaron speaks to the people for God, he wears the robes of the high priest, but when he speaks to God for the people, he wears simple, unadorned linen.

Our minds are taken to another mediator, another high priest, who humbled himself. Paul writes in Philippians 2: "[Jesus], being in very nature God, did not consider equality with God something to be grasped, but made himself nothing, taking the very nature of a servant, being made in human likeness. And being found in appearance as a man, he humbled himself and became obedient to death, even death on a cross!"

Christian brothers and sisters, humility should be your tradecraft. Even in a competitive business, in the dog-eat-dog world of politics, in prideful academia, humility should be your trademark. Don't put yourself forward, even when it's misunderstood as weakness. Clothe yourselves in humility. Ask yourself, "Am I willing to be wronged?" Be like Jesus in this regard.

Second, God provides veiling smoke. Leviticus 16:12–13 reads, "He is to take a censer full of burning coals from the altar before the LORD and two handfuls of finely ground fragrant incense and take them behind the curtain. He is to put the incense on the fire before the LORD, and the smoke of the incense will conceal the atonement cover above the Testimony, so that he will not die." The atonement cover had to be concealed because, as the Lord had told Moses earlier, "no one may see me and live." So incense is brought into the Most Holy Place, and it hides the atonement cover. Ever since the fall of Adam and Eve in the garden, and their rejection from the immediate presence of God, there has been a need for a visible separation to exist between a holy God and sinful man. As the prophet Habakkuk would later say to the Lord, "Your eyes are too pure to look on evil; you cannot tolerate wrong" (Hab. 1:13). This is why Jesus is all the more amazing, because we read in John 1 that no one has ever seen

God, but that God the only Son, who was at the Father's side, has made him known.

Brothers and sisters, pray that you will grow in your relationship with God and in your love for him, but realize that it can be dangerous to have unrealistic expectations about our fellowship with God in this world, in this life. The curse is not reversed until the Lord returns. Only when he returns will our fellowship with him be complete. Until then, we understand that we are in a fallen world and, therefore, as a church, we want to be honest about our limitations and at the same time joyous about the access God has given us to him in Christ.

Third, at the center of God's plan to reconcile sinners to himself are sin offerings. Aaron begins by making atonement for his own sins first. In verse 3 he is told that he is to enter the sanctuary by bringing with him a young bull and a ram. Then, in verse 11, Aaron is to offer the bull for his own sin offering to make atonement for himself and his household: "Aaron shall bring the bull for his own sin offering to make atonement for himself and his household, and he is to slaughter the bull for his own sin offering."

It's interesting that Aaron is to begin by making atonement for his own sin. Even Aaron, by office the most "holy" man in Israel, the high priest, is so sinful that he needs sacrifices for his sin. He needs atonement for his own sin. This word, *atonement*, is *kippur* in the Hebrew, as in *Yom Kippur*. The word has various shades of meaning: forgiveness, cleansing, ransom, averting God's wrath. All of them really are at play here in verse 11 and throughout this chapter. The bull had to die because God would not relate amicably to one who, like Aaron, was marked by sin. He would not make peace with sin.

Aaron's offering was simply to prepare the way for him to make the offering for Israel's sin as a whole. It happens in verses 5 to 9: "From the Israelite community he is to take two male goats for a sin offering and a ram for a burnt offering. . . . Then he is to take the two goats and present them before the LORD at the entrance to the Tent of Meeting. He is to cast lots for the two goats—one lot for the LORD and the other for the scapegoat. Aaron shall bring the goat whose lot falls to the LORD and sacrifice it for a sin offering." So the Lord's goat is sacrificed in order that the sins of the unrighteous nation would be forgiven. As verse 16 says, "In this way he will make atonement for the Most Holy Place because of the uncleanness and rebellion of the Israelites, whatever their sins have been." When I read this, I cannot help but think of what Peter wrote: "Christ died for sins once for all, the righteous for the unrighteous, to bring you to God" (1 Pet. 3:18). So this is the picture: Israel had sinned against God. And what should be done about that? How could so many people find forgiveness? Through atonement. Through the death of a substitute in their place, a sacrifice that would take the penalty due to them. And why would God teach people such a thing? Because he was preparing them to understand the great truth, as Hebrews says, that "Christ was sacrificed once to take away the sins of many people" (9:28).

We should also notice the distinctive sin offering of the Day of Atonement. The scapegoat is what really sets it apart. Have you ever heard that word, *scapegoat*? This is where it comes from—Leviticus 16. In verse 7 Aaron is told to present two goats to the Lord. The two were separated by casting lots, and the scapegoat was chosen. Some translations have left the word in Hebrew, untranslated, as *azazel*. We don't know exactly what that means. This word, *azazel*, is used three times in the Hebrew Bible, and that is most all of Hebrew literature that we have. All three of those instances are found here in this chapter. This is the only place it's used, in verses 8, 10, and 26. We do know, however, how the goat functioned, so that's how the name has often been translated, "scapegoat." He would be the one that carried off the people's sin into the wilderness, symbolically doing away with it. This was a terrible fate. Sometimes people think that the one poor goat was sacrificed while the other goat got to escape, but that's not the image at all. The other goat was led out into the wilderness and released, and it is understood that he would most certainly die. It is a symbol of being cut off, of being thrown out. The symbol assumes death.

Verse 10 says, "The goat chosen by lot as the scapegoat shall be presented alive before the LORD to be used for making atonement by sending it into the desert as a scapegoat." And then in verses 20 to 22: "When Aaron has finished making atonement for the Most Holy Place, the Tent of Meeting and the altar, he shall bring forward the live goat. He is to lay both hands on the head of the live goat and confess over it all the wickedness and rebellion of the Israelites—all their sins—and put them on the goat's head. He shall send the goat away into the desert in the care of a man appointed for the task. The goat will carry on itself all their sins to a solitary place; and the man shall release it in the desert." And then Aaron makes offerings for the Israelites.

The symbol of the scapegoat, performed just before the sacrifices, is a powerful image of what is happening. The goat is confessed over and then sent away. Look again at what God says is to be done: "Lay both hands on the head of the live goat." That symbolizes the transfer of guilt from Aaron and all the people he represents to the goat. It would carry on itself their sins, and thus the people were freed from the penalty that their sins deserved.

The New Testament graphically picks up this imagery in talking about Jesus Christ. Paul says in 2 Corinthians 5 that "God made him who had no sin to be sin for us, so that in him we might become the righteousness of God" (v. 21). What he means is that Jesus has become our scapegoat. He has taken our sins and their penalty on himself so that we might be free. The great Puritan Thomas Goodwin once said:

> Lay hold on Jesus Christ with both hands. That is, with all your might and then confess all your sins, particularly over Him, as the High Priest did over the head of the live goat, who by His resurrection and ascension into heaven has escaped from death and wrath for sins and in confessing them, transfer them from off yourselves, and implore Him to take them upon Himself. Discharge yourselves of them by desiring Him to take them, Who knows what to do with them. Not now to suffer for them, He hath done that once perfectly forever, but to carry them away to an utter forgetfulness and to be thy advocate to God to remember them no more, seeking of God not to impute thy sins to thee, but to Him that was made sin that thou mayest be made the righteousness of God in Him and so to make an exchange with Christ. He, to take thy sins and to bestow His righteousness upon thee.

Christian brothers and sisters, exult in the cross of Christ. See what God has done for us in him. As David said in Psalm 103, "As far as the east is from the west, so far has he removed our transgressions from us" (v. 12). If you are truly trusting in Christ, you can't confess a sin for which God has not provided forgiveness in Jesus. Indeed, if you work at the discipline of confessing your sin, it should not lead to despair at all, but rather to rejoicing over the extent of God's love to you in Christ. This scapegoat was there to prepare us for that, to remind us of and point us to the sacrifice of Christ.

Fourth, the Lord stresses to Moses the role of the atoning blood.
Notice Leviticus 16:14–15:

> He is to take some of the bull's blood and with his finger sprinkle it on the front of the atonement cover; then he shall sprinkle some of it with his finger seven times before the atonement cover. He shall then slaughter the goat for the sin offering for the people and take its blood behind the curtain and do with it as he did with the bull's blood: He shall sprinkle it on the atonement cover and in front of it.

The oddity here is that nobody aside from the one sprinkling the blood can see this blood. Only the high priest is in the room, and the whole thing is filled with incense smoke anyway, to "conceal the atonement cover above the Testimony, so that he will not die" (v. 13). Now what's the use of that? What's the use of sprinkling blood that nobody can see? The answer is that the meaning of the blood was far more than symbolic. God would see the blood.

Verses 18 and 19 instruct Aaron further: "Then he shall come out to the altar that is before the LORD and make atonement for it. He shall take some of the bull's blood and some of the goat's blood and put it on all of the horns of the altar. He shall sprinkle some of the blood on it with his finger seven times to cleanse it and to consecrate it from the uncleanness of the Israelites." The sacrifices are here performed in the outer sanctuary area only, but the blood is brought into the Most Holy Place as evidence of the sacrifice. This makes it clear that God will recognize this sacrifice for the people in an area that only God can see. The blood is then to be sprinkled on the altar as well, as "proof" of the atoning sacrifice. The Lord explains this a little more in 17:11 when he says that "the life of the creature is in the blood, and I have given it to you to make atonement for yourselves on the altar; it is the blood that makes atonement for one's life." The penalty of sin is death, and the blood represents the death of the victim.

Thank God for what he has done for us in Christ! "He did not enter by means of the blood of goats and calves; but he entered the Most Holy Place once for all by his own blood, having obtained eternal redemption" (Heb. 9:12).

Consider the seriousness of our need and God's love for us if he has done all of this to bring about our redemption! This is why our congregations are to be centered on this wonderful message of Jesus

Christ offering himself. Do we disagree on things among ourselves? Yes. We disagree about the Sabbath. We disagree about the particulars of the second coming. We all believe in it; we just disagree on how it's going to happen. We have a lot of disagreement among ourselves, but we have no disagreements on this. Friends, this is Christianity. This is our only hope. This is our message and our joy.

Fifth, we notice here the representative mediator. Look at the second sentence in verse 16, which shows that Aaron is acting as the representative for all others. He, that is Aaron or his successor as the high priest, "is to do the same for the Tent of Meeting, which is among them in the midst of their uncleanness. No one is to be in the Tent of Meeting from the time Aaron goes in to make atonement in the Most Holy Place until he comes out, having made atonement for himself, his household, and the whole community of Israel." Atonement is made in the Tent of Meeting for the whole community of Israel, a point stressed in verse 17 when it's said that no one is to be in the Tent of Meeting. That highlights the fact that Aaron and his successors would be acting as a representative for all the others. There are to be no others in attendance when Aaron performs the sacrifices of the Day of Atonement. This role was an awesome one. The high priestly duties on the Day of Atonement were the climax of the sacrificial year. Aaron, in fact, is in great danger himself, as the sacrifice must be done correctly. So important was this that the high priests would have practiced for these things for a week. Tradition tells us that the high priest would be separated and that he would literally go through his moves, day after day, to make sure he did this just right. All this shows one person acting for the good of the whole. If the high priest succeeded in his duties, he would then throw a celebration feast for his friends to celebrate his relief that he'd returned safely.

In verse 24 the high priest completes his duties by offering the rams for the people. The rams are mentioned in verses 3 and 5. Verses 24–25: "He shall bathe himself with water in a holy place and put on his regular garments. Then he shall come out and sacrifice the burnt offering [the ram] for himself and the burnt offering for the people, to make atonement for himself and for the people. He shall also burn the fat of the sin offering on the altar." It's interesting that in all this the Lord has one person to act for the good of the whole. Why would he do that? Because he is teaching them. In all of this, he is teaching them what his plan is. All of this activity is pointing ahead to Christ as the ultimate atoning sacrifice.

Friend, if you are not a Christian, can you conceive of someone doing something this wonderful for you? This is what the Bible tells us Christ has done for us. "For this reason Christ is the mediator of a new covenant, that those who are called may receive the promised eternal inheritance—now that he has died as a ransom to set them free from the sins committed under the first covenant" (Heb. 9:15).

How much Christ must care about us to do what he has done! I pray that we will follow his example as far as we are able, not in providing atonement but in using ourselves up for the good of others. In mediating the good things God has given us to those around us, we perform our duty as a kingdom of priests. There is, of course, no longer any high priest other than Christ himself, no special "priesthood" among Christians at all, in fact. No, the New Testament is clear that we are *all* priests, and we *all* bear witness to Christ, whereas in the Old Testament there was one high priest acting for the good of all. We are praying for others, we are sharing the gospel with them, we are caring for them, we are modeling God, and we are teaching as we have opportunity about the great news of the gospel. This is what we are about, together as churches and individually, bearing witness to the truth about Jesus Christ to the world around us, bearing witness to the truth about the only true mediator between God and man.

Sixth, these sacrifices were to be performed annually. This is clear in verses 29 to 34:

> This is to be a lasting ordinance for you: On the tenth day of the seventh month you must deny yourselves and not do any work—whether native-born or an alien living among you—because on this day atonement will be made for you, to cleanse you. Then, before the LORD, you will be clean from all your sins. It is a sabbath of rest, and you must deny yourselves; it is a lasting ordinance. The priest who is anointed and ordained to succeed his father as high priest is to make atonement. He is to put on the sacred linen garments and make atonement for the Most Holy Place, for the Tent of Meeting and the altar, and for the priests and all the people of the community. This is to be a lasting ordinance for you: Atonement is to be made once a year for all the sins of the Israelites.

What we have here is a summary of the day. Note particularly what the Lord tells them in verse 29 and then in 34. *Yom Kippur,* Day of

Atonement, is to be annually repeated. The Day of Atonement was an annual sacrifice, not just a one-time thing. Other nations had sacrifices in the ancient Near East; Israel was not unique in this. But other nations did these kinds of sacrifices when things weren't going well. They were trying to appease the gods. But the Israelites had to do it regularly—every year at the same time. The regularity and repetition of it shows that they were in a state of sin, that the sacrifices were not ultimately sufficient. The writer to the Hebrews explains that none of these animals actually made a perfect sacrifice. None of them actually took away sins. Thus, the Day of Atonement was to be a regular reminder for them, a regular proclamation to them of their sin and of God's grace. All this, of course, pointed ultimately to what Jesus Christ uniquely did. As the author of Hebrews put it, Jesus "has appeared once for all at the end of the ages to do away with sin by the sacrifice of himself." He "offered for all time one sacrifice for sins," and then "sat down at the right hand of God" (Heb. 9:26; 10:12).

Friend, do you have any other solution for your sin? Is there any other way you'll be able to face a holy God? What responsibility do you feel for those sins that you have fathered and nurtured and cuddled in your own life?

Christian brothers and sisters, all this elaborate work was required again and again, year after year after year after year, and every time it was repeated it pointed to the work of Christ. Now that Christ's work has been done, it need never be repeated again. In fact, the idea that Christ's work needs to be repeated again and again is a misunderstanding that goes to the very heart of what Christ was doing. His sacrifice was "once for all." O the joy we have in knowing that the work of atonement is done! Christ's sacrifice does not need to be repeated, because it was complete. It is complete. We don't need to wonder whether we can be saved or whether we will be saved if we are trusting in Christ. I have heard it said that every other religion in the world is the religion of "do" but that Christianity alone is the religion of "done."

So What Does This Leave for Us to Do?

The seventh thing to notice is the last sentence in the chapter: "And it was done, as the LORD commanded Moses." The Israelites believed and obeyed. Some have asked, "Does this mean that *all* Israelites' sins were forgiven?" I think the answer is clearly no, as Paul later wrote to the Romans, "Are all Israelites, Israelites? No, they are not all true children of Abraham. The ones who believed the promise are the true Israelites. Those who are trusting in God's promise are the true children of Israel."

But friends, more than the academic question of whether this means that all Israelites' sins are forgiven, why don't you think about the question, "Are all of *your* sins forgiven?" If so, why is that? And if you're not sure, how could you be sure? We read in Hebrews 10:

> Therefore, brothers, since we have confidence to enter the Most Holy Place by the blood of Jesus, by a new and living way opened for us through the curtain, that is, his body, and since we have a great priest over the house of God, let us draw near to God with a sincere heart in full assurance of faith, having our hearts sprinkled to cleanse us from a guilty conscience, and having our bodies washed with pure water. Let us hold unswervingly to the hope we profess, for he who promised is faithful. (vv. 19–23)

Friend, you should repent of your sins and have faith in this promise of God in Jesus Christ. This is the way to be confident that your sins are forgiven. We are to help one another to hear and obey. How are you doing at work and in your home at holding firm—holding unswervingly—to this hope that we profess? Do you realize that out of Christ's once-forever act, we have a constant obligation and a constant opportunity to bear witness, to trust and obey, to show all those around us that God is utterly trustworthy? So we keep believing and we keep obeying.

Ever since our first parents in the garden of Eden lost sight of God, we have desired again to be in his presence. Here in Leviticus, God was concerned to dwell among his people, but it was a difficult thing to do. The prophet Ezekiel later held out a wonderful vision of God's presence being restored, when he gave them the vision at the end of his book of a restored Jerusalem. The final line of his prophecy is this: "The name of the city from that time on will be: The LORD is There" (Ezek. 48:35). Amazing! But how will we get there? Not by having our sins disregarded by God, but by having them rightly judged in the person of a substitute.

The holiness achieved through such means as the Day of Atonement is what we might call a tentative holiness. Its very repetition showed that it foreshadowed something more. There needed to be something additional. Its very efficacy was based on the sacrifice of the Lamb slain before the foundation of the world. Jesus Christ is the true High Priest of his people. He alone has entered behind the curtain and seen God face-to-face. He has brought the blood of the Lamb, his own blood, into God's presence, and he has done so once for all time, never to be repeated. Now, how good is that news? Jesus Christ is *the* way back into the presence of God. We are restored to God by the substitutionary punishment taken by Christ.

CHAPTER THREE

CRUSHED FOR OUR INIQUITIES

Isaiah 52:13–53:12

MARK DEVER

One popular objection to the idea of substitutionary atonement is that such an image of forgiveness is quite simply meaningless today. It employs a vocabulary of sin and punishment, it is argued, that we don't use and that we don't understand. Now, if substitutionary atonement were simply an image, perhaps we might indulge such a conversation. But there is a difference between an image and the reality that image represents. The substitutionary atonement of Jesus Christ is not merely an image, one perspective, or one way among many that we might choose for thinking about forgiveness. Penal substitution is presented in Scripture as reality. God has substituted someone for us to take the penalty that we deserve, a truth we have seen in the last two studies from the books of Moses.

Now we go from the Pentateuch, the first five books of the Bible, written by Moses, to a book of prophecy written several hundred years later. Thus we pass by Joshua and David and Solomon. The kingdom of Israel is founded, flourishes, divides, and declines. And then we come to the prophet Isaiah. Reading through the book of Isaiah, it becomes clear that God's great plan for his people and for his world seems to turn on a person. Thus Isaiah 28:16: "See, I lay a stone in Zion, a tested stone, a precious cornerstone for a sure foundation; the one who trusts will never be dismayed."

There was an innate sense of this even in the way that God's people looked to a king for protection and deliverance (either a foreign king, or one from David's line). And God revealed to Isaiah the prophet that a Messiah-King would come. (Actually, all the kings of Israel and Judah were "messiahs" in the sense that they were anointed, which is what the word means. But Isaiah prophesies of a Messiah to end all others). So we read in Isaiah 32:1: "A king will reign in righteousness and rulers will rule with justice." As we read this prophecy, however, we get the sense that this coming king will be more than just a good king. Remember the famous passage in Isaiah 9:6–7, which is quoted so selectively every year around Christmas:

> For to us a child is born,
>   to us a son is given,
>   and the government will be on his shoulders.
> And he will be called
>   Wonderful Counselor, Mighty God,
>   Everlasting Father, Prince of Peace.
>
> Of the increase of his government and peace
>   there will be no end.
> He will reign on David's throne
>   and over his kingdom,
>   establishing and upholding it
>   with justice and righteousness
>   from that time on and forever.

In addition to the king, Isaiah also prophesies that another would come: a servant. And God seems to specially call this one "My servant" (see 42:1–4; 49:6–7; 50:4–10). Now, if this servant is exalted, could this servant also be this king? Could they be one and the same?

Throughout this prophecy and prediction about God's provision, the question crying out is: How will a holy God forgive and restore sinners? That question is answered in the famous passage we come to now, to what one writer has called the jewel in the crown of Isaiah's theology. Isaiah 52:13–53:12 is known as the song of the Suffering Servant.

Even atheistic scholars who study this passage tell us that Jesus' contribution to theology was a combining of the teaching about a coming Messiah with this teaching of the Suffering Servant here in Isaiah.

As far as we can tell from history, Jesus was the first one to teach that these two figures were the same person. This is what he taught his disciples. Jesus clearly knew and relied on this song to understand and explain his own ministry. In Matthew 8:17, Matthew quotes Isaiah 53:4 to explain Jesus' exorcisms and healings. He clearly applied the servant passages to Jesus, just as Jesus had taught him to do.

The song is divided into five stanzas, which can be understood like this: (1) this Servant is appalling; (2) we have despised him; (3) God laid our sins on him; (4) this Servant accepted his substitutionary suffering; and (5) the Servant would be satisfied.

1) This Servant Is Appalling (Isa. 52:13–14)

The song of the Suffering Servant is introduced in verse 13 with a summary: "See, my servant will act wisely; he will be raised and lifted up and highly exalted." The language used here, of being "highly exalted," is used elsewhere in the Bible only of God himself. So from the very beginning, the careful reader finds some things that surprise and shock, things that maybe he doesn't even understand. There is something unique about this Servant's nature and his fate. The Servant is going to do something unique, and God will exalt him uniquely.

But then in verse 14, the song turns strangely dark. We learn that many were shocked by the Servant's appearance. Look at verse 14: "Just as there were many who were appalled at him— his appearance was so disfigured beyond that of any man and his form marred beyond human likeness—so will he sprinkle many nations, and kings will shut their mouths because of him. For what they were not told, they will see, and what they have not heard, they will understand." This surprising message is about the Suffering Servant who will prepare the world to worship God.

So who is this servant? He is Jesus Christ. The references here to his appearance—"appalled . . . disfigured . . . marred"—are not to some native deformity in Jesus but rather to the horror of his crucifixion. It is this horror connected with the Servant that makes his effect described here so surprising. That mention of the sprinkling of many nations in verse 15 refers to the Old Testament religious practice of splashing water on an object in order to ceremonially cleanse it so that it can be admitted to the worship of God. This is the image Isaiah uses to describe how the Servant will prepare many others to be admitted to the worship of God. By means of the message about him, the Servant will have not just a ministry for Israel but for all the nations of the world! "For what they were not told, they will see, and what they have not heard, they will understand." Even the Gentiles, who were not studying the Jewish Old Testament, would hear, and see, and believe.

Jesus came not to be served, but to serve. He came to bring salvation to the world. As his self-styled followers, what do we do? Do we exalt ourselves around family, friends, and coworkers? Are we willing to risk our carefully cultivated reputations in order to tell them about Christ? This may not seem at first like the most obvious application of this passage, but in Romans 15, when Paul is explaining his ambition to take the gospel where it has never gone before, he says, "It has always been my ambition to preach the gospel where Christ was not known, so that I would not be building on someone else's foundation. Rather, as it is written: 'Those who were not told about him will see, and those who have not heard will understand'" (Rom. 15:20–21). Paul longed to join in the Servant's work of taking the message places where it had not been heard. That was his desire, his ambition.

What about you? My brothers and sisters, have you considered how you are helping in that task? Have you considered how you are ordering your life, how you are making decisions about what you will do, where you will live, whom you will befriend, what you will put your time and resources into? What are you doing to see the gospel spread to the nations? You can choose to live, work, or shop in a certain community, and part of your reason for doing that should be to get to know people so that you might share the gospel with them.

Anyway, we begin this song with the surprising, even shocking, news of the Servant's disfigurement. The camera, if you will, is squarely on the Servant, and then on the further surprise of his mission to the nations.

2) We Despised the Servant (Isa. 53:1–3)

Not only do we find that the Servant is appalling, but in this next stanza of the song, *we* appear. Now the nation of Israel seems to speak, and we find that the message to be delivered to the nations is a message about God's salvation of his people. Verse 1: "Who has believed our message and to whom has the arm of the LORD been revealed?" The message is shocking both in its means, this disfigured Servant, and in its end, the whole world.

This question implies much unbelief. The message strikes many as incredible. So in John's Gospel (12:37–38), he tells us: "Even after Jesus had done all these miraculous signs in their presence, they still would not believe in him. This was to fulfill the word of Isaiah the prophet." Then John quotes this verse, Isaiah 53:1. Paul, too, turns to this verse to show the widespread rejection of this message among his fellow Jews, saying, in Romans 10:16, "But not all the Israelites accepted the good news. For Isaiah says, 'Lord, who has believed our message?'"

Why would this message be so incredible? Because, as Isaiah's already begun telling us, the Servant will not be humanly attractive. The Servant will not be the type of person you would want to approach and talk to at a party. Look at verse 2: "He grew up before him like a tender shoot, and like a root out of dry ground. He had no beauty or majesty to attract us to him, nothing in his appearance that we should desire him." Have you ever noticed how telegenic many religious teachers who succeed on TV are? These verses show that the Servant would look different from the actors that turn up playing Jesus or Superman in movies. The Servant will be unexpected and unattractive. In that sense, Isaiah here is reinforcing what he told us in the first stanza.

But have you noticed how *we* have all of a sudden entered the story there in verse 2? "He had no beauty or majesty to attract *us* to him, nothing in his appearance that *we* should desire him." In verse 3 it's even clearer that the servant will be despised: "He was despised and rejected by men, a man of sorrows, and familiar with suffering. Like one from whom men hide their faces he was despised, and *we* esteemed him not." The song thus begins to implicate *us* in the guilt of not valuing God's Servant, of considering him of no account.

I wonder if you think, "I really have no opinion of Jesus. I'm not a Christian, but I have nothing against Jesus. Seems like a fine guy. I just am not particularly interested." Friend, Jesus didn't leave an "independent" category of response to him. You have to choose. As Jesus said, "He who is not with me is against me" (Matt. 12:30; Luke 11:23).

As the song goes on, the identification of this Servant with Jesus Christ becomes even clearer. Jesus Christ *is* the despised Servant. So how can we, his disciples, be surprised when we are despised and rejected for being Christians—among family, or friends, or at work? How do we cultivate in our own souls, in our children's hearts, this idea that our main responsibility is faithfulness not to someone else, not to the crowd, not even to ourselves, but to God?

Praise God that he has revealed himself to us and grown a desire in us for him, when we had no such desire ourselves! Has he not been good to us, and kind? He clearly picked us, for we would never have picked him on our own. We didn't esteem Jesus; we looked down on him and spurned him. How many times have non-Christian friends told us that perhaps they could believe, if only they could have known Jesus personally? Yet this prophecy was fulfilled. Reading the New Testament, we see that Jesus was despised; people avoided him and hid their faces from him. They passed him by and turned away from him. If we know the truth about ourselves, we know that this has been our response as well.

All this is why we must be very careful not to add worldly attractions to try to make this gospel seem attractive. We are not to do anything artificial to try to get people interested. We want to be honest about ourselves and our sins, and part of the message we've been called to bring is to call people honestly to confess sins. How can we engage in a call to confession and in flattery at the same time? It's not possible. So we try to be faithful, telling people, "You have sinned. You need a Savior."

3) God Laid Our Sins on the Servant (Isa. 53:4–6)

It is in this song's third stanza that we find perhaps the clearest statement in the whole Bible about how God deals with our sins. Some have suggested that Christ took up our infirmities in the sense that he was incarnate and joined us in our sufferings. But to join us is not the same thing as to help us, let alone to heal us and bring forgiveness for our sins and peace with God.

One of the earliest post–New Testament expressions of Christ's atonement comes from Clement of Rome. He said, "Because of the love he had for us, Jesus Christ, our Lord, in accordance with God's will, gave his blood for us, and his flesh for our flesh, and his life for our lives."[1] That's what we see in this central, climactic stanza of this Servant Song. In these verses is the answer to the riddle of the Old Testament—how a holy God can forgive sinners, how mercy and justice can meet, how a righteous God could, as Paul put it, justify the ungodly.

This song is full of words signifying suffering and anguish. Why? Why such anguish? It is because the Servant bore our infirmities. Look carefully at verse 4: "Surely he took up our infirmities and carried our sorrows, yet we considered him stricken by God, smitten by him, and afflicted." What an amazing statement! Note that it was God who struck and smote him. This was not, however, because he in any way deserved it. No, it was because we deserved it. Some of the verbs here are passive, showing what God did, and others are active, showing that the Servant himself has acted to take up our suffering and to carry our sorrows. The Servant may in some sense be a victim, but he is no *mere* victim. This was his action. As we'll see in verse 12, he poured out his life and bore the sin of many. Do you see this amazing combination? God's will and the Servant's willingness. This is no cosmic child abuse of a heavenly Father gone terribly wrong, abusing his trembling child who shrinks back from his Father's strokes. This is the eternal, triune God—Father, Son, and Holy Spirit—determining from eternity past that he would deal with our sins.

Verse 5 is the climax of the song. The Servant's suffering brought us salvation: "But he was pierced for our transgressions, he was crushed for our iniquities; the punishment that brought us peace was upon him, and by his wounds we are healed." What a picture! Those words "pierced" and "crushed" indicate a violent death. The Lord prophesied in Genesis that the offspring of the woman would crush the serpent, and here the Servant, Jesus, would be crushed so that by his death he might destroy death (Heb. 2:14).

Why would we need to be so delivered? Because of our sins. As Isaiah says in verse 6, we have sinned, yet God laid our sins on the Servant: "We all, like sheep, have gone astray, each of us has turned to his own way; and the LORD has laid on him the iniquity of us all."

The Israelites had been taught for hundreds of years, on their two great national holidays, Passover and the Day of Atonement, about

[1] "The Letter of the Romans to the Corinthians," in *The Apostolic Fathers: Greek Texts and English Translations*, ed. Michael W. Holmes (Grand Rapids, MI: Baker, 1999), 85.

God's holiness, their sin, and their need for a God-appointed substitute. Every spring and fall they were taught this. For centuries God was drilling into their minds the facts that he was holy, that they were not, and that they needed a substitute whom he would provide. Now, however, they see that that substitute is the Servant, a God-appointed person. This is what people had not been told before. The Servant is substituted for the sheep. The Servant is slaughtered so that the sheep—you and I—are saved.

This image of sheep is strange to us. If you've never lived in the country around sheep, sheep might seem like a fine thing. They're clean animals, little squishy things you give your kids stuffed versions of. But if you've lived in the country around sheep, you realize that sheep are dumb and dirty. It's not a compliment to be called a little sheep. It means you are helpless, that you'll kill yourself without intending to. You're not a confident creature but a dirty one, and you are kind of ornery. This is not a complimentary image. Yet as sheep, we've gone astray—all of us! Human beings are not represented as some great, proud animal, confident and to be feared—though I fear many religious teachers are telling their congregations that's how they should think of themselves. That's not the truth according to the Bible. I don't care who's flattering you; they're lying to you. According to the Bible, we all, like sheep, have gone astray. We need someone to save us from the sins we have committed.

My friend, if you're not a Christian, you have sinned, and you are responsible before God for your actions, for your life, for what you have done. You will give account to him for every sin you ever have or will commit. You can bear God's just punishment of you for your sins, yourself, or you can trust that someone else has suffered for your sins and paid the penalty for them. Trust the claims of Jesus Christ, that he has paid that penalty, and turn from your sins to follow him. God made us all in his image, to know and love him, and yet we all like sheep have gone astray. We have sinned against him. God would be completely just to allow us to go our own way and be destroyed, but in his mercy and love he has not. He has found a way that mercy and justice can act together, and that's in the eternal Son of God being made flesh, living a perfect life among us—the life you and I should have lived—and dying a death he didn't have to die.

Jesus did not sin; he died the death we deserve in order to bear our iniquities and our transgressions, to bear God's correct and right penalty against them. When that work was done, God raised him from the dead and highly exalted him to show that he accepted the sacrifice and that all of Jesus' claims were true. Now he invites us to turn from our sins and to trust in Jesus Christ. Friend, God's answer for your guilt is not to explain it away by circumstances that have victimized you, but to call you to own your sins fully and to entrust them all to Jesus Christ by faith. Jesus Christ is our substitute. He has taken our penalty.

Brothers and sisters, do you realize that all your disobedience is not ultimately disobedience to another or to yourself, but to God? Your sins will never be taken care of any other way—not by success in your marriage or family, your friendships, or your work. Christ alone is the way God has appointed to bear our sin. He died for us. Luther said, "We all walk around with His nails in our pockets." It was our sins that put him there. Consider what God did here. Remind yourself of his sovereignty in all of this, and return to the cross daily. Meditate on this passage. Consider what the Son of God has endured on your behalf.

4) The Servant Willingly Accepted His Substitutionary Death (Isa. 53:7–9)

Verse 7 says that although the Servant was oppressed, he did not cry out. "He was oppressed and afflicted, yet he did not open his mouth; he was led like a lamb to the slaughter, and as a sheep before her shearers is silent, so he did not open his mouth."

Consider here the Servant's humble acceptance of his role. He was quiet. He allowed himself to be brought like a lamb to death. Can't you see Jesus in Pilate's hall? Remember him in the garden a little before telling his disciple to put away his sword. He was like a sheep being shorn. He chose not to open his mouth to dispute, to denounce, or to prevent. Jesus Christ accepted this because it was God's plan.

The speaker here is either Isaiah prophetically describing the Servant's oppression, or again the Lord himself. Either way, verse 8 makes it clear that the Servant was killed because of the sins of the people. "By oppression and judgment he was taken away. And who can speak of his descendants? For he was cut off from the land of the living; for the transgression of my people he was stricken." In God's amazing providence it was these very verses that the Ethiopian official in Acts 8 just happened to be reading as he was returning from Jerusalem to

Ethiopia. The Holy Spirit brought Philip to the official, and he asked Philip, "'Tell me, please, who is the prophet talking about, himself or someone else?' Then Philip began with that very passage of Scripture and told him the good news about Jesus" (Acts 8:34–35).

Back in Isaiah 53:9 we see yet another prophecy that was fulfilled in Jesus' life and death. Though without sin himself, the Servant died and was buried: "He was assigned a grave with the wicked, and with the rich in his death, though he had done no violence, nor was any deceit in his mouth." The verse makes it very clear that this Servant had done no violence. That is, his suffering was not caused by his own sin. He had no wickedness and no injustice to account for himself. As it says in verse 11, he was righteous, different from what we've all confessed about ourselves in verse 6.

If you remember the accounts of Jesus' trial, even Pilate himself testifies to Jesus' innocence. It was as if he had read this prophecy in Isaiah and was following the script. As Peter wrote in 1 Peter 2:22, "He committed no sin, and no deceit was found in his mouth." Yet Jesus Christ, our Passover Lamb, was slain for our salvation.

Some have thought that Jesus' example of nonresistance here should serve as an example for Christians never to resist injustice. But I think this is a misreading of the importance of the text here. Jesus is certainly an example for us, but he was also undertaking the unique work of our salvation. There are many callings in life in which we have and should exercise authority, even to correct or punish. We know this in our homes, and we know this in our jobs. But while this does not teach that we should always practice nonresistance, it does teach us that we should always be humble.

Brothers and sisters, don't retaliate for wrongs done against you. Yes, if you can prevent them, do so, but follow the example of Christ here. If this Righteous One was so humble, surely we should be even more humble. Do you feel very righteous sometimes? Perhaps I'm the only one. Let me put it this way: I feel so righteous sometimes, for instance, when I forgive someone who has done something wrong against me. I feel like I have this great bank account of moral credit, and I've just inflated it still further. How false is that? I am a debtor to God's mercy alone. When I act even in the greatest act of forgiveness toward someone else, I have done so little compared to what God has done to me in Christ.

Brothers and sisters, when we act out the kind of love we see in the Servant Jesus Christ, we act not out of some great store of virtue and merit that we have, but rather out of our knowledge of how much more greatly God has forgiven us. We must constantly remind ourselves of God's mercy to us, and out of that mercy deal with those who have sinned against us. If we have been shown mercy, how can we not, in turn, show mercy to others? Pray that there would grow and flourish in your church a God-honoring culture of forgiveness and nonretaliation. Because we want our lives to reflect the humility of this Servant who accepted his special substitutionary suffering out of his love for us, and for his glory, we want to have that kind of life of forgiveness among ourselves.

5) The Servant Will Be Satisfied

In this last stanza of the song, Isaiah says that it was the Lord's will to crush the servant and yet cause him to prosper. Verse 10: "Yet it was the Lord's will to crush him and cause him to suffer, and though the Lord makes his life a guilt offering, he will see his offspring and prolong his days, and the will of the Lord will prosper in his hand."

To understand this, you need to understand that most of the offerings of the Old Testament weren't totally consumed by flame. Most of them were killed and eaten, and that was considered an offering. The guilt offering was the one big exception. The guilt offering would be wholly consumed by flame, and it was the only Old Testament sacrificial suffering that was intended to atone for sin (cf. Lev. 5:16, 18; 7:7). The Servant's death is presented as just such an atoning sacrifice, and that is how we as Christians understand Jesus' death.

The Suffering Servant will justify many and be satisfied. Look at verse 11: "After the suffering of his soul, he will see the light of life and be satisfied; by his knowledge my righteous servant will justify many, and he will bear their iniquities." The Servant's knowledge referred to here is his wisdom, shown not only in his relationship with God but also in his leading others to have such a relationship. That's what the Bible calls wisdom. It's not having a PhD or a certain position. It's not being an expert in this field or that. It's knowing God and bringing others to know God. That's the essence of wisdom in Scripture. That's the Servant's knowledge. As Paul writes to the Romans (5:19), "For just as through the disobedience of the one man the many were made sinners, so also through the obedience of the one man the many will be made righteous."

We noted in verse 11 that the Servant's death was a guilt offering, but it was a new kind of guilt offering, because this Servant would be wholly consumed (as guilt offerings were) and yet satisfied *after* his suffering. How could that be? Remember what was said in 52:13: he will be raised and lifted up and highly exalted.

The last verse summarizes the song, concluding that because the Servant bore the sin of many, God would reward him. "Therefore I will give him a portion among the great, and he will divide the spoils with the strong, because he poured out his life unto death, and was numbered with the transgressors. For he bore the sin of many, and made intercession for the transgressors."

This Servant would be an atoning penal substitute for the people whose sins he bore. Note the background of this. Just as we saw in Leviticus 16 in the last chapter, there is one who bore our sins. Those animals in Leviticus were signals and signs pointing forward to the one who would truly bear our sins, to the Suffering Servant of the Lord. John the Baptist recognized Jesus as this one, and when he "saw Jesus coming toward him [he] said, 'Look, the Lamb of God, who takes away the sin of the world!'" (John 1:29). John the Baptist saw that here was coming the Servant who would bear away our sins, not just the sins of those in Israel, but the sins of anyone from any nation in the world who would turn from his sins and trust this Lamb instead of trying to defend his own record before God.

At the Last Supper Jesus quoted this phrase, "numbered with the transgressors," and said, "This must be fulfilled in me. Yes, what is written about me is reaching its fulfillment" (Luke 22:37). Part of what would be fulfilled was the prophecy that God would reward him. The Servant's life can be summarized as *suffering, then glory.* Isaiah 53:11 uses the interesting language of being satisfied: "After the suffering of his soul, he will see the light of life and be satisfied." The Servant who has suffered will come to know joy. He will enjoy the many who have been justified, whose sins have been borne. Again, this key passage on penal substitution does not present the Servant as one abused by the Father but as one who shares the will of the Father—the Father's will is his will, the Father's plan is his plan, the Father's joy is his joy.

Friend, if you are not a Christian, I want to point out to you that all the good things this prophecy says will come to the Servant come to him only after he pours out his life unto death. This chapter presumes the resurrection from the dead of the Servant. If you want to understand who this Servant is, you must grapple with the idea that we Christians actually believe that Jesus was raised from the dead. That's how he fulfills this prophecy.

The wonderful news of this chapter is that not only will we be forgiven but Jesus Christ will be satisfied in it. He will have accomplished his end in all his actions connected to it. He's not waiting to be satisfied based on what *you* do or by how *you* act in this or that situation. The glorious news is that he *is* satisfied based upon what he has done. We are not laboring under the hope that somehow we might satisfy this unbending, merciless God. No, that's not the picture in the Bible at all. God is satisfied based upon what he has done, and we should follow his example in this. Our ultimate satisfaction should not be found in marriage or family, friends or work, but in God himself. If you struggle with the thought of God's loving you, consider the Savior's sacrifice of himself. Consider the joy that he finds in having fully satisfied himself with his own sacrifice. The cross is no contradiction to God's justice, and it is the pinnacle of God's love for us. What greater thing could he do to show you that he loves you?

Friends, if you are spending your Christian life right now looking for those sweet little circumstances that will give you satisfaction, abandon that search. The last circumstance lied to you; the one just over the horizon is lying to you also. Satisfaction is to be found in Christ. So pray that God will help you to be satisfied in Christ, even as Christ himself was satisfied in his action.

This wonderful passage is, as you can appreciate, especially controversial in the Jewish community. In the public reading through the Scriptures in many synagogues, this passage is simply left out. In their lectionary readings through the Prophets, the rabbis will literally read up to Isaiah 53:12 and on the next Sabbath day pick up with 54:1. Why? "It is too easily misunderstood," it is suggested. It has simply too often and for too long led people to think that Isaiah prophesied the coming of Jesus Christ to die as a substitute, bearing the penalty for the sins of many. Well, I think there's good reason for that. This is what Christians have always understood Isaiah to mean here, because Jesus taught us that's what it means. It is an idea that is both ancient and modern. So united are Christians' understanding of this that words from antiquity sound like the meditations of the Christian's heart just this morning. Here's what one early Christian said:

> O, the surpassing kindness and love of God! He did not hate us, or reject us, or bear a grudge against us. Instead, he was patient and forbearing; in his mercy he took upon himself our sins. He himself gave up his own Son as a ransom for us—the holy one for the lawless, the guiltless for the guilty, "the just for the unjust" (I Peter 3:18), the incorruptible for the corruptible, the immortal for the mortal. For what else but his righteousness could have covered our sins? In whom was it possible for us, the lawless and ungodly, to be justified, except in the Son of God alone? O the sweet exchange! O the incomprehensible work of God! O the unexpected blessings, that the sinfulness of many should be hidden in one righteous man, while the righteousness of one should justify many sinners![2]

Many commentators say that the last of the Servant Songs in Isaiah is found in Isaiah 61:1–2a: "The Spirit of the Sovereign LORD is on me, because the LORD has anointed me to preach good news to the poor. He has sent me to bind up the brokenhearted, to proclaim freedom for the captives and release from darkness for the prisoners, to proclaim the year of the LORD's favor." This is the Servant speaking again, the one who would be satisfied in the salvation he brings. With all this in mind about the Servant and his sacrificial death, consider that when Jesus began his earthly ministry:

> He went to Nazareth, where he had been brought up, and on the Sabbath day he went into the synagogue, as was his custom. And he stood up to read. The scroll of the prophet Isaiah was handed to him. Unrolling it, he found the place where it is written: "The Spirit of the Lord is on me, because he has anointed me to preach good news to the poor. He has sent me to proclaim freedom for the prisoners and recovery of sight for the blind, to release the oppressed, to proclaim the year of the Lord's favor." Then he rolled up the scroll, gave it back to the attendant and sat down. The eyes of everyone in the synagogue were fastened on him, and he began by saying to them, "Today this scripture is fulfilled in your hearing." (Luke 4:16–21)

---

[2] "Epistle to Diognetus," in *Early Christian Writings*, rev. ed., ed. Andrew Louth, trans. Maxwell Stamforth (London: Penguin, 1987), 148.

Think of everything that must have gone through Jesus' mind when he said that. He knew what it meant. He knew the life of the Servant, and he knew the Servant would suffer. Did he swallow hard before he said that sentence? Perhaps those words were a preview of the garden of Gethsemane, a kind of "Let it begin!"

CHAPTER FOUR

RANSOM FOR MANY

Mark 10:45

MARK DEVER

Steve Lambert, a member of our congregation here in Washington, wrote this a few years ago:

In no other manner are the differences between Muslims and Christians more sharply contrasted than in the difference between the characters and legacies of their prophets. Perhaps the contrast is best symbolized by the way Mohammed entered Mecca and Jesus entered Jerusalem. Mohammed rode into Mecca on a warhorse, surrounded by 400 mounted men and 10,000 foot soldiers. Those who greeted him were absorbed into his movement; those who resisted him were vanquished, killed, or enslaved. Mohammed conquered Mecca, and took control as its new religious, political, and military leader. Today, in the Topkapi Palace in Istanbul, Turkey, Mohammed's purported sword is proudly on display. . . .

Jesus entered Jerusalem on a donkey, accompanied by his 12 disciples. He was welcomed and greeted by people waving palm fronds—a traditional sign of peace. Jesus wept over Jerusalem because the Jews mistook him for an earthly, secular king who was to free them from the yoke of Rome, whereas Jesus came to establish a much different, heavenly kingdom. Jesus came by invitation and not by force. One of Jesus' disciples, the Apostle Peter, learned this lesson even during Jesus' apprehension by the Roman authorities. When Peter saw Jesus being taken away by the Roman legionaires and temple guards, he drew his sword and attacked one of the Jewish high priests' servants, cutting off his ear. Jesus, stopping Peter's aggression, healed the wound, and told him to put away his sword: "Put your sword back in its place," Jesus said to Peter, "for all who draw the sword will die by the sword." Shortly thereafter, Jesus was arrested, tortured, and crucified.[1]

So one of the largest religions in the world has a conqueror as its founder and hero. I think we can understand this easily enough. Humans naturally respect strength. We call autocratic kings and conquerors "the Great," from Alexander to Peter and so on.

But the strange fact to the nonreligious must be that nearly twice as many people claim to follow not the conqueror but this other man. The world's largest religion is centered on an execution, a crucifixion. Have you considered before how strange that is? A religion with a cross, an instrument of torture and humiliation, at the center. What is the significance of such a crucifixion? We understand easily what a conquest is about, but what is Jesus' death about? What did the cross mean?

In recent centuries that question has been under much dispute even among those who call themselves Christians. In fact, much of historic Christian doctrine has been recast and, really, rejected in these last few decades. Here's how one writer summed it up:

> With the advance of science and the growing acceptance of Darwin's theory of evolution, key theologians and churchmen concluded by the early twentieth century that the old faith had been essentially disproved. They began to imagine a more reasonable Christianity—one less insistent on miracles, resurrections, and a transcendent God who directed human history from a heavenly remove. Higher Criticism informed a new understanding of the historical Jesus; the Hegelian dialectic shaped a new image of an immanent and impersonal God, an unknowable force whose will was worked through human progress.[2]

This "more reasonable Christianity" would, of course, mean a new understanding of the central doctrine of the Christian faith—our understanding of the cross and of Christ's atoning death. One of the leading proponents of this new, revised Christianity has been John Shelby Spong, formerly Episcopal bishop of Newark, New Jersey. He "published a provocation he called his 'Twelve Theses'—a call to a new Christianity that rejected the divinity of Christ, the virgin birth

[1]Stephen Lambert, "To Gain Strategic Perspective" (August 2005), unpublished paper.
[2]Peter Boyer, "A Church Asunder" *The New Yorker*, April 17, 2006.

and bodily resurrection, and most of the traditional Christian doctrine. The central belief of Christian orthodoxy—the substitutionary atonement of Christ on the Cross—Spong . . . pronounced (quote) 'a barbarian idea based on primitive concepts of God.'"[3]

Now, today, such reworkings of Christianity are occurring even among many who call themselves "evangelical," that is, who say that they believe in the full trustworthiness of the Bible. So the idea of substitutionary atonement is now dismissed and even attacked not just by Muslims or unbelievers, not only by "liberal Christians," but by those who formerly held to it staunchly.

In this chapter we come to Jesus' own teaching about his death, to his own words in the Gospel of Mark (10:45). Before we look more closely at that verse, however, let's spend a moment noticing the context of the story to this point. The first half of Mark's Gospel is basically spent following Jesus' ministry in Galilee. Then in chapters 8 to 10 Jesus travels to Jerusalem for his final week, and it is on his way to Jerusalem that Mark records three predictions that Jesus makes about his own death (8:31; 9:30–37; 10:32–45). As Jesus nears Jerusalem, the request of James and John for certain privileges is surrounded here in Mark 10 by Jesus' teaching about his own death. In fact, their request sets up perfectly Jesus' teaching on what he is going to do, and, therefore, on what it would mean for you and me to follow him.

As you look down through Mark 10, you'll see that Jesus perceives this problem among his followers: they want to exercise authority over each other. So we come to what many consider the central theological verse in Mark's Gospel: "For even the Son of Man did not come to be served, but to serve, and to give his life as a ransom for many" (v. 45).

This verse is a large, clear window into the theology of Jesus. We see what he intends. I think, in fact, in this short saying we see the hues and shades of eight different complementary aspects of who Jesus Christ is and of what he came to do.

Jesus Is Our Fellow Man

First, Jesus is our fellow man. The phrase "Son of Man" was clearly a *human* designation that Jesus used for himself. He was calling himself

[3]Ibid.

a son of Adam. What he meant was that he was physically present. He was able to suffer, as the disciples had seen. Jesus was fully human. Athanasius once speculated in his famous book *On the Incarnation of the Word* why it might be that God saved sinners through a human incarnation, with all the pain and agony that involved. "Why not have the Son of God incarnated as a donkey?" his imaginary questioner asked. But would God give us a mediator who would understand us, who could communicate with us? Yes, he would give us a mediator who would share our nature and be able to share our sins. This sacrifice would be no dumb, mute slaughter. God was sending a talking sacrifice, who even as he gave himself was explaining *why* he was doing so.

The figure of the Son of Man appears scores of times in the Old Testament. Usually it refers merely to a human being, a man. Ezekiel in the Old Testament prophecy is many times addressed as "son of man." So Jesus certainly meant to affirm to his disciples here that they should understand him to be their fellow man.

If you're not a Christian, this aspect of Christian belief may come as something of a surprise to you. We Christians are so intent on praising Jesus Christ and exalting him that you could be forgiven for not understanding that we really do believe that Jesus was fully man, that he was wholly human. But we do. As the writer to the Hebrews says, "We do not have a high priest who is unable to sympathize with our weaknesses, but we have one who has been tempted in every way, just as we are—yet was without sin" (Heb. 4:15). Jesus sympathizes with our weaknesses because he felt them; he experienced them.

My Christian brothers and sisters, isn't God kind to give us sympathy, to teach us what it means to have the capacity to feel with others, to create us so that we can laugh with others and cry with others? Have you realized that this is one of the reasons God created marriage? He did it so that those sympathetic feelings are drawn out of yourself for someone else, so that you can learn the truth from outside of yourself. Through our friends, and especially through our families, God calls us out of ourselves so that we might get our hearts tangled up with others. He has made us in his image. He has shown us that he is like this, as God, and he has made us in his image to be like that, too. Brothers and sisters, marvel at God's love to us in this. The eternal Son of God took on flesh. He left all the privilege and honor that he knew to come down to us!

Notice here, though, that Jesus was not merely "a" son of man, but rather "the" Son of Man. That brings us to our second point.

Jesus Is Our God

Mark 10:45 says that he "did not come to be served." This would be an unusual way of talking about a mere human being. It implies deliberate *purpose* in Jesus' coming. In fact, it implies that unlike you and me, he *chose* to come into this world. Now, that would seem to imply that he existed before he was conceived in the Virgin Mary. That's why we refer to Jesus' incarnation, his taking on flesh, in a way we wouldn't refer to our birth. We have flesh, too, but we've always had flesh. There was no "us" apart from this flesh. We are created beings, but there was never a time when the eternal Son of God was not. And yet he came. Think of that—of what Jesus Christ laid aside in that coming!

So Jesus is our fellow man, but he is also our God. This is clear in his use of the term "Son of Man," as well. That was not only a designation of humanity, but it also referred back to a Messianic title from the Old Testament. In fact, in Daniel 7 the Son of Man is "given authority, glory and sovereign power; all peoples, nations and men of every language worshiped him. His dominion is an everlasting dominion that will not pass away, and his kingdom is one that will never be destroyed" (v. 14).

This great one chose to be born, to come, in a way that you and I never chose. The eternal God—Father, Son, Holy Spirit—purposed before the foundation of the world that the Son should be sent. Jesus knew that he had been sent, and that is why he speaks of his purpose in this way. Thus, Jesus had said in Mark 1:38, "Let us go . . . to the nearby villages—so I can preach there also. That is why I have come." Again in Mark 2:17: "I have not come to call the righteous, but sinners." Jesus Christ, the eternal Son of God, came with a purpose.

And what was that purpose? Jesus says it clearly here. He came with the purpose of *not* being served. Jesus makes his point in a typical, emphatic way, stating it negatively first and then positively. Remember the context. The disciples were fighting for honor and glory and comparative greatness and authority, and in the middle of all this, as the disciples were angling for power and prominence, Jesus turns and tells them that he came *not* to be served.

When you read the prophecy in Daniel about the Son of Man, this is not how you would think of that divine figure. If anyone ever has come with a right to be served, surely it's this one, and yet Jesus says he came for exactly the opposite reason.

Jesus Is Our Servant

Third, Jesus is our servant. Jesus came not to be served but to serve. Do you see Jesus' humility in such a purpose? What an amazing thought. Jesus, our God, the Danielic Son of Man—this one would minister to us? He would wait on us? He would be *our* servant, *our* help, *our* slave? Then again, is it really any surprise that Jesus, who clearly knew and considered the Servant Songs in Isaiah, would identify himself as a servant?

The word here (Mark 10:45) for *serve* is the word from which we get *deacon*. It generally means "to wait on tables," which is very humble work. This is the antithesis of what James and John were jostling for. They wanted to be the ones sitting at the table being waited upon. But Jesus sought no place of great honor, no service from others. He came to fulfill a role of great service. Indeed he would say to his disciples just a few evenings later, when he was washing their feet: "I have set you an example that you should do as I have done for you" (John 13:15). He came to serve.

Now if you live long in this world, you know that that is precisely what some people hate about Christianity: it is a religion that promotes and exalts service. Friedrich Nietzsche famously called Christianity a slave religion. Christianity's exaltation of service enraged Nietzsche. He despised it. In his 1888 book, *The Antichrist*, he said, "I call Christianity the one great curse, the one great intrinsic depravity, and the one great instinct of revenge, for which no means are venomous enough, or secret, subterranean and small enough—I call it the one immortal blemish on the human race."[4]

But Jesus taught differently—that those to be honored most are those who serve. As a result, unlike Nietzsche Christianity has long helped to create a culture unlike the one in which it arose. Christianity lifts up and honors service in a way that was repugnant to the power-worshiping Romans and wisdom-worshiping Greeks.

[4]Friedrich Nietzsche, *The Antichrist* [1888], cited in James A. Haught, *2000 Years of Disbelief* (Amherst, NY: Prometheus, 1996), 178. Instead, Nietzsche lionized "the dynamic person—the Übermensch, the hyper, 'higher man,'" 177.

As Christians, therefore, Jesus calls us to labor for the good of *others* at work, rather than just for ourselves. He calls us to sacrifice our own interests for the benefit of some other person in the office, because we are his followers. It's as if we are seeing a reality that others don't see and are responding to things that they don't understand. And indeed we are. We are following this one who, though in very nature God, took on the form of a servant.

Jesus Is Our Sacrifice

Fourth, Jesus is our sacrifice. We've seen that Jesus, fully man and fully God, came to serve. But how would he do that? As he neared Jerusalem for this final time, what did his service to us really mean? The answer comes in the very next words: "to give his life" (Mark 10:45). These words are used in a parallel with the phrase "to serve," showing more specifically what kind of service Jesus was referring to. Here was Jesus' specific service—fully giving himself. His life, his soul, his very self he would give up and hand over. As Isaiah had prophesied:

> Yet it was the LORD's will to crush him and cause him to suffer,
>   and though the LORD makes his life a guilt offering,
>   he will see his offspring and prolong his days,
>   and the will of the LORD will prosper in his hand.
>
> After the suffering of his soul,
>   he will see the light of life and be satisfied;
>   by his knowledge my righteous servant will justify many,
>   and he will bear their iniquities.
>
> Therefore I will give him a portion among the great,
>   and he will divide the spoils with the strong,
>   because he poured out his life unto death,
>   and was numbered with the transgressors.
>   For he bore the sin of many,
>   and made intercession for the transgressors. (Isa. 53:10–12)

Here in Mark, almost at the gates of Jerusalem, we see Jesus identifying himself as the Suffering Servant of Isaiah 52–53. He interpreted his own approaching death in that light. Jesus knew that he was going to Jerusalem not to experience a tragic surprise that would take his life but rather to persevere in a long obedience in which he would finally lay down his life. From the moment of Peter's first confession of Jesus as the Messiah in Mark 8:29, Jesus' teaching more and more seems to concentrate on his death. He becomes, one might almost say, preoccupied with it. He talked about his death very little before that, but once Peter confesses him as the Messiah, once Peter realizes and announces who he is, it's as if Jesus then knows that now is the time. "They have come to understand who I am, and now I must fully act out this final full measure of my coming." The cross was looming larger with each step he took.

Friends, we will never justify ourselves by our faithfulness at work or at home or even at church. These are not crowns that we'll be able to present to God in order to be made right in his sight. All our works, all our faithfulness, is woefully insufficient for that. No, we need something more. As the sinless Son of God, Jesus' life had infinite value, and he would pay even that price in order to serve us.

Jesus Is Our Ransom

Fifth, Jesus is our ransom. The word "ransom" here in Mark 10:45 means quite simply that Jesus' death purchased our life. We don't often encounter the idea of ransom today in the same way people did in the ancient world. We don't think of it that often. But the word really conveys the same idea as the word we Christians so often use—*redemption*. It refers to something being bought back for freedom out of captivity, a price being paid for someone's or something's release. It's the unpleasant language associated with hostages. Why would Jesus understand his death that way—just a week or so before the cross? What was going on in his own mind that would make him think this way?

The idea of ransom and redemption is deeply founded in the Bible, as we've already seen. From the exodus to the sacrifices to the Suffering Servant of Isaiah, Jesus understood his own death as a substitutionary ransom for his people, purchasing their freedom from the bondage of sin. So Jesus becomes our ransom. He wins our release from sin and judgment by giving his life, by dying. His death would pay the price so that his people might be released. Instead of his people continuing in bondage, Jesus would give himself in exchange for them.

The idea of ransom was used of buying back a prisoner of war, or a slave, or a debtor from debtors' prison. Brothers and sisters, through Jesus Christ *we* are those prisoners and slaves that have been redeemed. We are those who have been brought out by what Jesus has done. Jesus told his disciples plainly that "everyone who sins is a slave to sin" (John 8:34). Now he has come to ransom us from sin, from Satan, from the penalty due us for breaking God's law, from the wrath of God, and from the eternal death we deserve. Oh, Christian, meditate on what you have in your redemption. God has loved us extraordinarily.

People sometimes speak of ransom as a "theory" of the atonement, over against penal substitution. But excluding the unrelated and clearly unbiblical theory whereby Jesus actually pays the ransom *to* Satan, the idea of ransom is not a theory that stands in opposition to the idea of substitution. Substitutionary atonement is the reality of how God has brought reconciliation through Christ, and ransom, understood rightly, is one image, one metaphor that the Bible uses to describe that. Penal substitution itself, though, is no metaphor. It is the reality. That is what in fact happened, and the Bible uses many different metaphors to explain, describe, and extol that fact—including this metaphor of ransom.

Jesus Is Our Substitute

Sixth, Jesus is our substitute. That's what we see in the little word "for," *anti* in the Greek. Jesus died in the place of many—in their stead, as a substitute for them.

Many a commentator has decried finding "a crude substitutionary idea" here in Mark 10:45, even in the word "for."[5] Some have raised a question about the word used here and whether it should be translated "for." But most commentators agree that this word, especially taken together with the other words Jesus uses here, must mean "in the place of." Jesus is talking about substitution. In fact, this verse may be the first time Jesus so clearly taught this idea of substitutionary ransom and redemption to his disciples. He certainly predicted that he would die, but this is the first time he makes it so clear that he would die *for* them, in their place. He didn't just die *on behalf of* or *for the benefit*

---

[5]So A. W. F. Blunt, *The Gospel According to St. Mark* (Oxford, UK: Clarendon, 1929), 221.

of, but he literally died *in their stead*, or in their place. They deserved death, but because he has died *for* them, now they will not die.

We see this substitutionary idea in various places throughout the Gospels (though with different words). So in Mark 8:37 Jesus says, "What can a man give in exchange for his soul?" And it's there, even more clearly, throughout the Bible. As we've seen, God had been preparing us to be taught this. In the Passover meal, in the Day of Atonement, even in the Genesis 22 account of Abraham's sacrificing the ram instead of Isaac (Gen. 22:13) or in Judah's wanting to remain Joseph's captive in the place of Benjamin (Gen. 44:33), this idea of exchange and substitution is deep in the stories of the Bible.

Friends, we need such a substitute because we are by nature guilty, and God has determined that he will accept the sacrifice of Christ as a sufficient substitute for our sins. Augustine's teacher Ambrose told him:

> It is profitable to me to know that for my sake Christ bore my infirmities, submitted to the affections of my body, that for me and for all he was made sin and a curse, that for me and in me was he humbled and made subject, that for me he is the lamb, the vine, the rock, the servant, the Son of a handmaid, knowing not the day of judgment, for my sake ignorant of the day and the hour.

Friends, either we understand and embrace this idea of substitution, or we begin to slip into a religion of self-salvation. If you don't believe this, you don't believe Christianity.

Occasionally some will accuse evangelicals of being too atonement-centered. But I don't know what it would mean to be too centered on the Suffering Servant suffering for us for our salvation. That's what makes us a people. That is our identity. Just as we saw in the last chapter, Jesus clearly understood Isaiah 53 to be talking about *his* life and about *his* death. He knew that his sufferings were vicarious, that they were endured in sinners' stead. Thus, in just a few nights he would look into his disciples' eyes at the Last Supper and say, "This is my blood of the covenant, which is poured out for many" (Mark 14:24). As Paul would later put it, "Christ died for our sins according to the Scriptures" (1 Cor. 15:3). What would you suggest we put at the center of our focus instead of the cross?

Jesus Is Our Savior

Seventh, Jesus is our Savior. Notice the word "many" in Mark 10:45. If you have repented of your sins and trusted in Christ, then you are one of these "many" for whom Christ gave his life as ransom.

We now come to the question, "For whom did Christ die?" Jesus says that he gave his life as a ransom "for many." So who is in that "many?" There is an age-old battle here between Calvinists and non-Calvinists. Calvinists tend to say, "Look! It says *many*, not *all!*" The Arminians respond, "Yes, but there are a lot of other verses." Well, let me help out our Arminian friends for a moment, at least in part. I don't think this text is addressing the question of "many versus all." *Many* simply means "a whole bunch of" as opposed to "one" or "a few." Jesus is not just laying down his life for "a few"; he's laying it down for a lot. That's what's going on.

But who did Jesus die for? Well, I think Scripture is very clear on that. In Isaiah 53 we are told that the Servant would bear the sin of many (v. 12) and that he would "justify many, and he will bear their iniquities" (v. 11). That says to me that the Servant dies for and bears the iniquities of the very same ones he justifies. Moreover, in verse 11 we read that this justifying Servant would be "satisfied" with the results of his labor. Presumably he would not be frustrated at his inability to deliver some that he'd really love to deliver. The word found here in Mark 10:45 for "many" shows us that Jesus had a great host in mind, an innumerable host for whom he would cheerfully undertake this work of redemption, and so he did. He prosecuted it diligently and faithfully, and we can trust that he finished it completely.

How can we measure the power of Christ's death? Surely it's sufficient for the salvation of all, if you want to ask the question that way, but it is, as the theologians say, efficient for the salvation of "many." Christ knew those for whom he was laying down his life, and they were the same ones that the Father had elected, the ones to whom he would give the gifts of repentance and faith and whom the Spirit would regenerate.

If you are not a Christian, I would beg you to repent of your sins, turn from them, and trust in Christ. See that he is this fully sufficient Savior. Your own sins have put you in God's debt and separated you from God. We could use image after image to describe it, but your conscience knows what I'm talking about. And the answer for all that is to trust that Christ has borne the punishment you deserve for your sin.

Jesus Is Our Example

Eighth, Jesus is our example. In those first two words, "For even," Jesus is making himself an example for his disciples to follow. He employs a typical form of argument here: if the *greater* one (Jesus), then how much more should the *lesser* one (the disciples) do this, too? Jesus was calling the disciples to follow his example by giving their lives for the good of others, *not* in atoning for sins (obviously none of us can do that) but in humble service to other people.

This is really an extraordinary moment. For Jesus to use his atoning death as an example of something, that something must be incredibly important. Yet it's simply this: self-sacrifice in humbly serving others. It is nothing more extraordinary or apparently supernatural than that. What a small thing, we may think, to be commended by the most extraordinary act in all of history. Yet Jesus was using his death to draw a contrast between his own attitude and that of his grasping disciples.

So, friends, what would we be like at work? If there was a videotape of your dating or courting relationship, would we see you give yourself to serve the other person, by working carefully to protect him or her, to center that person on God, or would we see you serving yourself first? C. J. Mahaney writes: "Ultimately our Christian service exists only to draw attention to *this* source—to our crucified and risen Lord who gave Himself as the ransom for us all."[6] Have you thought of the service you've given this last week in those terms? Every bit of humble service you gave was a pointer to Jesus' humble giving of himself on the cross, and so it's far more important than you may have thought. Such service won't save you, but it will point the way for you and others to that one act of service that *will* save—Jesus Christ's giving of himself as a ransom for many.

We should humbly seek to serve, not grab prideful places of honor. We don't want to be James and John, asking for the best positions in the kingdom, or the blindly self-righteous ten who then become indignant with them (as if they were any different). We want to be a

[6]C. J. Mahaney, *Humility: True Greatness* (Sisters, OR: Multnomah, 2005), 48.

people typified, in just a few moments, by the same attitude that was in Christ Jesus as he gave himself in humble service to others.

In an interview once, the philosopher Ayn Rand said that faith is the "negation of reason." She said that "friendship, family life and human relationships are not primary in a man's life. A man who places others first, above his own creative work, is an emotional parasite; whereas, if he places his work first, there is no conflict between his work and his enjoyment of human relationships." And then she said this:

Now you want me to speak about the cross. What is correct is that I do regard the cross as the symbol of the sacrifice of the ideal to the nonideal. Isn't that what it does mean? Christ, in terms of Christian philosophy, is the human ideal. He personifies that which men should strive to emulate. Yet, according to the Christian mythology, he died on the cross not for his own sins but for the sins of the nonideal people. In other words, a man of perfect value was sacrificed for men who are vicious and who are expected or supposed to accept that sacrifice. If I were a Christian, nothing could make me more indignant than that: the notion of sacrificing the ideal to the nonideal, or virtue to vice. And it is in the name of that symbol that men are asked to sacrifice themselves for their inferiors.

I wonder if Ayn Rand had considered other religions, religions of strength and this-worldly power? You can find them easily. Some preachers even attempt to turn Christianity into such a self-centered religion, but it never seems to work very well.

By meditating on this one verse, we've seen that Jesus Christ is, in fact, almost nothing like Mohammed. One came to kill and conquer, the other to give up his life to serve others. You have never been crucified, and I am pretty sure you have never conquered a city, but if your friends were telling you honestly about your life, which man would they say you are more like? Would they say that you are using yourself for the good of others, or using others for the good of yourself?

How will you serve others?

How will you live a life that points to Jesus Christ's service to you?

The even more important question is this: How will Jesus Christ serve you?

In Mark 10:27, Jesus told his disciples that salvation was impossible without God but possible with God, and here he tells them how

God would bring about that incredible salvation. Is Jesus Christ *your* ransom? Spurgeon said:

> Dost thou believe? "I believe," says one, and he begins to repeat what they call the "Apostles' Creed." Hold your tongue, sir! That matters not; the devil believes that, perhaps more intelligently than you do; he believes and trembles. That kind of believing saves no man. You may believe the most orthodox creed in Christendom, and perish. Dost thou trust—for that is the cream of the word "believe"—dost thou trust in Jesus? Dost thou lean thy whole weight on him? Has thou that faith which the Puritans used to call "recumbency" or "leaning"? This is the faith that saves—faith that falls back into the arms of Jesus, a faith that drops from its own hanging-place into those mighty arms.[7]

Friends, is your faith in Christ flourishing? What more could he do for you? "For even the Son of Man came not to be served, but to serve, and to give his life as a ransom for many."

[7]C. H. Spurgeon, *Metropolitan Tabernacle Pulpit*, vol. 62 (1916), 477.

CHAPTER FIVE

FORSAKEN

Mark 15:33–34

MICHAEL LAWRENCE

Recently the pages of our local newspapers were filled with the images of four girls. In the photos their smiling, hopeful faces betrayed no hint of the fate that awaited them. Cruelly neglected for months, they were finally killed by their emotionally and surely mentally unstable mother.[1] Our hearts break and our stomachs turn at the mere thought, much less the reality, of the abuse of a defenseless child by the very person intended to protect and cherish that child. Our minds reel—what kind of monster must someone be in order to hurt or kill her own child?

Yet we must stop right there and ask, "Is that not what Christians teach that God the Father did to God the Son?"

The seeming incongruity of attributing violence to a loving God has long led liberal theologians to reject the idea that the violence of the cross was God's design, much less his doing. In contrast, conservative and evangelical theologians have argued that God's willingness and ability to punish evil is not only consistent with his love and goodness, but also necessary. After all, indifference may pass itself off as tolerance, but it is entirely unconvincing as the posture of love.

But even though God's judgment of evil is right, the object of the cross's violence was not a child abuser getting his just deserts. It was Jesus, to the world an example of goodness and kindness to be emulated, and to Christians the very Son of God incarnate to be worshiped.

[1] *Washington Post*, January 11, 2008, A.1.

Either way, the assertion that on the cross Jesus was the passive victim of violence he did not deserve, inflicted by his Father, has led some, even within evangelicalism itself, to recoil in horror and disgust at the idea of the atonement as penal substitution. Penal substitution is the Christian doctrine that, on the cross, Christ suffered the death, punishment, and curse we deserve because of our sin. Moreover, he suffered this penal violence at the hand of God the Father.

Stephen Chalke and Alan Mann, self-proclaimed evangelicals, have described this doctrine as "a form of cosmic child abuse."[2] Colin Greene, another theologian, suggests that penal substitution turns Christ into "the whipping-boy who appeases the wrath of God."[3] Joel Green and Mark Baker, both self-described evangelicals, insist that such an understanding of the cross is built on a picture of God as a Father who is "emotion-laden . . . ever on the verge of striking out against any who disobey his every will" with a rage he cannot control.[4] Other evangelical and conservative critics have suggested that penal substitution is inconsistent with the Father's love for the Son. What's more, they ask, doesn't it require us to accept a division within the Trinity, the setting of one divine person against another?

It's precisely because of such critiques in recent years, with their emotional and theological pull, that we are considering what the Bible says about the atoning death of Christ on the cross. Now we come to the thing itself, the crucifixion of Jesus Christ on the cross. All four Gospels record the event, but we consider now the earliest of the four, Mark's account. Specifically, we want to focus not so much on what Christ endured at the hands of Roman soldiers but rather the suffering he experienced from God the Father. Mark writes:

> At the sixth hour darkness came over the whole land until the ninth hour. And at the ninth hour Jesus cried out in a loud voice, "Eloi, Eloi, lama sabachthani?"—which means, "My God, my God, why have you forsaken me?" (Mark 15:33–34)

[2]Steve Chalke and Alan Mann, *The Lost Message of Jesus* (Grand Rapids, MI: Zondervan, 2003), 182.
[3]Quoted in Steve Jeffery, Michael Ovey, and Andrew Sach, *Pierced for Our Transgressions: Rediscovering the Glory of Penal Substitution* (Wheaton, IL: Crossway, 2007), 229.
[4]Joel Green and Mark Baker, *Recovering the Scandal of the Cross: Atonement in New Testament and Contemporary Contexts* (Downers Grove, IL: InterVarsity, 2000), 53.

What are we to make of Jesus' words? Is this an agonized plea for help to the Father who loves him, for help to be rescued from what's happening around him? Or does penal substitution turn Jesus' words into something like the uncomprehending and bewildered cry of terror from a child ineffectively shielding himself from his father's wicked blows?

Actually, what we need to understand is that these words of Jesus', spoken in anguish and agony, are neither a request to be rescued from the terrors of the cross nor a cry of terror itself. Rather, what we see in these verses is that on the cross Jesus was forsaken, and he knew himself to be forsaken. Let's consider three questions about this cry of Jesus' on the cross.

Who Forsook Jesus?

First, who forsook Jesus? The simple answer is *everyone*. In fact, it would be much easier to say who *didn't* forsake him.

Jesus was forsaken by his government, the institutional authority that should have protected him as an innocent man. The Jews didn't have the authority to put anyone to death on the cross, so the fact that Jesus hung on a cross must be traced back to Roman authority. That's exactly what we see in Mark 15:15–20. It was Roman soldiers acting on the orders of the Roman governor, Pilate, who first flogged Jesus and then crucified him.

The Romans had been crucifying people for over three centuries. As the cruelest form of capital punishment Rome exercised, it was reserved for the worst of the worst: traitors, rebels against Caesar, slaves, and foreigners. Citizens were immune to this particular penalty, and polite people didn't even use the word *cross* or *crucify*. Because of that there are very few descriptions of them, despite the thousands of crucifixions that happened in antiquity. Literate people didn't like to talk about such things. The charge against Jesus was rebellion against Caesar, but it was a sham. Pilate admitted he had no basis for a charge against Jesus, and yet he abandoned Jesus to the will of the crowd anyway. He executed a man he knew to be innocent in order to curry favor with the crowds. On the cross, Jesus died unjustly.

But Jesus was not only forsaken by his government; he was also forsaken by his own people, the Jews. Though they'd welcomed him as their king a week earlier, he didn't turn out to be the savior-king they'd hoped for. So first the crowd shouted for Jesus' blood, and then, as he hung on the cross, they mocked and insulted him, throwing his own words back at him in derision. Jesus claimed to be the one sent by God to save Israel. In his death, the ones he came to save refused him. On the cross, Jesus died rejected.

Perhaps worst of all from a human perspective, Jesus was forsaken by his followers. For three years Jesus had poured his life into a small group of disciples. He had taught them, lived with them, and shared his life with them. But at his arrest the night before, betrayed by one of his own, Mark tells us they'd all deserted him and fled. In his death, Jesus was abandoned by his closest friends. On the cross, Jesus died alone.

Does it surprise you that one so good should be left so forsaken? It shouldn't. As Christians, we understand that we live in a fallen world that is characterized by sin, both externally in our institutions and internally in our hearts. We are saddened by sin as Christians, but we are not surprised at it. If you are not a Christian, I wonder how it is that you explain the presence of such good and such evil in this world?

Forsaken by the human instruments of justice, forsaken by those he'd come to save, forsaken by his friends—it is hard to imagine a more desolate scene. But if we stop there, we have failed to grasp the true nature of the forsakenness Christ experienced on the cross. When human justice failed him, Jesus was silent. When his people mocked him, he did not reply. Even in response to Peter's denial of him, there was only a look. But Jesus was also forsaken by God himself, and it was this and this alone that drew forth his anguished cry, "My God, My God, why have you forsaken me?"

When Jesus utters those words, he is quoting Psalm 22:1. Mark lets us know that in the extremity of Jesus' soul, he speaks not in the *lingua franca* of Greek but in his native Aramaic. A psalm of David, Psalm 22 had long been understood to be a messianic psalm, yet there is no exact event in David's life that it seems to correspond to. The psalm appears to be describing an execution, yet as it proceeds we see that the Suffering Servant-King's prayer has been answered: he is delivered. Help is given. By the end of the psalm, not only is the King delivered, but that deliverance has resulted in the deliverance of the people of Israel, and not just them, either. In fact, the nations are brought to worship the Lord as a result of this deliverance. Some have suggested that though Jesus is quoting Psalm 22:1, he doesn't really mean that God has forsaken him, nor is he displaying what appears to be almost despair. Instead, they say, he is really thinking of the end of the psalm, the victory and the deliverance.

Maybe.

That would certainly make Jesus' words easier to understand and swallow. But to me that explanation has the sound of special pleading about it and the desire to avoid something very difficult. No, rather than explain away the offense and difficulty of these words, we must grapple with the force and pain of what has been described as Jesus' cry of dereliction, if we are to understand the cross. For at this point, what had been a plea for help in David's mouth has become on Jesus' lips a rhetorical question, a statement of fact, as the rest of the psalm and the description of his crucifixion make very plain. We will unpack that fact in three steps.

First, on the cross Jesus Christ was forsaken *by God*. This, of course, is what the crowd around him assumes. They know their Old Testament. They know that the law declared God's curse, God's forsaking, of anyone who hung on a tree. They also know the promises that God had made about his anointed one, the Messiah, and it's clear that these promises aren't being applied here. What about the promise in Psalm 22, that God would not hide his face from his anointed or despise his suffering, or the promise in Psalm 16 that God would not abandon his servant to the grave? Yet isn't that exactly what is happening here? For his enemies, Jesus on the cross was proof that God had rejected his claim to be Messiah and that God had forsaken him.

But, surprisingly, it's not just his enemies that understood it this way. This is, in fact, what the entire Bible teaches about the cross, from the Old Testament to the New. As we saw in Isaiah 53, "it was the LORD's will to crush him and cause him to suffer" (v. 10). And this is not just the idiosyncratic view of one prophet. The prophet Zechariah declares in Zechariah 13:7, "'Awake, O sword, against my shepherd, against the man who is close to me!' declares the LORD Almighty. 'Strike the shepherd, and the sheep will be scattered.'" In Mark 14 Jesus quoted those very verses, that they were about to be fulfilled about himself and about his disciples. In the New Testament Peter says, in Acts 2:23, "This man [that is, Jesus] was handed over to you [Israel] by God's set purpose and foreknowledge." Paul told the Corinthians that "God made him who had no sin to be sin for us" (2 Cor. 5:21), and he told the Roman Christians, "God presented him as a sacrifice of atonement" (Rom. 3:25).

In fact, this is surely what Jesus himself understood to be the case. On the night of his betrayal Jesus prayed in agony in the garden of Gethsemane, "Abba, Father, everything is possible for you. Take this cup from me. Yet not what I will, but what you will" (Mark 14:36). That is an extraordinary prayer, for in acknowledging that everything is possible for God, Jesus is acknowledging that God's purpose in the cross had not somehow been forced upon God by some external logic, nor was it a last-second reversion to some sort of plan B. No, Jesus is acknowledging that the cross is God's free decision made of his own will.

There have been many who have sought to rescue God from the scandal of the cross. They think it is unworthy of his character, inconsistent with his love for Christ. But as we've seen, the Bible will not let us do that. The cross was God's idea, his set purpose and plan from before the foundation of the world. On the cross Jesus Christ was actually forsaken by God the Father.

Friends, what does this tell you about God? It tells you how much a God of love he really is. God did not stop loving the Mediator when he forsook him on the cross. Rather, on the cross he demonstrated the nature of his love for us. I don't know what you think about the relationship between Jesus and the Father. Sometimes people think of Jesus as the really loving one and the Father as the grudging, miserly one whose love must somehow be won for us in Jesus, but nothing could be further from the truth. It was the Father's love that planned the cross from the beginning.

Second, we need to understand that on the cross, *Christ* was forsaken by God. From the beginning of Christianity many have tried to save Christ from the horror of God-forsakenness on the cross. In the early centuries of the church, Docetists of various forms and types claimed that Christ's sufferings weren't real but only appeared to be real. Hence, they were called "Docetists," *doke* being the Greek word for "appearance." Others claimed that it wasn't really Jesus who died on the cross but that, at the last second, God rescued Jesus, whom he loved, and put someone else there, the most popular substitute being Judas. This idea especially was later picked up by Islam and popularized in the Muslim world. By the Middle Ages the rescue attempts had taken on more sophisticated forms. The Roman Catholic

Church began to teach that though Christ did suffer God's forsaking wrath on the cross, he did so only in his human nature, not in his divine nature as the God-man. Quite naturally this led to a focus and an emphasis on the physical sufferings of Jesus the man, reflected in the piety of the crucifix, with the body of Christ still on the cross, and of the mass, in which the body of Christ is supposedly crushed again in our mouths.

But despite all these attempts, the first to take the path of trying to rescue Christ from the horrors of the cross was not some early mistaken follower, but his oldest enemy, Satan himself. It was Satan who first tempted Christ in the desert to take a shortcut in his ministry that would avoid the cross altogether. Jesus tells us in Mark 8 that it was Satan who used Peter to try to dissuade him from laying down his life. Surely it was Satan, too, who was inspiring the mockers on that terrible day to tempt Christ to save himself and to come down from the cross.

But, friends, it was Christ who was forsaken by God on the cross, not some substitute. The preaching of the apostles was always and only *Christ* crucified, *Christ* made sin, *Christ* offered as a sacrifice. As we've already seen, crucifixion was so offensive that it's absurd to think the disciples would have preached a crucified Messiah if they'd had any other option. But they didn't. It was Christ who was crucified, and it was Christ, *the God-man*, who was forsaken by God on the cross, not merely Jesus in his human nature. As Hebrews 9:14 says, "Christ . . . through the eternal Spirit offered himself unblemished to God." Though it was his human nature that suffered the pains of physical death, it was his divine nature that gave his suffering its infinite value and dignity, so making it effective as a ransom for many.

Christ was forsaken by God, and he endured that suffering not as the unwilling victim of cosmic child abuse but as the willing and obedient Son of his Father. We see it in his prayer in the garden of Gethsemane: "not my will, but yours be done." We see it in Jesus' teaching in John 10: "No one takes [my life] from me, but I lay it down of my own accord" (v. 18). We see it even here in the cry of dereliction: Jesus doesn't say, "Oh God"; he says, "*My* God, my God, why have you forsaken me?" To the end, to the bitter end, Jesus is willingly obedient to the will of the Father.

As Christians, this is why we understand that Christ is uniquely able to save those who repent of their sins and put their trust in him. There is no other mediator between God and man. As Peter says, "Salvation is found in no one else, for there is no other name under heaven given to men by which we must be saved" (Acts 4:12). That's why we as a church are committed to taking the message of the cross to the ends of the world, particularly to those places where it's never been heard before. It's not because we're neocolonial cultural imperialists, though some would accuse us of that. It's not because we're bigots, or because we want to impose some kind of worldwide intolerance. No, it is because we believe people spend eternity in hell apart from faith in this Christ, and so we want to spend ourselves, our money, and our time to see this saving message taken to the world. This is the kind of church we want to be, because Christ was forsaken by God on the cross.

But we cannot finally understand the cross until we understand what it means that Christ was *forsaken* by God. That brings us to another question.

What Does It Mean to Be Forsaken?

Second, what does it mean to be forsaken? To be forsaken is to be abandoned. This is what Paul says Demas did to him (2 Tim. 4:10). He forsook him. Paul goes on to say that *everyone* forsook him at his first trial and defense. Paul uses the same word that's found in Hebrews 10:25, where we are told not to "give up meeting together," but rather to "encourage one another—and all the more as you see the Day approaching."

But even though I could point you to other verses in the Bible that talk about people being forsaken, we in one sense cannot understand the God-forsakenness of Christ because, as one theologian has noted, "it has no parallel in human consciousness."[5] His physical agony we can appreciate, because we have all felt pain. Even his emotional grief we can sympathize with because we too have known human injustice, and we have all known people who have betrayed us, friendships that have been lost. But to be utterly forsaken by God is to know "the judicial stroke from eternal justice."[6] Friend, if you yet draw breath today, then you have not known that stroke. You have not known that forsakenness—and may you never know it.

[5]William G. T. Shedd, *Dogmatic Theology*, 3rd ed., ed. Alan W. Gomes (Phillipsburg, NJ: P&R, 2003), 718.
[6]Ibid.

At this point we come to some deep theology. Here we reach the deepest point of the deep theology of what it means that the second person of the Trinity was forsaken by the first. We cannot understand this sympathetically, but there are things the Bible tells us that we must understand. To begin with, the God-forsakenness that Christ experienced on the cross is not merely the absence of God's favor and blessing, though it is that. It is also the positive infliction of God's wrath for sin. On the cross, Jesus Christ bore the penalty for sin. This is extraordinary, of course, for he had no sin of his own. The sin that he bore was the sin of others, the sin of those he had come to save. Yet God made him who had no sin to be sin (2 Cor. 5:21); he endured a cursed death because God had made him to become a curse (Gal. 3:13). There on the cross, bearing sin, Christ endured the wrath of God that sin deserves. God's wrath at that point was not personal anger. He was not angry at Jesus. He was angry at sin, and Jesus bore it. Christ experienced a judicial wrath.

Friends, the Bible is clear that sin makes God angry. Maybe you don't like to think of God as angry. Neither do I. The thought of an angry God is a scary thought, but just because it's scary doesn't mean it's not true. Since it is true, we need to deal with it. Sin makes God angry, not with anger like ours, as when our sense of pride has been insulted or our rights have been infringed, but rather with the righteous anger of perfect justice and the holy anger of perfect love. Sin is an attack on God's character, a denial of God's truth, an affront to his very being. God is right to be angry at sin and to punish it as it deserves. As Paul says in Romans 1, "The wrath of God is being revealed from heaven against all the godlessness and wickedness of men" (v. 18). We see God's wrath in hints and echoes of all sorts in the trials of our own lives, but the place where we see it most clearly is right here on the cross.

This means that on the cross, before Jesus experienced physical death, he endured spiritual death in his God-forsakenness. Jesus died spiritually before he died physically. I do not mean that some part of the divine nature died. Nor do I mean that the Trinity itself was torn apart. Rather, I mean that on the cross Jesus Christ experienced the death that Adam and Eve experienced immediately upon their rebellion in the garden and the death that you and I are all born into. He experienced in the consciousness of the God-man what it means for

God to be opposed to those who are by nature objects of his wrath.[7] This is the whole point of Paul's argument in Colossians 1 and 2, where he says that on the cross, in his body, Christ reconciled us to God by nailing the requirements of the law to that cross. Those requirements of the law were separation from God for sin and being cut off from him. That is what Christ knew. His soul, not just his body, knew the torments that God has stored up for sin.

Most importantly, all this means that Christ experienced what the Bible calls the "second" or "eternal" death. Unless Christ returns first, all of us will experience the death of our bodies. But the Bible tells us that our souls do not die; our souls were created to be immortal. God created them to live forever. The Bible also tells us that the day will come, which Paul calls the Day of the Lord, when our bodies will be resurrected and reunited to our souls, and we will give an account to God for how we lived (1 Thess. 4:13–5:2). Paul says, "For those who are self-seeking and who reject the truth and follow evil, there will be wrath and anger" (Rom. 2:8). In the book of Revelation, John is given a vision of that day. Anyone whose name is not found in the book of life is cast, body and soul, into hell. This is described as a second death, an unending death, a death of eternal conscious torment as finite creatures attempt for all eternity to pay an infinite debt against an infinite and holy God (Rev. 20:11–15).

It is this eschatological judgment, this final judgment, that Christ endured in his person, body and soul, on the cross—not in extent of time, but in fullness of experience.[8] This is the point of verse 33, this darkness that covered the land from the sixth until the ninth hour, that is, from noon until 3 PM. This was no natural eclipse, which was physically impossible at this time of the month (the Passover was always attended by a full moon); nor was this darkness a symbol somehow of God's sadness at the tragic spectacle of his Son's crucifixion. No, this darkness was a supernatural act of God, and it was the portent of his wrath (cf. Joel 2:31; Amos 5:20). The Day of the Lord had arrived, and it was crashing down on Jesus on the cross. Like the three-day plague of darkness that preceded the judgment against the firstborn of Egypt (Ex. 10:21ff.), this darkness is the darkness of judgment, prophesied by Amos:

[7]Herman Bavinck, *Reformed Dogmatics, vol. 3: Sin and Salvation in Christ*, ed. John Bolt, trans. John Vriend (Grand Rapids, MI: Baker, 2006), 389–90.
[8]cf. Shedd, *Dogmatic Theology*, 738.

"In that day," declares the Sovereign LORD,
   "I will make the sun go down at noon
   and darken the earth in broad daylight.

"I will turn your religious feasts into mourning
   and all your singing into weeping.
I will make all of you wear sackcloth
   and shave your heads.
I will make that time like mourning for an only son
   and the end of it like a bitter day." (Amos 8:9–10)

Over the centuries, many have taught that after Christ's physical death on the cross, he descended into hell. But the Bible never teaches that. What the Bible says is that Jesus made atonement for sin on the cross where we could see what was happening—not hidden away somewhere in some other spiritual reality, but *publicly* he bore the judgment of God. Jesus' descent into hell happened in those three hours on the cross, as he experienced the torments of hell reserved for those who have been forsaken by God.[9] For three hours he endured those torments as eschatological darkness covered him, and at the end he cried out, "My God, my God, why have you forsaken me?" In those three hours, he bore the infinite wrath of God against sin to the very end of that wrath.

Why Did God Forsake Christ?

Third, why did God forsake Christ? This last question hangs there on the lips of Jesus, unanswered. But though it stands in our text as a declaration of what Christ endured, it must be answered. It demands an answer, and, praise God, the answer is as simple as it is profound. Christ was forsaken by God so that we who have put our faith in him will never be forsaken. Christ was forsaken by God so that we would not have to be. This is the message of the cross that the apostles and the prophets preached. "God made him who had no sin to be sin for us, so that in him we might become the righteousness of God" (2 Cor. 5:21). "Christ redeemed us from the curse of the law by becoming a curse for us, for it is written, 'Cursed is everyone who is hung on a tree'" (Gal. 3:13). "He was pierced for our transgressions, he was

[9]cf. John Calvin, *Institutes of the Christian Religion*, 2.16.10.

crushed for our iniquities; the punishment that brought us peace was upon him, and by his wounds we are healed" (Isa. 53:5).

Penal substitution does not turn God into a cosmic child abuser. It does not reduce Christ to the passive victim of some divine injustice. It does not pit the Trinity against itself. No, in the God-forsakenness of Christ on the cross, the love of God and the justice of God are revealed on our behalf. United in purpose, Father and Son act in concert to save God's people. The sinless Son of God bears our sin, and then God pours out the wrath that our sin deserves, and Jesus the Son endures it so that we, who deserve that wrath, might never encounter it. This is the gospel, the good news of the cross, and it calls us to forsake our sin, to turn away from it and embrace Christ, the forsaken one, so that we may not be forsaken.

Christian, what sin are you cherishing these days that you should not be? What sin do you feel like you just can't forsake? What obedience do you feel like you just can't make? Oh, Christian, remember that Christ was forsaken for you. In light of that, what can you not forsake? Friend, if you're not a Christian, consider what a small thing it is to forsake your sin, to forsake the whole world even, in exchange for never being forsaken by God.

CHAPTER SIX

TO SAVE THE WORLD

John 3:14–18

MICHAEL LAWRENCE

What do you think is the great need of the hour? That question is ban-
died about often by political and social leaders, and it seems just about
everyone has a different answer. I suppose the way you answer it depends
on what you think the problem is. In 1907, President Teddy Roosevelt
thought the great need of the hour was government investment in the
railroads.[1] A century later, the secretary-general of the United Nations
says the need of the hour is tolerance.[2] How times have changed!

I wonder what you consider to be your greatest need? I'm sure it's
not more investment in the railroads. Perhaps, like many Westerners,
you think your greatest need is material—more money, a better job,
a more secure future for yourself and your children. Or perhaps you
consider your greatest need to be psychological—personal authenticity,
healthy self-esteem, respect, wholeness. If you're not from the West,
perhaps you define your greatest need in social rather than individual
terms—respect and security for your family or people, the removal
of shame due to historic injustice, political self-determination, social
vindication. All of us have a sense of what the great need of the hour
is, though it may differ wildly.

[1] "At Indianapolis, Ind., May 30, 1907," in *Presidential Addresses and State Papers, January
16, 1907–October 25, 1907* (Whitefish, MT: Kessinger, 2006), 1264.
[2] Ban Ki-moon, "Remarks to Alliance of Civilizations Group of Friends Ministerial Meeting,"
New York, Sept. 26, 2007.

For 2,000 years Christians have also had an answer to the question, "What is the great need of the hour?" The answer is that each of us, individually, needs to be saved—saved from our sins and the penalty those sins have incurred before God. This is what we believe Jesus Christ came to do. He came to meet sinners' greatest need—to save them from the wrath of God—and he did it by enduring that wrath himself on the cross.

We come now to a passage that speaks of Jesus saving people, and it answers two questions. What do we need saving from, and how are we saved from it? Look at John 3:14–18:

> Just as Moses lifted up the snake in the desert, so the Son of Man must be lifted up, that everyone who believes in him may have eternal life. For God so loved the world that he gave his one and only Son, that whoever believes in him shall not perish but have eternal life. For God did not send his Son into the world to condemn the world, but to save the world through him. Whoever believes in him is not condemned, but whoever does not believe stands condemned already because he has not believed in the name of God's one and only Son.

There is perhaps no more beloved or familiar verse in Scripture than John 3:16. Even many who didn't grow up in the church know it by heart. So as we turn now to consider this verse and its context, we're approaching something like the *Mona Lisa* of the Bible. What could possibly be said about it that you haven't already heard and that you don't already know? Even so, let's simply walk through this passage and observe what it teaches us about why Jesus was sent from heaven to die on a cross. These verses teach us five very important things.

We See the Need for the Atonement

First, we see the *need* for the atonement. In the beginning of John 3, Jesus and Nicodemus, a religious leader in Israel, have been discussing how somebody gets into the kingdom of heaven. Jesus has insisted that the only way into the kingdom is to be born again; that is, to be given new life through the supernatural work of the Holy Spirit. Nicodemus's response, naturally enough, is, "But that's impossible!" to which Jesus replies by saying that he knows what he is saying is true because he himself has come from heaven. Then in verses 14 and 15, he goes on to explain why he's left heaven and come to earth.

Jesus says that what happened in the desert to the Israelites 1,500 years earlier must happen to him. He's referring to the story in Numbers 21, in which the people of Israel complain and grumble against Moses and God. There's no water; there's no bread, and they're sick, they say, of manna, the miraculous food God has been sending them from heaven. It's not enough that God has rescued them from Egypt, nor that he is supernaturally providing food and water in the wilderness. As far as they are concerned, it's taking too long to get to the Promised Land, and the room service along the way isn't up to snuff. This is a perfect picture of prideful discontent, of ungrateful and selfish hearts. These Israelites were fully convinced that they could do a better job managing their situation than God was doing. In judgment for their rebellion and grumbling, God sent poisonous snakes among them, and Numbers tells us that many of them died.

The point of comparison Jesus is making here is not just what will happen to him, which we'll come to in a moment, but the condition we are all in. Like the Israelites in the desert, we stand under the wrath and judgment of God. Our circumstances may be different, but our hearts are the same. God has placed us in the world that he has made and provided us with everything we have. Thus, he has every right to expect that we will respond to him with trust, thanks, and worship. But, instead, all of us grumble and decide to take charge of things ourselves. Our grumbling varies; some of us don't like what God says about our sexuality; others don't like the idea of any authority outside ourselves; still others chafe at what God says about our money; and all of us find it intolerable that God made us to love him rather than ourselves.

Whatever form it takes, we are all guilty of rebellion against the God who made us, and we stand under his judgment. The snakes, the evidence of God's wrath, may not have arrived yet in your life, but don't let the delay fool you, and don't let the comforts of this life lull you into a false sense of security. The judgment of God has already begun in our spiritual separation from him, and the day will come when final judgment will be delivered—eternity spent in conscious torment, not from snakebite but from the wrath of God himself. Friends, the great need of the hour is to be saved from God's wrath. We need atonement, a way to be forgiven by God and reconciled to him.

The Nature of the Atonement

That brings us to the second thing these first two verses teach us, and that is the *nature* of the atonement. In response to God's judgment, the Israelites in the desert asked Moses to pray that God would take the snakes away. They knew that they couldn't remove God's judgment. Only God could do that. In reply, God told Moses to make a bronze snake and lift it up on a pole or standard. Anyone who was bitten and then looked at the uplifted bronze snake would not die but live.

Why a bronze snake? The text isn't explicit, but the logic seems to be the same as every other means of atonement God provided the Israelites. There was nothing magical about it. Like the Passover lamb or the sacrifice on the Day of Atonement, the bronze snake was a symbol of Israel's condemnation and judgment. Thus, by looking at the snake the Israelites were acknowledging the justice of God's judgment, but they were also depending on the promise itself, that if they looked in humble, repentant faith they would not die.

Jesus goes on to say that just as Moses lifted up that snake, so the Son of Man must be lifted up. When he speaks of the Son of Man, Jesus is referring to himself as the one sent from heaven to save his people. But what must have been shocking to Nicodemus was not just Jesus' claim to be the messianic Son of Man but the rather unambiguous statement that the Son of Man must be crucified. That's what the Greek word for *lifted up* meant. And Jesus says this must happen. He doesn't mean that some external logic is forcing this on God; he's referring to the fulfillment of Scripture. As Isaiah said of the Suffering Servant in Isaiah 52:13, "See, my servant will act wisely; he will be raised and lifted up and highly exalted." According to Jesus, that bronze serpent in the desert was just a picture of the true atonement that would be made when he was lifted up on the cross, not merely as a symbol or emblem of our judgment but as the substitute who would actually suffer our judgment in our stead.

So this is the nature of Christ's atonement: he would be lifted up on a cross and condemned as a criminal in our stead in order to suffer the penalty we deserve. This *must* happen, Jesus says, and yet he suffers willingly in order to fulfill God's purpose laid out in Scripture.

Contrary to what liberal theologians like to say about the symbolic meaning of the cross, the good news is that there is nothing symbolic about it. The symbols were in the Old Testament; they were given so that when the real thing happened, we'd know what we were looking at. When Jesus was lifted up on the cross, he wasn't making a symbolic statement about the power of faith over the meaninglessness of life. No, he was making atonement for sin, as only he could do.

Parents, have you thought about this in relation to your children? We talk a lot about training our children and raising them up in the nurture and admonition of the Lord, and we should be doing that. But we must never forget that we cannot train sin out of our kids. Their sin must be atoned for. We also talk a lot about the importance of spiritual discipline and being in the Word regularly, about training ourselves in godliness and righteousness. We should do that, too. But friends, we must not forget that we cannot discipline ourselves out of sin. Our sin must be atoned for.

Parents, as you work with your children, and Christians, as you go about your own spiritual disciplines, do not forget to apply the gospel to your life and to your children's lives. It is the atoning death of Christ that they need and you need. Do not depend on training; depend on the work that Christ did. And realize that this is a work that only Jesus Christ could do. Only Jesus can make atonement for sin.

Jesus is unique. Fully God and fully man, he alone did not stand under God's judgment; he alone never grumbled against God and never sought his own will over against the Father's. This is why he alone could offer himself as a substitute. Because Jesus obeyed his Father's will, not only was he lifted up on the cross, but God lifted him up to heaven and has highly exalted him. Jesus died on the cross, but he didn't stay dead. He got up from the grave and ascended to heaven, and, as Paul declared, "Therefore God exalted him to the highest place and gave him the name that is above every name, that at the name of Jesus every knee should bow, in heaven and on earth and under the earth, and every tongue confess that Jesus Christ is Lord, to the glory of God the Father" (Phil. 2:9–11). Jesus was mocked and despised on that cross, but God has already and will in the future vindicate his Son.

Have you ever noticed the difference between the way the followers of Mohammed and the followers of Jesus react when one or the other is insulted? When Mohammed is insulted, Islam says the offender is to be killed by the faithful, but when Jesus is mocked, Scripture teaches us to pray that God would have mercy on the mocker. Why the difference? Do Muslims hold Mohammed in higher esteem? Not at all. It's simply this: Mohammed oppressed and slaughtered some of those that resisted his message and taught his followers to do the same. But Jesus died for his enemies and taught us to love our enemies as well, so that we would be like our Father in heaven. Now, I ask you, which religion sounds as though it came from heaven, and which was made here on earth?

The Motivation for the Atonement

Why would God send his beloved Son to die for sinners? That brings us to the third thing we see in these verses: the *motivation* for the atonement. According to Jesus, the motivation for his substitutionary death on the cross is the love of God the Father for the world. So often we read John 3:16 as if it's telling us something about the intensity or quantity of God's love: God loved the world sooooooo much! Of course that's true, but that's not actually what it says. A more precise translation might be: "God loved the world in this way." The intense love of God is not just emotion. It has a content, and what an amazing content! How do we know that God loves the world? We look at the cross. How do we know what God's love looks like? We look at the cross. On the cross God gave his Son as a sacrifice for a sinful world in full-tilt rebellion against him, and the person God gave for the world wasn't just anybody; it was his one and only Son, the incarnate second person of the Trinity, whom the Father had loved from all eternity and with whom he was well pleased. This is the one God gave, and he did it because of his love for the world.

The world thinks of love as mere sentiment and emotion, but that's not the biblical definition of love. It is so much more than that. When the Bible says that God is love, this is what it means: an active giving of oneself, of one's best, for the good of another, even for the good of one's enemy.

Children, how do you measure your parents' love? Is it by how much you're getting your own way, what you want, when you want it? That's not a good measure. Sometimes, love opposes what you want and prevents you from getting your way. I fear that too often we measure God's love the same way children measure their parents' love. If life is going well and we are getting what we want, then God loves us. If not, then he doesn't love us. Friend, that's a deceitful measure. Do not trust the yardstick of your emotion. Perhaps right now God is loving you as a wise Father by *not* giving you what you want, even by making your life difficult, so that you might stop your headlong descent into destruction and reach out to him for forgiveness in Christ.

As Christians we understand that we are called to imitate this kind of love by spending our lives in sacrifice for others. We don't do this to earn God's love. How could we earn the cross? No, we love others because we have been so well loved, and now our greatest joy is in introducing others to that love, by displaying that love to the world. So, spouses, how will your mate see your Christlike love this week? Children, how will your schoolmates see your Christlike love? How will people at the office or in the neighborhood see your Christlike love this week? The cross didn't happen on a whim. God planned it. What kind of planning are you doing so that people will see the love of Christ in you?

As a society we would do well to reconsider our reduction of love to mere sentiment. That idea may sound romantic, but its effect is corrosive and destructive. If love is merely sentiment, then when we don't feel loving, we don't have to act loving anymore. Sentiment does not make promises or keep commitments. It merely describes the present. But if sentiment is all we have, how will we ever maintain a marriage, a family, a civil society? How do we do all that if all that motivates us is how we are feeling at the moment?

The Effect of the Atonement

There is a fourth thing to consider, and that's the *effect* of the atonement. What did Christ's death on the cross accomplish? If the only statement we had on the matter was John 3:16, we might think that Christ's sacrificial death made salvation possible but stopped short of actually accomplishing it. However, John 3:17 will not allow us to draw that conclusion: "For God did not send his Son into the world to condemn the world, but to save the world through him."

The purpose of God in sending Christ into the world was not to make salvation a mere possibility; much less was it to condemn the world. No, God sent his son to *save* the world, and salvation was accomplished through him, that is, through the death of Christ as a sacrificial substitute. Our faith does not accomplish our salvation; good works or viewing Christ as a model for our life does not rescue us from God's wrath. No, if anyone is saved, it is through him. Christ's death on the cross is effective, and it's effective in two ways, negatively and positively.

On the one hand, negatively, it endures God's condemnation so that we are not condemned. It exhausts God's wrath so that he is not angry anymore. It pays the penalty so that justice is satisfied and we are not punished. As a result of Christ's death on the cross, sinners do not perish.

On the other hand, though, positively, like the Israelites in the desert who looked to the bronze snake, we are given life, the "eternal life" Jesus talks about in John 3:15–16. What's eternal life? It's life that doesn't end. But more than that, when the Bible describes life as eternal, it's not talking so much about duration as about the quality or even the source of that life. Eternal life is the life of the age to come; it's the life of heaven, and it's found only in Christ. Not only will our current life come to an end, but while it lasts it is characterized by mortality—weakness and frailty, change and decay, shame and sin. But not so the life that is found in Christ! As Paul says in 1 Corinthians 15, the immortal life found in Christ will be characterized by glory and power. It will be imperishable and incorruptible, and though we don't know exactly what we will be like, we know that we will be like him, Jesus, the firstborn from the dead.

Christian, are you living with that life in view, or is your gaze distracted by the life of this world? Oh, that you could only see this world for the tawdry Vanity Fair that it is! Do you remember going to the carnival or the fair as a kid? It was amazing. But now think about taking your kids to the fair as an adult. Same thing, different eyes. There is much that is beautiful and sublime about this world, but in comparison to the life to come, we need to see this world as it is, through adult, not kids' eyes. Oh, Christians, set your eyes on heaven.

If you're not a Christian, I hope you understand that this is why we make such a big deal about Jesus. It's why we're always talking about him. I was recently talking with one of my family members who had stopped going to church. I asked him why. He said that he believed there were only about thirty sermons out there and that continuing to attend was only to hear those thirty sermons over and over again. We had a good conversation, but I found myself saying, "Oh, no, brother, there's really just one sermon." And it's all about

Jesus. Jesus is not just your role model or example. He's not there just to give you existential hope. We keep talking about Jesus because Jesus accomplished salvation. Jesus, and Jesus alone, saves us from God's wrath. Why would we talk about anything else?

This is why Christians go to every corner of the globe and risk their lives as missionaries. It's not that they have a death wish. It's not that they're culturally insensitive spiritual megalomaniacs. It is simply the certain knowledge that Jesus, and Jesus alone, saves sinners from the wrath of God and grants them eternal life. Having received that life, Christians hold their mortal lives cheap in comparison with the riches of seeing Christ glorified through the salvation of those who otherwise would not hear the message.

But it's not just as individuals that we do this. It is as churches that we spread this message of salvation through the death of Christ. As a church we want to be faithful to the only work he's given us. The world would applaud us if we would spend ourselves on social action. The world might even fund us if we'd commit our resources to the work the world deems worthy. But this we know: "God was reconciling the world to himself in Christ, not counting men's sins against them. And he has committed to us the message of reconciliation" (2 Cor. 5:19). Here is our proper work as a church. It's not that we don't care about those other things the world cares about. It is that like our self-giving, self-sacrificing God, we love the world, not the way it wants to be loved but the way it needs to be loved—through the appeal of the gospel of Jesus Christ.

I don't know if this story maps onto your story, whatever you think your story is. But I know this maps onto the Bible, and therefore it maps onto reality. This is what the world needs.

Our Response to the Atonement

This brings us to the final thing we learn from these verses, our *response* to the atonement. Look at John 3:18: "Whoever believes in him is not condemned, but whoever does not believe stands condemned already because he has not believed in the name of God's one and only Son."

The substitutionary death of Christ on the cross stands as a sharp division in the history of this world and in each of our lives. There is no neutral place to stand in relation to God and the cross. Jesus could not be clearer on this point. Like the bronze snake set up as a standard and sign in the middle of the camp, so the cross stands before you today. It is not an insurance policy that you can turn to when and if you decide you need it.

Do you understand that the cross would never have happened if this world wasn't already under God's judgment? There would have been no need for it. It is a declaration that you are already condemned and under the wrath of God for your rebellion and sin.

You can look away from the cross; you can refuse to acknowledge the truth about your own heart; you can continue to plead the merits of your own so-called good life; you can continue to convince yourself that believing in God is folly, that the dead don't rise and that there will never be a final accounting. But if you do, if you refuse to believe in the name of God's one and only Son, if you refuse to believe that he is who he said he is and that he did what he came to do, you will perish in your rebellion just as surely as those Israelites died in the desert. It is a death that will last for all eternity.

Or you can look to Jesus. You can believe that the death he died, he died for you. You can rest in the knowledge that his death satisfied the penalty you have earned. It doesn't matter how bad you've been or how great your sin is. Jesus says that whoever believes will not perish; whoever believes is not condemned. Everyone who believes is given eternal life. You are included in that wide-open *whoever* if you will turn away from your rebellion and put your faith in the God whose love is measured not by your feelings but by his actions—a love measured by the span of a wooden beam and nail-pierced hands. Oh, friend, look to Jesus today and be saved.

CHAPTER SEVEN

BETTER THAT ONE MAN DIE

John 11:47–52

MICHAEL LAWRENCE

Irony: the use of words to express something other than, and especially the opposite, of their literal meaning; often but not always, humorous.

Dramatic irony: the incongruity between a situation and the accompanying words or actions that is understood by the reader or audience, but not by the characters.

History is replete with irony. For example, isn't it ironic that Adolf Hitler was of Jewish ancestry? And isn't it ironic that Joseph Stalin first studied for the priesthood?

Politics and history aren't the only place where irony abounds, whether or not we see it. Take Christianity, for example. As a religion, Christianity is known for its concern for justice, so isn't it ironic that Christianity began with a tragic miscarriage of justice? An innocent man condemned and executed as an enemy of the state. But, of course, the irony deepens, for Christians actually claim that this injustice, Christ's death on the cross, actually secures the forgiveness of sinners, people who are not innocent, people who justly deserve God's judgment. In fact, this is a core tenet of Christian doctrine—the voluntary penal substitutionary death of Jesus Christ—which means, of course, that we now have the irony of one injustice securing a second apparent injustice. Christians assert all this with a perfectly straight face, apparently unaware or unconcerned with the irony of it all.

Well, not all Christians. Some Christians are deeply troubled by the irony present here, so troubled, in fact, that they simply deny the doctrine of penal substitution to be rid of the irony. Theologically liberal Christians have long been troubled by this teaching of the substitutionary death of Christ, but recently a number of theologically conservative evangelical pastors and theologians have begun to raise objections on precisely these grounds. Stuart Murray Williams, for example, simply asserts, "Punishing an innocent man—even a willing victim—is fundamentally unjust."[1] Tom Smail explains why, saying, "Guilt and punishment are not like fines, things that can be incurred by one person and settled by another. . . . Even though I, who am innocent of the offence, should be willing to bear the punishment you have incurred . . . it would be an unjust judge that would permit, let alone organize, such an illegitimate transfer."[2]

These critics confront us with the irony of traditional Christian teaching on the cross. But this is no laughing matter. For these critics, such irony at the very core of our faith is not just tragic; it's intolerable. Therefore, they suggest that we have badly misunderstood something, and, as a result, we should be talking about what Christ did on the cross in very different terms.

The questions these critics raise are important and, at least on this point, reasonable. Has the doctrine of penal substitution turned the primary demonstration of God's love for the world into a monumental miscarriage of justice? Is it time for us as evangelicals to reread our Bibles and reconsider our theology?

Another passage that speaks eloquently—and ironically—to this question is John 11:47–52:

> Then the chief priests and the Pharisees called a meeting of the Sanhedrin. "What are we accomplishing?" they asked. "Here is this man performing many miraculous signs. If we let him go on like this, everyone will believe in him, and then the Romans will come and take away both our place and our nation." Then one of them, named Caiaphas, who was high priest that year, spoke up, "You know nothing at all! You do not realize that it is better for you that one man die for the people than that the whole nation perish." He did not say this on his own, but as high priest that year he prophesied that Jesus would die for the Jewish nation, and not only

---

[1] Quoted in Steve Jeffery, Michael Ovey, and Andrew Sach, *Pierced for Our Transgressions: Rediscovering the Glory of Penal Substitution* (Wheaton, IL: Crossway, 2007), 241.
[2] Ibid.

for that nation but also for the scattered children of God, to bring them together and make them one.

In these verses, we come to the most ironic passage in a Gospel that is known for being full of irony. What we see is that in a world full of sin, there is no salvation that is not an ironic salvation. That's not, however, because one injustice secures another injustice. No, it's because of who needs saving and who must do the saving.

As we walk through this passage, which is all about the decision to execute an innocent man for the sake of others, we should appreciate the irony of it all, for it's in that irony that we come to see the meaning of Christ's death. Let's consider, then, three ironies that are present in this scene and what these ironies finally result in—a perfectly just but deeply ironic salvation.

The Dramatic Irony

First, consider the irony of the scene itself, the *dramatic* irony:

> Then the chief priests and the Pharisees called a meeting of the Sanhedrin. "What are we accomplishing?" they asked. "Here is this man performing many miraculous signs. If we let him go on like this, everyone will believe in him, and then the Romans will come and take away both our place and our nation." (vv. 47–48)

John 11 records for us the account of Jesus' raising Lazarus from the dead. Now Jesus had raised people from the dead before, but this event stands out. To begin with, Lazarus had been dead for four days, so there was no chance that this was merely some sort of resuscitation. Then there's the fact that Lazarus lived in Bethany, a village just outside of Jerusalem. Many of the people who lived in Jerusalem would have known the people who lived in Bethany, and vice versa. So this wasn't just making local news; this was making national headlines. Then there's the timing of it. The Passover was very close, which meant that not only is Lazarus's rising from the dead making news in Jerusalem, but Jerusalem is filling with people from around the country, and expectations are running high. Everyone is already wondering if this would be the year that Jesus would finally come out into the public and announce himself to be the Messiah. Of course, raising a dead man is only going to heighten that expectation.

Inevitably, someone makes sure that the Pharisees, the popular religious leaders, know what has happened. It's obvious, in light of such an event, that the Sanhedrin must gather, so that's exactly what they do. The Sanhedrin was the official and semi-autonomous governing body of the Jews under Roman rule. It was composed of Pharisees, along with the chief priests from leading families, and it was led by the high priest. As the text makes clear, there is no question in their minds about whether Jesus actually raised Lazarus. The chief priests and Pharisees have been talking to the people who saw it happen; for that matter, they've been talking to the people who have been talking to Lazarus! They know this is a real event. So the only question in their minds is the one they ask: "What are we accomplishing?" Literally, "What are we doing?" This is a question full of irony, because in the very asking of it they are admitting their ineptitude, their ineffectiveness in opposing Jesus. But why would anyone want to do that, oppose a man who can raise the dead?

Let's just step back a moment and think about this. A man comes along and raises the dead, and the question on the minds of the Sanhedrin is, "What are *we* doing?" It's not the right question. The question they should be asking is not, "What are *we* doing?" but "What is *he* doing?" And "Will he do it again?" And "Will he do it for *me*?" So the irony deepens.

The members of the Sanhedrin can clearly see that Jesus is no ordinary man. Though they've admitted that they don't know what they're doing, they know precisely what he's doing. They tell us he's doing miraculous signs. But in those words the irony deepens yet again. Many of the Old Testament prophets had done miracles, but the miracles that Jesus is doing, these are no run-of-the-mill miracles. No, they're *signs*. That's what the Sanhedrin calls them. What are signs? Signs were what God specifically gave Moses in Exodus 3 to prove that God had sent him to speak for God to the people. Signs are what the Messiah would do to demonstrate and prove his identity as the Son of God, sent from God. As John makes clear later on in his Gospel (20:31), these signs were recorded "that you may believe that Jesus is the Christ, the Son of God, and that by believing you may have life in his name." The Sanhedrin recognizes the signs, they recognize that Jesus is doing the signs, and they're worried. "Oh no, if he keeps this up, everyone will believe in him!"

Isn't that ironic? The whole point of the religious leadership of Israel was to care for the people, and the way they could have cared for them best was to teach them God's word and prepare them to recognize and accept the Messiah when he finally showed up. Now here comes Jesus performing the miraculous signs of the Messiah. He's claiming to be the Messiah. And they're *worried*. Shouldn't they be excited?

The explanation is found in the final phrases of John 11:48: "Everyone will believe in him, and then the Romans will come and take away both *our* place and *our* nation." Ah, so there we have it. In the Greek, the word "our" comes first. It is emphasized. The Sanhedrin is worried that if the people believe in Jesus, there might be a revolt, and then the Romans would come and crush it, and the result—and here's the rub—would be that they would lose their privileged place as rulers of the temple and of the nation.

Just to summarize then: a man shows up claiming to be the Messiah and doing miraculous signs to prove that he's the Messiah. The leaders, naturally, call a meeting. That makes sense. But the motivation for the meeting isn't that they're worried that the people aren't going to get it. They're worried that the people *are* going to get it, and if they do, these leaders will lose their place of privilege.

What we're seeing here in this scene is the irony of sin, for at the heart of sin lies self-interest. The fact is that regardless of how we're feeling about the Pharisees at this moment, we're not all that different from them. We reject God's standards for our lives because we're convinced that our own standards will lead to a better quality of life; in fact, we think we ought to be able to define that quality. We don't love our spouses, our friends, or our siblings as we should because, honestly, we're too busy loving ourselves, and that consumes most of our energy. We don't want to believe in Jesus because that would mean giving up control of our lives and therefore the freedom to pursue our self-interest.

This is what sin is all about. Sin is all about promising us satisfaction, but it never keeps its promises. It can't, because we weren't made to satisfy ourselves. No, all sin does is blind us to the truth, just as it seems to have blinded the Sanhedrin to what they were looking at. We were made to find our satisfaction in a loving relationship with God, but sin convinces us to spend our lives in a self-loving relationship with ourselves. The tragedy is that in the end it doesn't even work.

Sin leaves us bitter, empty, and filled with regret. Worst of all, it leaves us outside the love of God, the one thing that could have satisfied us. It leaves us exposed to his righteous anger that was provoked by our decision to love anything and everything except him, the one and only who was worthy of our love.

Christian, I wonder what self-interested lies you are tempted to believe today. Is it the lie of lust, the lie that says that satisfying your cravings—whether for sex, food, power, recognition, or whatever it is—will make you happy? Is it the lie of circumstances, that if only you were married, if only you were married to someone else, if only you had kids, if only you had different kids, if only you had a better job, a better house, a different career path, then you'd be fulfilled? Is it the satanic lie of doubt, that if you weren't a Christian, life would be better, or that if God really loved you, life would be better? Christian, stop measuring your life, stop ordering your life by this cramped and distorted ruler of self-interest. You were created to find your joy and meaning in something much bigger than yourself. Recognize your sin and confess it. Then set your eyes on Jesus, who alone will satisfy you.

If you're not a Christian, I wonder how your program of self-satisfaction is going. Is it going to survive the next election? How's it going to do if the economy stays sour? Will it survive the process of growing old, of becoming irrelevant through retirement or even of becoming a burden to your family? Jesus Christ raised the dead, and he got up from the dead himself. That's why he could say to Martha, Lazarus's sister, "He who believes in me will live, even though he dies; and whoever lives and believes in me will never die" (John 11:25–26). Does that sound like somebody who has your best interest in mind?

The Personal Irony

Second, consider the irony of the characters themselves, the *personal irony*: "Then one of them, named Caiaphas, who was high priest that year, spoke up, 'You know nothing at all! You do not realize that it is better for you that one man die for the people than that the whole nation perish'" (vv. 49–50). This man Caiaphas is the leader of the Sanhedrin, the high priest, so he obviously waited to speak last. Appointed by Pilate to be the high priest in the year AD 18, he would serve until AD 36, when both he and Pilate were deposed. The high priest had many responsibilities, but two of them stand out in our context.

First, the high priest had religious duties in the temple, foremost of which was that he alone was responsible to enter the Most Holy Place once a year and offer the sacrifice of atonement for the forgiveness of the sins of the whole nation. To enter into the Most Holy Place was a dangerous activity, for it was to enter into the very presence of God. For a week in advance, the high priest would go through an elaborate series of sacrifices and rituals designed to ceremonially cleanse him. He would also make sacrifices to atone for his sins and the sins of his family. Even after all that, Jewish tradition records that a rope would be tied to the high priest before he went into the Most Holy Place, which was separated by a curtain, lest God strike him dead so that his body would need to be dragged out. It was dangerous being a high priest. As the mediator between God and his people, the high priest was to be the very picture of holiness.

Second, as leader of the Sanhedrin, the high priest was something like the chief justice of the Supreme Court and the president, all rolled into one. It was his responsibility, finally, to see that that justice was both determined and executed.

So the Sanhedrin is in a state of panic. It looks like the Messiah has finally appeared, the people are going after him, and they are terrified at the prospect of losing their privileged position when the Romans react to the commotion. What does the high priest, this human picture of both God's holiness and God's justice, say to calm these guys down and bring them to their senses? Well, first he calls them idiots. What the NIV has translated politely as "You know nothing at all" is, literally, "You don't know nothing." In other words, "You guys are stupid." That's what he says—not exactly a model of leadership. Then he shares with them his considered judgment. He tells them they should condemn a man whom they know to be innocent and sacrifice him on the altar of political expediency. The word "realize" in verse 50 literally means "calculate." Never was there a crasser example of political calculation than this. They know Jesus had done nothing worthy of death; in fact later they'll have to bribe witnesses to get a guilty judgment. But it doesn't matter. They're convinced, and Caiaphas is convinced that if they sacrifice him for the people, not only will the nation avoid Roman destruction, but it will be better for *them* because they will get to keep their place of privilege.

So the supreme court of Israel is going to publicly and officially condemn Jesus to death, and the high priest of Israel understands himself to be sacrificing an innocent victim for the benefit of the people and for himself.

What could be more ironic? This man who should personify holiness is convincing others to conspire with him in unholy murder. The man who should stand for justice is arguing for injustice on the grounds of political expediency. But the irony goes even deeper. There is another unnamed character in these verses—Jesus, whom John tells us is the Lamb of God, who takes away the sins of the world. Hebrews tells us that he is the true High Priest, who alone mediates between God and man by offering himself as a perfect sacrifice for sinners. Jesus himself tells us in John 5 that he has been given all authority to judge, and that his judgment is just because he does not seek to please himself but to please his Father, who sent him.

So this is the scene: the Judge of the world condemned by a corrupt court. The true High Priest to be murdered by an unholy counterfeit. The Lamb of God sacrificed by the high priest as a political scapegoat.

People today might not like the idea of Christ's death on the cross being a penal substitution, but the fact is, that's exactly what the people who instigated his execution thought they were doing. Their logic is clear, even if corrupt. Either Jesus dies or the nation perishes under the Roman boot. If Jesus dies, the nation lives. So Jesus is publicly and judicially condemned and then suffers the punishment of that condemnation on a Roman cross. This happens so that the nation does not perish. That's what the people who accomplished this miscarriage of justice thought they were doing. Of course, after reading this, it's easy to think it should have been the despicable Caiaphas they strung up on the cross rather than the innocent Jesus, but then that wouldn't have accomplished anything, would it?

It's at just this point that the irony gets very personal. With which character do you most relate in these verses? If it's the innocent Jesus, then you have missed the point and the force of the irony, for we have far more in common with Caiaphas than we do with Jesus—not that we've corrupted justice to have an innocent man murdered, but that we've corrupted our lives so that we can serve ourselves rather than God. You and I need an effective sacrifice, one that will avert the condemnation of God that we so richly deserve because of our corruption. That means we need *spiritually* what Caiaphas thought he was providing *politically*. We need a substitute. We need a sacrifice that will bear our punishment in our stead in order to save us, not from political anger but from the judgment of God.

On the cross Jesus publicly bore the judgment we deserve. He was sacrificed not for his own sin, but rather to save others. In their own twisted way, even the people who put him to death understood that.

But, friends, cynicism gains no benefit from Christ's sacrifice, nor does self-sufficient pride or a vain hope that at least I'm not as bad, well, as Caiaphas, for example. No, the only people who benefit from this substitutionary sacrifice are those who put their faith in him, those who understand that "yes, Jesus is *my* substitute, for *my* sins, bearing *my* punishment, that *I* deserve."

Christian, I want you to consider the extraordinary love of God for you in this ironic reversal of roles. You and I have a hard time humbling ourselves just a little bit in order to love someone else. But Christ, the Judge of the world, the true High Priest, the spotless Lamb of God, submitted to the mockery of this small, corrupt, wicked man, for you. Would he have done this for any reason other than love?

Children, do you know what the love of God looks like for you in your life right now? I want to suggest to you that it looks like the humility of your parents. "The humility of my parents?" you ask. "I didn't know that my parents were humble." Well, think again. Do they cook for you? Do they wash your clothes? Do they give you rides? You think, "Yes, but those are things they're supposed to do." If you ask me, though, those sound like things a servant does. Perhaps there's more humility and more love in your parents than you realize. Children, God wants you to see that humility and that love in your parents and think of him and his Fatherly love for you in Christ. It's not a love that gives you everything you want, but it is a love that serves.

I wonder if, when you have read this passage previously, you saw all the various ironies that I've been pointing out. John doesn't spell them all out, but he assumes that his readers will see them. That's because he assumes we will be familiar with the Old Testament; that's where all the ironies really come from. That is why churches should be committed to preaching through the whole Bible—and every part of the Bible—on a regular basis.

A Divine Irony

Finally, consider the irony of the plot itself, which turns out to be a *divine irony*:

> He did not say this on his own, but as high priest that year he prophesied that Jesus would die for the Jewish nation, and not only for that nation but also for the scattered children of God, to bring them together and make them one. (vv. 51–52)

At the end of verse 50 it appears as if cynicism and corruption have won the day, but in the plainest of understatements John upends the entire scene with the opening phrase of verse 51, "He did not say this on his own." The plot is ultimately God's idea, not Caiaphas's. It is accomplishing God's purpose, not the Sanhedrin's.

There are a couple examples of the high priest prophesying in the Old Testament, but John's point is not that this was regular and to be expected. Rather, his point is that "that year" (v. 51), that fateful year in which the Messiah would be crucified, the high priest prophetically declared the meaning and the purpose of Christ's death. As one commentator put it, "When Caiaphas spoke, God was also speaking, even if they were not saying the same things." Here is divine irony. Caiaphas had declared that his fellow priests knew nothing. In fact, Caiaphas knew even less. Yet in a mocking judgment of this cynical, political priest, God causes him to speak the very words that would explain what was going on. He causes him to speak words that were truer than he knew.

This divinely inspired and orchestrated irony goes even further. Our passage is framed by the Greek word for "gather." We see it there in verse 47, where the Pharisees and chief priests "called a meeting"; literally, they "gathered" the Sanhedrin together, the purpose of which was to figure out how to save themselves, ultimately by killing Jesus. Then, at the end of our passage, John tells us what the true result of that first gathering was: Jesus' death was not only for Israel but also to bring, literally to "gather together," the scattered children of God and to make them one. John is talking here about the Gentiles, the nations of the world scattered and divided since the judgment of Babel and excluded from the promises of God since Abraham. But God had promised Abraham that through his seed all the scattered nations of the world would be blessed. So Jesus, the promised Son, comes to die not just for the ethnic children of Abraham but also for the scattered children of God among the nations, wherever they are. As Jesus himself said just one chapter earlier:

> The good shepherd lays down his life for the sheep. . . . I have other sheep that are not of this [Jewish] sheep pen. I must bring them also. They too will listen to my voice, and there shall be one flock and one shepherd. The reason my Father loves me is that I lay down my life—only to take it up again. No one takes it from me, but I lay it down of my own accord. (John 10:11, 16–18)

Caiaphas thought he had hatched quite a plot, but the fact is that he was just playing the bit part God had assigned him from eternity past. From eternity past, the triune God—Father, Son, and Spirit—had a plan of his own, one in which the Son, at just the right time, would take on human flesh so that he could represent sinners like you and me before the bar of God's justice. Then, having taken on our flesh, he lived a perfect life to demonstrate that justice had no claim on him, and then, as our text says repeatedly, he willingly died for the people, for the nation, for the scattered children of God.

If Jesus were an unrelated third party to God's just complaint against us, we might have reason to balk at the apparent injustice of his substitutionary death on the cross for us. But Jesus was no disinterested observer. As the second person of the Godhead in his divinity, he stood in perfect union with God, the very one who has the complaint. As fully man in his humanity, he stands in perfect solidarity with us, being like us in every way except without sin. And as the Scriptures make clear, through faith, sinners like you and me are brought into union with Christ so that our sins are credited to him, and his righteousness is credited to us. How does that happen? It happens through union with him, a union of love, like marriage. When you marry, you get all of your spouse's assets and all of your spouse's debts. Well, union with Christ is a union of love that faith accomplishes—a real union even as it is a spiritual union that we can't see. Here's how the apostle Paul put it in Romans 6, using baptism as a picture of our faith that creates this union:

> Don't you know that all of us who were baptized into Christ Jesus were baptized into his death? . . . If we have been united with him like this in his death, we will certainly also be united with him in his resurrection. For we

know that our old self was crucified with him so that the body of sin might be done away with, that we should no longer be slaves to sin. (vv. 3–6)

So Caiaphas was right after all. Either Jesus dies for us, bearing our sin and the punishment it deserves, or we die, bearing our own sin all the way to the bar of God's justice. How will we ever pay back to an infinitely holy God the debt that we owe? If we die outside of this union with Christ, it will be an eternal death in order to satisfy an infinite wrath.

Here is the irony of salvation: not that one injustice secures another, but that a holy God would take on himself the sins of his unholy people and pay the penalty of those sins through the death of his holy and only-begotten and well-beloved Son, all in order that unlovely people like you and me might become his beloved children. This is the irony of the gospel, and it confronts each one of us. What will you do with this irony? Will you simply add to the irony by walking away, having seen the sign? Having seen Christ crucified, will you simply walk away to pursue your own interest, though that pursuit is a pursuit unto death? Or will you die to your own interests, repent of your sins and believe in him, and so discover the true irony of Christianity? What an irony it is, that in death—in the death of Jesus Christ—we find what is best for us, for in his death we find life.

CHAPTER EIGHT

PROPITIATION

Romans 3:21–26

MARK DEVER

In his commentary on Romans, Cambridge professor C. H. Dodd wrote years ago that God's wrath meant "not a certain feeling or attitude of God towards us, but some process or effect in the realm of objective facts."[1] "'The Wrath of God,'" he says, "is taken out of the sphere of the purely mysterious, and brought into the sphere of cause and effect: sin is the cause, disaster the effect." Wrath describes "not . . . the attitude of God to man, but . . . an inevitable process of cause and effect in a moral universe."[2]

This kind of God without wrath has been promoted in many Christian institutions, including churches, for decades now. In a popular book published just a few years ago, the authors write, "The Bible never defines God as anger, power, or judgment—in fact it never defines him as anything other than love."[3] Many modern scholars, even at schools known as "evangelical," have suggested that emphasizing the "penal substitution" of Christ is a terrible idea. It seems inherently, they say, to contain these ideas of God and his character—wrath, anger, judgment—that are not noble. They object that an emphasis on Christ being condemned in our place in order to deliver us from God's wrath obscures other images that the Bible uses to describe what

[1]C. H. Dodd, *The Epistle of Paul to the Romans* (New York: Harper and Brothers, 1932), 22.
[2]Ibid., 23.
[3]Steve Chalke and Alan Mann, *The Lost Message of Jesus* (Grand Rapids, MI: Zondervan, 2003), 63.

Christ did for us on the cross. And besides, they argue, penal substitution is really an irrelevant idea today. People simply don't understand the idea of sacrifice in a world where few people have seen an animal being killed and offered to a deity. All this makes the good news not very good, these critics say, and in fact the idea of penal substitution seems to sanction a kind of divine child abuse.

Here's how Steve Chalke has put it. In *The Lost Message of Jesus* he quotes John 3:16 and then asks, "How then have we come to believe that at the cross this God of love suddenly decides to vent his anger and wrath on his own Son? The fact is that the cross isn't a form of cosmic child abuse—a vengeful Father, punishing his Son for an offence he has not even committed. Understandably, both people inside and outside of the Church have found this twisted version of events morally dubious and a huge barrier to faith."[4]

So what about it? Does the Bible teach that God planned to present his own Son as a sacrifice? If not, what was going on at the cross? If so, was that what Jesus wanted? Was it child abuse, or did he lay down his life willingly? What was the end to be accomplished? Why would God have done all this?

All these questions and more are addressed in the next passage of our study, Romans 3:21–26. As we move from the Gospels where the teaching of Jesus is recorded to the letters in the New Testament, you may be saying something like, "Well, we've done the best part. We've seen what Jesus himself taught." But I'd like to challenge that. Just as the Old Testament books of Exodus, Leviticus, and Isaiah were inspired by God's Spirit to teach us what he would do with his Son, so these New Testament letters are also inspired by God's Spirit to explain to us the significance of what he did at the cross.

This is the pattern we typically find in Scripture. God doesn't mutely act, like some pagan deity capriciously throwing down random lightning bolts. When the God of the Bible acts, he acts with purpose. God predicts, God acts, and then he interprets his actions. This is what we see with the great redemption episode in the Old Testament, the exodus. God predicted it, he taught about it, he did it, and then for centuries afterward he referred back to it, interpreting it and explaining its significance to the people of Israel. He did this with the great redemption episode in the New Testament as well, the cross.

[4]Ibid., 182.

He predicted it, did it, and then he interprets and explains it. This is what the letter to the Romans is doing.

Looking back to the beginning of the epistle, Paul has been building a careful and sustained argument about mankind's position before God. In 1:16–17 he announced the gospel, a summary announcement of what he was about to explain in the rest of the letter. Then from 1:18 through 3:20 Paul makes clear that God's wrath is revealed against all who sin, both Gentile and Jew. Thus Paul argues us all into his conclusion in 3:19–20:

> Now we know that whatever the law says, it says to those who are under the law, so that every mouth may be silenced and the whole world held accountable to God. Therefore no one will be declared righteous in his sight by observing the law; rather, through the law we become conscious of sin.

So Paul has set up the problem: no one will be declared righteous by observing the law. If anyone is to be declared righteous before God, it will have to be otherwise than by doing good and observing the law. It will require this gospel that he announced back in 1:16.

Leon Morris called Romans 3:21–26 "possibly the most important single paragraph ever written."[5] It is the heart of Paul's great letter to the saints in Rome, and in it he describes the way of salvation. Here in the heart of Romans, in one of the greatest passages in all of Scripture, we see how the one triune God would save us:

> But now the righteousness of God has been manifested apart from the law, although the Law and the Prophets bear witness to it—the righteousness of God through faith in Jesus Christ for all who believe. For there is no distinction: for all have sinned and fall short of the glory of God, and are justified by his grace as a gift, through the redemption that is in Christ Jesus, whom God put forward as a propitiation by his blood, to be received by faith. This was to show God's righteousness, because in his divine forbearance he had passed over former sins. It was to show his righteousness at the present time, so that he might be just and the justifier of the one who has faith in Jesus.

There are three specific questions we should ask of this text.

---

[5] Leon Morris, *The Epistle to the Romans* (Grand Rapids, MI: Eerdmans, 1988), 173.

What Is Our Situation?

First, what is our situation? In a word, it is dire—very bad. Chapters 1 to 3 have shown that everyone is in trouble, separated from God and sinful. We are all spiritually enslaved, spiritually dead, and spiritually condemned. As Paul says here in verse 23, "All have sinned and fall short of the glory of God." Look back through the preceding chapters and you find lists of godlessness and wickedness that we know, if we are honest and if we know ourselves well enough, describe us— judgmentalism and hypocrisy, faithlessness and unrighteousness, sin and all-around rejection of God. It's all there.

This letter makes it clear that we are depraved. Indeed the whole of the Scriptures warns us that we have rejected God with our hands and in our hearts, by what we do and what we love. Eugene Peterson put it this way in *The Message*: we've "proved that we are utterly incapable of living the glorious lives God wills for us." There is something in us that resents God and that resents being told what to do. You know that is true. Look at your own life. Look at the way marketers appeal to you; they depend on it.

Recently in *The New Yorker* magazine, for example, I ran across a BMW advertisement that amounted to a little booklet glued into the pages with "No" written across it, and of course the booklet was sealed. What do you think I immediately wanted to do? I had the booklet lying on the table of my study when one of our interns walked in. He saw the booklet immediately and lunged forward to seize it and open it just before I stopped him and said, "No, it is a sermon illustration." I still haven't opened that little booklet. I'm assuming it will try to sell me some neat BMW car. But the ad makers at BMW are tapping into something more there than mere curiosity. There is something in us that doesn't want to be told no.

The etymology of the word used for *sin* here is "missing the mark." It refers not merely to what *we* want to hit but to what *God* calls us to hit. Many Christian pulpits today have watered down the reality of sin, saying that sin is simply a failure to reach full human potential. It is true as far as it goes; sin causes one not to reach full human potential, but it is still a lousy definition of sin. Sin is not fundamentally about our failing to reach our potential; it is about our relationship with God. Sin is about what we have done against God, not just against his laws but against him. We have rejected God and so no longer relate to him as our loving Father. Because God is good and holy, we now face his opposition and his just wrath against us for our sins.

People are sinners, individually and universally. We have been removed from God's presence; he is invisible to us. His glories and goodness are gone from our experience, and the result is the ravages of the fall: strife and war, ruin and misery, an eagerness for hatred even to the point of murder. This is the dark picture of the human situation.

I wonder if you think I'm overdrawing the situation. If you're not a Christian, all this may surprise you. You might think Christians are just sweet people and that they think of everybody as basically good. But they do not think that way because that's not the way the Bible presents it. We don't see the Bible teaching that everybody is basically good. Have you thought you deserve good things to happen to you? Well, that is not how the Bible presents it. I once was talking to a Hare Krishna outside a store called Marks and Spencer in the center of Cambridge, England. The man was standing outside trying to sell a magazine. When he offered it to me, I said, "No thank you."

"Why not?" he asked. "It is for good Christian camp work."

I said, "I don't think what it is saying is true."

He seemed surprised by this, and asked, "You don't think it is true? Why don't you think it is true?"

I said, "Well, I am a Christian." He seemed kind of relieved at that and replied, "Well, we are Christians too. We believe in Jesus."

"Yeah," I said, "but you believe in Jesus like my Hindu friends believe in Jesus—that God is in everything, right?"

"Sure."

"No, no," I replied, "we believe that Jesus is the one and the only true God. In that sense, you are totally unlike us in that. But don't worry," I continued. "If you and I both had megaphones and could tell the people around here what we both believe, and if they didn't know that I'm a Christian and you're a Hare Krishna, they'd probably mostly agree with you."

"What do you mean?" he asked.

"You think that people are basically good, right?"

"Sure, of course."

"Well, I think people are basically bad." This intrigued him, so I continued: "I believe that people have been made in God's image, but we've all turned in on ourselves. We serve ourselves. We reject

God by our actions. That is the truth of all of our lives and the lives of everybody on this planet." ·

The Hare Krishna and I kept talking a little bit longer, and he soon realized that I wasn't going to buy the magazine. But the longest bit of the conversation was about this idea of the basic sinfulness of human beings. He was surprised by that. He thought Christianity teaches that people are basically good. But Christianity doesn't teach that at all. Christianity tells you the truth about your heart in a way no other religion will. This is the strange truth about Christianity.

This is why, by the way, Christianity has tended to be a force for limited government powers, not in the sense of small-government versus big-government ideology but in the sense of preventing the concentration of power in the hands of sinful individuals. This kind of thinking has a long pedigree in Christian thought, from Calvin's "middle-magistrate" to Samuel Rutherford's book *The Law Is King*. Christianity is suspicious of giving much authority to a single sinful individual precisely because of this understanding of depravity. Moreover, Christianity is in that sense anti-utopian. It is not Christianity but rather various atheistic philosophies that have voiced the utopian lies to our world in the last century. As Christians we believe that no job, no relationship, no amount of money, no economy, no president will ever end the fallen state of our world. Good can be done, even great good. But until Christ returns, this world will always be fallen.

So, given that the Bible paints such a dim view of this world, is there any hope? Yes! It's seen in Romans 3:19–20:

> Now we know that whatever the law says, it says to those who are under the law, so that every mouth may be silenced and the whole world held accountable to God. Therefore no one will be declared righteous in his sight by observing the law; rather, through the law we become conscious of sin. But now . . .

But now! It's a new day. Up until this point Paul has described us in desperate terms, even more accurate than they are painful:

> They were filled with all manner of unrighteousness, evil, covetousness, malice. They are full of envy, murder, strife, deceit, maliciousness. They are gossips, slanderers, haters of God, insolent, haughty, boastful, inventors of evil, disobedient to parents, foolish, faithless, heartless, ruthless. (Rom. 1:29–31 ESV)

But now, the light of God's hope cleaves the dark sky of our own sin. After the darkness of 3:20, a lightning strike of grace has lifted forever the night of our condemnation.

Paul emphasizes that this new day, this new hope is "apart from law" (3:21). That way, the way of righteousness by law-keeping, has been blocked up. That's what the whole letter has shown so far. John Bunyan wrote in *Pilgrim's Progress* of a character named Mr. Legality, who, before he goes to the Wicket Gate, goes over to Mount Sinai, which looks very low from a distance and thus an easy way to the Celestial City. But as he treads this hill, it seems to get steeper and steeper until finally it seems to even bend over on him, and there is no way forward. The law is here to show us what we cannot do. It is here to drive us out of ourselves and show us that we need another way.

Friends, hear this carefully. Before we go on to investigate the way of salvation in this passage we need to know that there is *no* salvation apart from despair of our self-righteousness. If you are treasuring hope of your own righteousness before God, you have no room in your heart to treasure the righteousness of Christ as your only hope. Christ is not one among many options. You cannot have him as just one part of a mixed portfolio of religious trust. The only way to have faith in Christ is to realize your complete and utter need of him. We cannot be saved until we realize this. Jesus cannot be our help until we realize we are helpless. We will not see him until we acknowledge our spiritual blindness. We will not hear him until we know our rejection of his Words. We will not live until we have known and acknowledged our spiritual deadness. Conviction of sin always precedes conversion. D. Martyn Lloyd-Jones spoke about this:

> "But now" . . . is the essence of the Christian position; this is how faith answers the accusations of the Law, the accusations of conscience, and everything else that would condemn and depress us. These are indeed very wonderful words, and it is most important that we should lay hold of them and realize their tremendous importance and their real significance.[6]

Like the blind man, we Christians can say, "I was blind *but now* I see" (John 9:25). The result is that we live lives at work distinct from those still on the other side of the "but now." We Christians have this

---

[6]D. Martyn Lloyd-Jones, *An Exposition of Romans 3:20–4:25: Atonement and Justification* (Edinburgh: Banner of Truth, 1998), 27.

in common: we recognize that our greatest need has nothing to do with money or a job or our kids; it has to do with our sin. Polls subdivide the electorate every which way looking for votes, but Christianity says that we're all subsets of the one great set we inhabit together. We are sinners. We are single sinners, married sinners, sinners with kids, male sinners, female sinners—but all still sinners. Christ finds those who know that. Christians are those who *know* they are sinners and have confessed it and gone to Christ for salvation.

We outgrow many things as we age—habits, clothes, hobbies, or interests—but we never outgrow our sin. We do not escape our sin by growing up. We grow out of a habit or clothes, but we need another way to escape the grasp of sin, and that's what Paul writes about in this paragraph.

Well, if that is our situation by nature, and if there is now hope, what is that hope?

How Can We Be Saved?

The second question we should ask of our text in Romans 3 is how can we be saved? Paul has three things to say about this.

First, we can be saved only by God. God alone can save us, and he does so through his own righteousness. Paul refers in verses 21 and 22 to a "righteousness from God." That means that if you and I are saved, it is only because of God and his righteousness. "But now a righteousness from God, apart from law, has been made known, to which the Law and the Prophets testify."

The righteousness we are given in the gospel is from God. God has provided for us his own righteousness. Paul has already mentioned this in his gospel summary: "For in it the righteousness of God is revealed from faith for faith" (1:17 ESV). Before, there was the wrath of God revealed against the wickedness of men, *but now* there is the righteousness of God made known. This is the good news, that there is this righteousness from God that has been made known to us, supremely, in the life, death, and resurrection of Jesus Christ.

Paul says here also that this righteousness has been made known "apart from law." What law? Well, in 3:19–20 Paul is clearly referring to the first five books of the Bible (though earlier in 2:14–15 he showed that the naturally revealed law in everyone's heart, the moral law, also reflects God's character). Paul isn't referring to God saving us by a righteousness that is our own because we obeyed. No, this is a righteousness from God, and it is one "to which the Law and the Prophets testify."

Scripture tells us what this righteousness is to which the Law and the Prophets testify. It is the righteousness of the Lord Jesus Christ—his perfect life and his substitutionary, sin-bearing death. Peter preaches this throughout the early chapters of Acts. He tells Cornelius in Acts 10:43: "All the prophets testify about him that everyone who believes in him receives forgiveness of sins through his name." The law couldn't bring us righteousness, but it did bear witness to the one who would.

This is all by God's grace. Salvation is all of grace. You see that wonderful repetition of ideas in Romans 3:24: "freely by his grace. . . ." This righteousness, this salvation, is a gift. It is received only by God's grace.

Sometimes people will, in ignorance, represent the Christian gospel as a loving Son persuading an unwilling Father to show mercy. But that is not what the Bible teaches. God the Father was not reluctant. He planned our salvation and initiated it. He acted. It was his gift. It was only by his grace. God—Father, Son and Holy Spirit—is the author of our salvation. No one else could save us, and all others who claim to be able to save us from God's wrath, lie. God alone can save us from his wrath against us because of our sin. If we're to be saved, it must be by God's grace and according to his plan. As Paul says here in verse 25, it was *God* who presented Christ as a sacrifice of atonement.

We need God's grace. No nationality, no ethnicity, no vote, no gender, no marital status will ever entitle any of us to salvation. Parents, how are you modeling God's grace to your children? Are they seeing your dependence upon God, your awareness that you've not *earned* your relationship with God? Pray that God will help you model his relationship to your children by your relationship to them. We need to reflect the gospel.

Moreover, shouldn't thinking about the gracious nature of our salvation give us confidence? If salvation is based on what *we* do, we have reason to fear because we know we aren't doing it well enough, but if it is based on what *God* does, what a great ground for confidence and joy we have. We don't believe in some religion where we think we're always treading on the verge of hell. We're saved by God's grace toward us.

This should also make us quick to forgive. If God's Holy Spirit has convicted you of your unholiness, and if you have some sense of what you deserve and of how different what you're getting is from what you deserve, then shouldn't that quicken your spirit to be kind and forgiving toward others for their much smaller transgressions against you? The merciful are usually those who have themselves known mercy.

Knowing all this should also encourage humility. People who think they save themselves by their church attendance or their financial giving or their progressive attitudes or their careful honesty are proud people. They are people who don't know that salvation can never come by anything they do. I love the questions Paul put to the Corinthians: "Who makes you different from anyone else? What do you have that you did not receive? And if you did receive it, why do you boast as though you did not?" (1 Cor. 4:7).

One reason we should be excited as we sing words such as "Son of God, slain for us. What a love! What a cost! We stand forgiven at the cross" is that we don't deserve that forgiveness. There may be people with high-paying jobs who are worth every cent of their salary, who have *earned* what they get. But Christians are not a meeting of the religious elite, the moral minority who have earned their place in the pew. They are those who are properly astounded "that for *my* sake my Lord should take frail flesh and die!"

We can only be saved from the penalty our sins deserve by the very one we've sinned against—God himself.

Second, we can be saved only through Christ. God has set forth Christ alone to save us. So in Romans 3:24 we see the language of Christ's redemption of us: "by his grace through *the redemption* that came by Christ Jesus." This is the language of the marketplace, buying and selling. People in this age would talk about redeeming someone (or oneself) out of slavery. God speaks of redeeming Israel out of bondage in Egypt. Here in verse 24 it appears that God has graciously acted to save us by redeeming us in Christ.

There is also in verse 24 the language of justification: "justified freely by his grace through the redemption that came by Christ Jesus." Lloyd-Jones called this verse "a perfect synopsis of the Christian faith."[7] God saves us by justifying us—that is, declaring us to be righteous—in

7Ibid., 54.

Christ and because of Christ. This is the language of the law court and of relationships.

The language of justification has been fraught with controversy in the history of Christianity. When Paul says here that Christians are "justified," some have thought that he meant that we've been made righteous in ourselves with his help to be good, but that misses the point entirely. In Romans 4:5 Paul is explicit that the God who saves us is the "God who justifies the wicked." When Paul writes here of our being "justified freely by his grace through the redemption that came by Christ Jesus," he means not our *becoming* in and of ourselves righteous but our being *regarded* by God as righteous, *declared* righteous. This justification through Christ is a judicial pardon for all our sins. Because we are clothed in his righteousness through Christ, we are justified. It is God's positive declaration that we are pardoned from our sins.

It's even more than that. It is a positive declaration that restores us to fellowship with a holy God. Marcus Loane, a former archbishop of Sydney, puts it this way: "The voice that spells forgiveness will say: 'You may go; you have been let off the penalty which your sins deserve.' But the verdict which means acceptance [justification] will say: 'You may come; you are welcome to all my love and my presence.'"[8]

Brothers and sisters, if you are justified, you understand that it's not that God has merely let you off because the penalty has been paid, but that there are no longer *any* grounds for him to condemn you. All those grounds have been met and exhausted by Christ. Therefore, do not live trembling on the verge of hell. Live trembling on the verge of heaven, knowing that there is no longer any charge to be made against you, because Christ has taken it all. The punishment for your sin has already happened, and it has happened to Christ.

When the Protestant Reformers recovered this biblical gospel, the Church of Rome feared that if people began to believe that, they would live immoral lives. But that's only a danger if you think morality is driven by fear and guilt. The fact is that there is another morality, the one we find in the Bible. It is not self-centered and fearful but God-centered and hopeful; we run toward the one in whose image we are made. When our holiness is given to us in Christ, when his

[8]Quoted in John Stott, *Romans: God's Good News for the World* (Downers Grove, IL: InterVarsity, 1995), 110.

righteousness has been given to us as our own, then we run with great hope toward this one in whom we desire to spend all our days and in whom we place all our hopes. This is the basis for our Christian lives. Another way to say this is that justification marks the *initiation* of our sanctification, of our being made holy. In fact, this is the great surprise of Romans 4:5: "God who justifies the wicked." People sometimes say that God will make us righteous until we are finally righteous *enough*, and then he will justify us. But thank God that is not what the Bible teaches us. There is no hope for us there. Our hope is in the fact that, as Paul says in 5:6, Christ died for the ungodly.

In 3:25 Paul tells us exactly how that happened: "God presented him as a sacrifice of atonement, through faith in his blood." Blood is clearly central in Paul's thoughts about Jesus. Blood stands for Jesus' death, of course, and it is Christ's death that is said here to be the object of our faith. Death, according to Romans, comes as a result of sin. In Romans 1:32 Paul said that those who sin "deserve death." So Jesus' death is here thought to be deserved—a punishment for sin. But not his own sins. Jesus Christ had no sins. He lived just as the Father told him to live. No, those sins for which he died are *ours*. He bore *our* penalty. He was our substitute when he died on the cross, condemned by God for our sins.

This sacrifice of atonement is called in some translations "propitiation," a form of the word that was used for the cover of the ark of the covenant. This was the place where God's wrath would be propitiated—assuaged, satisfied—by the sprinkling of the blood of the lamb. The point is that Christ's death removed the penalty of our sin by removing the wrath of God. Our sin is not the primary object of this sacrifice. It is not merely an expiation, or covering of sin, that takes place. No, the main point of Christ's sacrifice is not covering over our sins, though he does that, but rather the satisfaction of God's right wrath against us because of our sins. That's what the word *propitiation* indicates—the satisfaction of God's holy anger against us. This wasn't just Paul's idea. Jesus taught his disciples about the prophecies of the Suffering Servant in Isaiah 53 being fulfilled in his death: "The LORD has laid on him the iniquity of us all" (v. 6). "Yet it was the LORD's will to crush him and cause him to suffer . . . the LORD makes his life a guilt offering" (v. 10a). "He bore the sin of many" (v. 12). That's what a propitiation is. It is a sacrifice that satisfies God in his wrath, thereby turning aside the wrath of God from us.

Contrary to what Professor Dodd taught, there is nothing dishonorable about God's being wrathful. In fact, if he were not wrathful against sin, we would question whether he is personally good. What would it mean for him to say that he is committed to oppose evil if he refused to judge it? But God is good, and he is opposed to evil, and it is personal. That commitment is shared by the Son, who willingly gave himself up.

Once again, do you see God's grace provided for us? We don't work to appease God's wrath, as if trembling next to a volcano and searching around the village for something we can give to appease the gods. That is not what the sacrifice of atonement is about. No, according to the Bible, God himself provides the way. God has done it himself. It says in Romans 3:25, "*God* presented him as a sacrifice of atonement." There is no pagan idea here of trying to find a way to sate the rumbling god of the volcano. John Stott said:

> It would be hard to exaggerate the differences between the pagan and the Christian views of propitiation. In the pagan perspective, human beings try to placate their bad-tempered deities with their own paltry offerings. According to the Christian revelation, God's own great love propitiated his own holy wrath through the gift of his own dear Son, who took our place, bore our sin and died our death. Thus God himself gave himself to save us from himself.[9]

So, Jesus Christ is our substitute. He took our penalty. He was bound that we might be freed. He was condemned that we might be accepted. He was killed that we might live.

I say "we," but of whom is this true? Who are the "we"? Most clearly, those who believe.

Third, we can be saved only through faith. The benefits of Christ's life and death come to us only through faith in Christ. Verse 22 says it: "through faith in Jesus Christ." Lloyd-Jones said of this faith: "It is this protest, it is this standing up in spite of everything that may be said against us on earth or in hell. We say, 'No, no one can finally convict me because of my new position in Christ Jesus. "But now" I am no longer in condemnation; I was once there but I am no longer there.'"[10]

[9]Stott, *Romans*, 115.
[10]Lloyd-Jones, *Exposition of Romans*, 28.

So, what is the nature of this faith? Surely it includes knowledge *about* something and also *agreeing* that something is so, but even further, it must include a *trusting* in that which we know to be so. Faith looks to Christ, believes him, and *trusts* him. Faith doesn't save us; it doesn't cause our salvation. Anytime we speak of "being saved by faith," we are, at best, speaking in a kind of theological shorthand. What we mean is "faith in Christ." Faith is the instrument that God uses to save us through Christ.

Note in verse 22 what comes through faith—righteousness. "This righteousness from God comes through faith in Jesus Christ to all who believe." Our need is not merely to have the record of our sins canceled, but to have a positive righteousness in order to be united to God again and be in fellowship with him. This comes through faith in Jesus Christ, or "in his blood," as Paul says in verse 25: "God presented him as a sacrifice of atonement, through faith in his blood. . . . He did it to demonstrate his justice at the present time, so as to be just and the one who justifies those who have faith in Jesus." This makes it clear that central to saving faith in Christ is faith in his blood. Central to the saving mission of Jesus Christ was his death on the cross. As we've seen, it's through Christ's death on the cross that God propitiates himself, and justifies and redeems us.

What a good thing this is for us, because it means that God saves *whoever* has faith in Jesus. There is no other qualification, no other work, no other standard to be met. This is Paul's point in the sentence that stretches over verses 22 to 24: "This righteousness from God comes through faith in Jesus Christ to *all who believe*. There is no difference, for all have sinned and fall short of the glory of God, and are justified freely by his grace through the redemption that came by Christ Jesus."

The amazing news here is that—after centuries of deliberate distinction—the way of salvation for Jew and Gentile was the same. There would be no distinction according to religious background or ethnicity, nationality or politics. Salvation, Paul says, comes to all who believe. Thus this call to believe is both exclusive (it is only through faith in Jesus) but also wonderfully inclusive, for it is offered to all. There are no other qualifications; you must simply believe in Jesus Christ and in his death for you on the cross. Believe, and you shall be saved, justified, and redeemed.

My non-Christian friend, this is a call for you. God has made you in his image, to know him, but you have sinned against him. What you read at the earlier part of this chapter is a description of your life and mine, and yet God, in his great mercy, sent his Son to live the life that we should have lived and to die the death that we should have died. And he raised him from the dead, showing that he has accepted the sacrifice, that his wrath was assuaged for all who would repent of their sins and trust in Christ, who would turn and have faith in him. Now, that is what you should do. You should turn from your sins and trust in Christ. You are not getting a good return on your sins now, and you will get a worse return on them in the future. Turn from your sins, trust in Christ. Believe him, have faith in him, and you will be saved.

Christ is the object of our faith, and faith can only come by hearing about him. It doesn't have to be in a church gathering. The Ethiopian governmental official was reading Isaiah 53 in his chariot when Philip shared this message with him. Saul was walking on the road to Damascus. Cornelius was sitting in his own home, and Lydia was in an outdoor Jewish female prayer meeting in Greece. Whatever the setting, whoever the messenger, it is *this* message you must hear and believe if you would be saved from your sins. This is the message that creates faith.

Brothers and sisters, do you want your coworkers to come to Christ? How will they do so if you never share this message with them? How will they have saving faith in Christ if no one ever tells them about Christ?

Is faith in Christ the most important thing in your life? Would your kids say so? Would your parents say so? Or do you have some other circumstance you've elevated to that place—some friendship or job or spiritual practice or good work?

If you want to give your faith a practical workout, relate more closely to those with whom you have Christ in common, and not much else. Figure out how you can more naturally reach out and care for Christians who are poorer than you. Don't be made nervous by their poverty in some worldly way. Reach out and care; include them more normally in your life. Invite those whose education intimidates you to do something with you and your friends. You might be surprised how much they enjoy doing it with you, commonly in Christ. American members, reach out to other members from Asia or Latin

America or Africa. Are the people you invite to your home for meals all white, single people? Friends, the fellowship we have together in Christ is sweet. Taste it and see.

That is the answer to our main question, "How can we be saved?" Only by trusting in Christ, or, as the Reformation put it, by grace alone through faith alone in Christ alone.

> Nothing in my hand I bring,
> Simply to the cross I cling;
> Naked, come to Thee for dress;
> Helpless look to Thee for grace;
> Foul, I to the fountain fly;
> Wash me, Savior, or I die!

Why Did God Save Us?

The third question we should ask of our text in Romans 3 is why did God save us? Some critics see the whole idea of Christ dying to satisfy God's wrath as irrelevant in the modern world, or even as making a mockery of Jesus' teaching to love our enemies. Here's what Paul said about it:

> God presented him as a sacrifice of atonement, through faith in his blood. He did this to demonstrate his justice, because in his forbearance he had left the sins committed beforehand unpunished—he did it to demonstrate his justice at the present time, so as to be just and the one who justifies those who have faith in Jesus. (vv. 25–26)

There was no adequate retribution for the sins God's people committed before Christ's death. They were in that sense unpunished, and God's having left these sins unpunished may have been used by some as evidence for a false conclusion that God would never punish sin. But in Christ's death on the cross, God was offering the solution to the problem of the fall. He was solving the ancient riddle of how he as a holy and good God could show mercy. Do you remember how it was stated in Exodus 34, at the end of the golden calf debacle?

> Then the LORD came down in the cloud and stood there with [Moses] and proclaimed his name, the LORD. And he passed in front of Moses, proclaiming, "The LORD, the LORD, the compassionate and gracious God, slow to anger, abounding in love and faithfulness, maintaining love to thousands,

and forgiving wickedness, rebellion and sin. Yet he does not leave the guilty unpunished." (vv. 5–7)

How could that be? How could God "forgive wickedness, rebellion and sin" and yet "not leave the guilty unpunished"? This really is the riddle of the Old Testament, indeed of the ages. Here in Romans we learn the answer of how God could save us, yet in a way that is consistent with his character. At the cross of Christ, God demonstrates his justice. He *is* good. He *will* take vengeance. No sin will go unpunished. Yet at the same time, at the cross God shows himself to be full of mercy, the one who is just and the justifier of those who have faith in Jesus.

We see in this our salvation and in the salvation of others we love. God is in all this for our salvation, yes, but he is also about something far larger—demonstrating himself. He has a larger end in mind—the display of his character in his creation, the theater of his splendor and glory. The fruit of God's Spirit in us is meant to confirm us in our faith and to show the truth to the universe around us:

What if God, choosing to show his wrath and make his power known, bore with great patience the objects of his wrath—prepared for destruction? What if he did this to make the riches of his glory known to the objects of his mercy, whom he prepared in advance for glory—even us, whom he also called, not only from the Jews but also from the Gentiles? (Rom. 9:22–24)

We Christians are walking demonstrations to the world of God's character, of his justice and mercy. Jesus said, "All men will know that you are my disciples, if you love one another" (John 13:35). We have his character stamped on us. We're made by it. His Spirit re-creates it in us. That's why Paul instructed the Philippians to "do everything without complaining or arguing, so that you may become blameless and pure, children of God without fault in a crooked and depraved generation, in which you shine like stars in the universe as you hold out the word of life" (Phil. 2:14–16).

This is why God does everything he does. God acts in order to get glory for himself, to make the truth about himself known. Throughout the book of Ezekiel, again and again the Lord says that he has done something so that all will know that he is the Lord. We read that God's "intent was that now, through the church, the manifold wisdom of God should be made known to the rulers and authorities in the heavenly realms, according to his eternal purpose which he accomplished in Christ Jesus our Lord" (Eph. 3:10–11). Have you realized that all this is going on in the church—in plain old you and me? Well, it is, because the real God is personal. His plans involve his person. His opposition to sin and evil is real and personal, and God desires to be and to be *known* to be, both just *and* the one who justifies those who have faith in Jesus.

CHAPTER NINE

DELIVERED OVER TO DEATH FOR OUR SINS

Romans 4:25

Mark Dever

Polly Toynbee, one of the most well-known opinion columnists in Great Britain and leader of the British Humanist Association, reviewed the 2005 movie *The Chronicles of Narnia: The Lion, the Witch and the Wardrobe.* In an article subtly entitled, "*Narnia* Represents Everything That Is Most Hateful about Religion," she stated, "Of all the elements of Christianity, the most repugnant is the notion of the Christ who took our sins upon himself and sacrificed his body in agony to save our souls." Then she adds the question: "Did we ask him to?"[1]

Like Polly Toynbee, today many people say they don't care so much about fussy old doctrines. They want experience, a church that's lively and friendly. They want a community of people that they can belong to, not doctrine. So we relax our grip, thinking that the main thing is belonging, not believing. Indeed, whole theologies arise that encourage us in our relaxation.

Even many pastors are diminishing the importance of doctrine today. For example, Rob Bell suggests in his book *Velvet Elvis* that the important thing is not doctrines (such as the virgin birth, he says) but living like Jesus lived.[2] Thinking that certain doctrines are essential, he argues, diminishes God. Such defensive confidences make God seem small and limited, and as if he is reliant on them.

[1]*The Guardian*, Monday, December 5, 2005.
[2]Rob Bell, *Velvet Elvis: Repainting the Christian Faith* (Grand Rapids, MI: Zondervan), e.g., 26–27.

Certain doctrines are treated with more than indifference; they're met with opposition and even contempt. That's not just by humanists like Ms. Toynbee but by those who call themselves Christian pastors. One pastor, in his recent book *Reimagining Christianity,* writes of a "thread of just criticism" that "addresses the suggestion implicit in the cross that Jesus' sacrifice was to appease an angry God. Penal substitution was the name of this vile doctrine. I don't doubt for one moment the power of sin and evil in the world or the power of sacrificial love as their antidote and the peculiar power of the cross as a sign of forgiveness and restoration, but making God vengeful, all in the name of justice, has left thousands of souls deeply wounded and lost to the Church forever."[3]

What do we say to all this? Is the doctrine of penal substitution—the teaching that Christ bore the penalty for our sins in our stead—really a "vile doctrine?" We turn now to Romans 4:25: "He was delivered over to death for our sins and raised to life for our justification."

In the first three chapters of Romans, Paul has shown that Jew and Gentile alike are all condemned before God because of sins. There is no way we will be declared righteous before God—no way we will avoid condemnation—by our actions. By 3:20, Paul has shut us up to a hopeless existence if salvation is based on our own actions and righteousness. But then verse 21 of chapter 3 begins, "But now . . ." Then Paul explains how now, apart from the law, God has presented Jesus Christ as a propitiation, a sacrifice of atonement, to assuage his right wrath against us because of our sins and to restore us to a right relationship with him. All this will take place if we will trust in Jesus, believing in him and the promises of God.

Then Paul makes the argument here in chapter 4 that all this is nothing new. It's always been the case that justification, being declared right before God, has been by faith. Even Abraham, the father of the faithful, was justified through faith, not works. Paul quotes Genesis to prove his point. Abraham believed God, and God credited it to Abraham as righteousness. Thus, Paul has called the best witness of all, Abraham, the progenitor of all the Jews, as an example of justification by faith alone. Then he summarizes this powerful chapter in

[3]Alan Jones, *Reimagining Christianity: Reconnecting Your Spirit without Disconnecting Your Mind* (Hoboken, NJ: Wiley, 2004), 168.

verse 25: "He [Jesus Christ] was delivered over to death for our sins and was raised to life for our justification."

This is such a concise statement of truth that many biblical scholars have wondered if it might actually be an early creed or part of an early creed with which the Roman Christians were familiar and which Paul here quotes. The verse is fairly straightforward, containing five basic facts about Jesus and his death and resurrection.

Jesus Was Killed

The first fact is that Jesus was killed. This is the most basic fact of all, and you have to begin here. There are plenty of people in the world who assume that Jesus, Socrates, Buddha, Confucius, and Mohammed all must have died peaceful deaths of old age in their own beds. That's true, more or less, for everyone on this list except for Jesus. Socrates was about seventy when he died (he committed a judicially mandated suicide). Buddha was eighty, Confucius was in his seventies, and Mohammed was in his early sixties. Jesus, however, is in stark contrast to all these. Jesus was the only one who was violently killed, and what's more he was in his mid-thirties. It wasn't an accidental death, either. He was killed by the state.

Now that would not have been a selling point to the earliest Christians. The fact is that Jesus' crucifixion made the incarnation—an idea already grotesque to the Greeks—downright grisly. Paul dealt in 1 Corinthians with how scandalous the Greeks would have found the idea of the supreme God not only taking on flesh, which was bad enough, but then suffering in this way. Yet it is the widespread offensiveness of this idea that also gives even the most skeptical historians confidence in the truth of it. This is not a story you would make up, certainly not if you were trying to concoct a religion that would honor the religion's leader. You just wouldn't say he was crucified, and if that were true you'd go out of your way to try to expunge it. But there it is: Jesus was killed.

Crucifixion was a severe punishment. There was great suffering. There was profuse bleeding. Jesus was scourged so severely before his crucifixion that he couldn't carry the crossbeam of his own cross. He had open wounds on his chest and back. It is gruesome for us to consider, but it was even more gruesome for those early Christians who had actually seen it happen. They knew what it was. Of all the punishments of the ancient Mediterranean world, crucifixion was especially detested. So, for example, in stories from ancient Mediterranean cultures, the hero is never crucified. No, the only reason the early Christians would have had to include a crucifixion in the story of Jesus is that it's true. Jesus was killed. He was crucified. Ropes and nails were employed to keep him, offender that he was to Roman rule, on the cross. Such a death was reserved for those whose crimes the state most wanted to discourage. Sometimes just the threat of some crucifixions could cause a besieged city to surrender. The punishment was both hated and feared, so the Romans used it to break the wills of those who resisted their rule. They would crucify rebels especially, particularly if they were of a lower, laboring class, or were foreigners. Jesus was both.

All this makes it even more amazing that Jesus would use an image such as he did in Luke 14:27: "Anyone who does not carry his *cross* and follow me cannot be my disciple." The cross was not a religious symbol then, but a word that was never to be used in polite company. Can you imagine the effect of that? Imagine a teacher saying to people in the Jim Crow South, "If you want to follow me, put on your own noose and follow me." Such a thing would have been shocking and offensive. Who would follow a person who says something like that? Yet that's what Jesus was saying, and he was saying it to people who would have been tragically aware of what such a cost was: extreme humiliation, shame, and even torture. That is how Jesus was killed.

If you're not a Christian, it is still likely that you know that Christ was crucified. Many churches even have physical representations of a cross prominent in their places of meeting, to remind them of that central event.

We don't have a cross prominently displayed at my church, Capitol Hill Baptist Church. Visitors sometimes ask me about that. Well, you can certainly find them if you look around. Some people wear them or have them on the front of their Bibles. There's a small one in one of our stained glass windows. But we don't have a cross prominently displayed. Yet we want our visitors to see the cross—just in a different way. We want them to hear the cross in our messages and in our songs that we sing. We want them to see the cross demonstrated in our lives—in the way husbands lay down their lives for their wives, for example, as Paul says in Ephesians 5.

Jesus Died for Our Sins

The second fact about Jesus and his death and resurrection is that he died for our sins. The fact that Jesus was killed is not much disputed, but *why* he was killed most certainly is. Many have touted Jesus as a great example of selfless love, and they portray his death as the highest example of such love. But if the idea of Jesus' dying as a substitute has been evacuated from our understanding of the cross, then in what way is Jesus' death loving? James Denney used the example of a man sitting on the end of Brighton Pier. Imagine him falling off into dangerous waters, and a second man comes along who jumps in to save the first man, and the second man perishes in the rescue. That is surely an example of heroic, selfless love. The man's self-sacrifice accomplishes the saving of the one who was in peril. So Christians believe that the cross accomplished something, and that's why it is an example of amazing, self-sacrificial love.

However, to disconnect Christ's death from any kind of saving substitution is to leave it hanging there with no purpose. We all know Christ's death is supposed to be about love, but the theology of too many people has left them unable to say how it is so. Really, these new theories of the cross are no better than if a man ran down Brighton Pier toward another man sitting there, safely fishing, and exclaimed, "I love you, and to show you how much I love you, I'm going to jump off this pier and drown." Really, what does such sacrifice accomplish? No one needs saving. So in what way is that showing love? What kind of example is it? The sacrifice of Christ is reduced to a purposeless suicide if it just *shows* something rather than *accomplish* something.

But Romans 4:25 tells us that Jesus' death did, in fact, accomplish something. He was delivered up to die on account of our trespasses. Those false steps we've made in life—he was sacrificed for them. Those offenses we have committed against God and against others— it's because of those that Jesus was handed over to die. He was given over to die in order to pay God's just penalty against us for the evil we have done. His death was a substitutionary death. He was put to death; he was killed, as Paul says here, for our sins.

We've seen this idea already in Isaiah's picture of the Suffering Servant. "He was pierced for our transgressions, he was crushed for our iniquities; the punishment that brought us peace was upon him, and by his wounds we are healed" (Isa. 53:5). John the Baptist, when he first sees Jesus, points to him and says, "Look, the Lamb of God, who takes away the sin of the world!" (John 1:29). Paul refers to God as "he who did not spare his own Son, but gave him up for us all" (Rom. 8:32). To the Corinthians Paul wrote, "God made him who had no sin to be sin for us, so that in him we might become the righteousness of God" (2 Cor. 5:21). To the Galatians he wrote, "Christ redeemed us from the curse of the law by becoming a curse for us, for it is written: 'Cursed is everyone who is hung on a tree'" (Gal. 3:13). The apostle Peter wrote, "Christ died for sins once for all, the righteous for the unrighteous, to bring you to God" (1 Pet. 3:18). And the apostle John wrote, "He is the atoning sacrifice for our sins" (1 John 2:2).

According to the clear testimony of the Bible, Jesus was delivered over for a purpose, for our salvation. He is our substitute. Again, as we read in Isaiah, "We all, like sheep, have gone astray, each of us has turned to his own way; and the LORD has laid on him the iniquity of us all. . . . He poured out his life unto death, and was numbered with the transgressors. For he bore the sin of many, and made intercession for the transgressors" (Isa. 53:6, 12).

So what do you think about this? Do you think you have any sins? Have you done anything morally wrong? Is there any person you've harmed, any grudge you've been bearing, anything you're even thinking about right now that you've done morally wrong, anything that a good God would condemn? What will you do about your sins? They are undeniably yours. The God who will act as judge knows all; there's no court of appeal from him. No evidence needs to be presented or argued. He knows the truth before you open your mouth. So what will you do with your sins? Jesus Christ has come to be your savior, if you will only turn from your sins and trust that he has died for you to pay the penalty for your sins.

Christian brothers and sisters, do you climb up the church steps every Sunday burdened with guilt, as if there's some way you need to perform on a Sunday morning in order for God to once again be sufficiently pleased with you to allow you to go on for another week? That's not the gospel; that's not the good news of Jesus Christ. Do you feel that there is something you still need to do to gain God's favor? There isn't. There is nothing else you need to do in order to gain God's favor. God has done that for you in Christ. God has provided a substitute to bear his correct punishment of us for our sins, to bear his wrath for us, and because of that we are left in this incredible state of freedom and acceptance. Indeed, for us to think there is something else we need to do is to take away from the sufficiency of Christ's substitutionary sacrifice. Friends, we don't gather on Sunday mornings in order to gain God's favor. We do so because Christ has saved us.

> This, the power of the cross;
> Son of God—slain for us.
> What a love! What a cost!
> We stand forgiven at the cross.

It Is God Who Delivered Jesus Up to Die

The third fact about Jesus and his death and resurrection is that God delivered him up to death. As we mentioned earlier, sometimes people misunderstand what was going on at the cross, thinking that it was the loving Son who saves us against the reluctance of a stern, displeased, difficult Father. But that is not at all the Bible's picture of the matter.

We know that Jesus willingly laid down his life. In the garden of Gethsemane, Jesus says that he will do his Father's will, not his own. He chose to do his Father's will (Matt. 26:42). First John 3:16 also says, "Jesus Christ laid down his life for us," and in John 10:18, Jesus said quite clearly, "No one takes [my life] from me, but I lay it down of my own accord. I have authority to lay it down and authority to take it up again."

But there is more. Here in Romans 4:25 the passive tense of the phrase "delivered up" indicates divine action. It implies that this action was done to Jesus, that he had received the action, and it implies that God was the one who did it. It was God who delivered Jesus up. Romans 3:25 is perhaps even clearer on this: "God presented him as a sacrifice of atonement." Paul even says in Romans 8:32 that God "gave him up for us all," the same verb that he uses here in 4:25. Of course, this idea that God delivered up the Messiah to die echoes what we read in Isaiah 53: "the LORD has laid on him the iniquity of us all" (v. 6).

Behind the anger of the crowds, therefore, lay the plan and purpose of God himself. This is undeniably what the early Christians preached. So Peter, who himself felt keenly responsible for denying Jesus in his hour of trial, preached and prayed this great truth. At Pentecost Peter preached, "This man was handed over to you by God's set purpose and foreknowledge; and you, with the help of wicked men, put him to death by nailing him to the cross" (Acts 2:23). Then in Acts 4 he prayed, "Indeed Herod and Pontius Pilate met together with the Gentiles and the people of Israel in this city to conspire against your holy servant Jesus, whom you anointed. They did what your power and will had decided beforehand should happen" (vv. 27–28). Friends, our theology has to be large enough to handle that, to understand the fact that human beings are responsible for their actions even as God rules over it all in order to accomplish his purposes.

Non-Christian friends, I wonder how this seems to you? You see, this is how we Christians understand that God can be both holy and good, both just and merciful. How else could God be both just and the justifier of the ungodly, both good and gracious? We think that this Christian message gives free rein to both justice and mercy. We minimize neither his holiness nor his love. What do you think about God? Obviously I'm not speaking about those of you who are atheists, but there are many who believe there is a God yet are not Christians. How does your understanding of God compare to the Christian gospel? Is your image of God as good as this, as holy as this? If so, how then do you keep him from becoming just a sort of stoic God far removed?

I understand how it could be tempting just to get rid of his justice and goodness, but then what do you have? You have a mercurial deity, unstable and unreliable. I also understand how it could be intellectually satisfying simply to get rid of his mercy and salvation, but then you wind up with a god closer to stoicism and indifference than to anything we see in the Bible. So how do you understand that there could be a God who is both just and merciful? How do you portray anything like the love and mercy that we see in Jesus?

The Bible clearly teaches that a holy God has made us in his image and that we have sinned and rejected him, and we are therefore culpable, guilty for those actions. Yet God in his most amazing love has come seeking us. The eternal Son of God took on flesh, lived a perfect life, and died on the cross, paying the penalty for the sins of all those who would ever turn from their sins and trust in him. God raised him from the dead, as this verse in Romans 4 says, "for our justification." Do you see how God's holiness is not compromised in that basic message of Christianity, and do you see how God's love is fully expressed there? How else could you understand God to be holy and yet so loving at the same time?

In 1888, an aging Charles Spurgeon said, in his Sunday night sermon to his congregation:

> Of late, I have heard things that I never dreamed of before, alleged even by professedly Christian ministers against the fundamental doctrines of God's Word; and some have even dared to say that the substitution of Christ, his suffering in our stead, was not just. Then they have added that God forgives sin without any atonement whatever; but, if the first be not just, what shall I say of the second? If God continually forgives sin without taking any care of his moral government, if there be nothing done for the vindication of his justice, how shall the Judge of all the earth do right? Then the very foundations of the universe would be removed, and what would the righteous do? Depend upon this, whatever modern philosophy may say, "Without shedding of blood there is no remission of sin," that is to say, without an atonement and an atonement consisting of the giving up of a life of infinite value, there is no passing by of human transgression.[4]

For those of us who are Christians, what should our response be to all this? Well, I think, among other things, we learn to trust God even in the darkest times—even as the Lord Jesus trusted his Father in the garden of Gethsemane. Jesus was right to trust God in the garden of Gethsemane, and therefore there is no way even to imagine a time so dark that God would be unworthy of trust. God overrules even the wrath of men to accomplish his greatest purposes of love. This is why, as a church, we begin our times together by praising this great God and celebrating him—it was God who planned our salvation and God who saved us.

Jesus Was Raised to Life

The fourth fact about Jesus was that he was raised to life. "He was delivered over to death for our sins and was *raised to life* for our justification."

Again, the verb in the phrase "was raised to life" is passive, which tells us that it was God who did the raising, just as he did the delivering up. That God would do such a thing as raising someone to life seems

---

[4]C. H. Spurgeon, *Metropolitan Tabernacle Pulpit*, vol. 40 (1894), 187.

extraordinary. It's certainly not normal in our experience. None of us has ever attended a funeral where we expected the person to get up in the next few days (unless, of course, the Lord were to return). Still, this is something that Jesus predicted many times—his own resurrection. So in John 2: "Destroy this temple, and I will raise it again in three days. . . . The temple he had spoken of was his body" (John 2:19, 21). More than anything else, it is Jesus' resurrection from the dead that sets him apart, that vindicates his claims. No such thing is claimed for Buddha or Confucius, for Socrates or Mohammed. Indeed, Muslims can even go to the place in Medina where Mohammed's body lies buried.

For me, it was staring at the resurrection of Jesus that God used more than anything else to move me from being an agnostic to being a Christian. Jesus was raised from the dead. How else could you explain the facts that are before us? Here are a few:

- The chief priests paid off the guards at Jesus' tomb to silence them.

- Many people claimed to have seen Jesus in the forty days after his crucifixion, and then such claims ceased.

- Matthew reported (28:17) that some doubted. That's a note of authenticity in the eyes of any historian. In a concocted tale, we would expect such a detail to be left out. Why record in a Gospel about Jesus that some people doubted the truth of the resurrection? The only plausible explanation is that Matthew knew it was true, and he was just trying to record, as a matter of fact, that some did doubt it.

- The disciples were transformed. *Something* happened to Peter. Just a few days earlier his hopes had been dashed and he had denied Jesus in front of a few people he had never met. Yet just a few days later, he was fearlessly preaching about Jesus and explaining Jesus' death to the very people who killed him. From dashed hopes to death-defying faith—not just in Peter, but in all the disciples.

- A denial of the resurrection does not figure in early anti-Christian apologetics. That would be the obvious thing to attack if you wanted to stamp out this fledgling religion, right? But no one attacks it. Why do you think that is? I think it was because too many people knew it was true. There may have been bewilderment about its significance, but the *fact* of Jesus' resurrection was never denied. Jesus was clearly raised from the dead. The argument was simply about what that could possibly mean.

- These first-century Jews—thousands and thousands of them—suddenly changed their normal day of worship from Saturday to Sunday. Sociologists tell us that the most ancient parts of a culture are found in its religious rites. They are the most conservative elements of a culture, the least likely and slowest to change. What then can account for this sudden change around the Mediterranean, among thousands of first-century Jews, from worshiping on Saturday to worshiping on Sunday?

I would suggest to you that the best answer to all these questions is that there is a God, that this God has chosen to become incarnate in Jesus of Nazareth, and that this Jesus was raised from the dead.

Christian brothers and sisters, don't forget this. Your job doesn't ultimately define you. The resurrection of Christ is the fundamental fact of the Christian's life. Does knowing the truth about Christ's resurrection make any difference in your life? How does knowing that the grave is not the end affect your life? How are you living differently because you understand that most of your life is going to be lived on *that* side of the grave? How does that cause you to approach your decisions, your values, and your priorities differently from how you would if you did not believe that? The death and resurrection of Jesus Christ and our own coming resurrection in him are the fundamental facts in our lives as Christians. Do you live like you believe in the resurrection?

Not only so, but it is only because of the resurrection of Jesus that there is unstoppable joy in Christianity. Sometimes people have the wrong idea that all religions are joyful. With all due respect to friends from other religious traditions, my experience with friends in other religions suggests that that's simply not true. I don't want to say that joy is the *unique* preserve of Christianity, but I will say that among the religions joy is the *distinctive* preserve of Christianity. That joy comes because our hope is completed in Christ. We're not left trying to follow the Five-Fold Path well enough, or in having eight practices done correctly for long enough. We as Christians are not laboring under some burden. As one person said, "All the other religions are the religions of 'do.' Christianity is the religion of 'done.'" That brings about a joy and confidence that are actually typical of Christianity as a religion.

Jesus Was Raised for Our Justification

The fifth fact about Jesus was that he was raised for our justification. "He was delivered over to death for our sins and raised to life *for our justification*."

This is the phrase that most draws attention to this verse. In the Gospels, Jesus repeatedly predicted that he would be raised to life, but we're never really told *why*. Yes, this phrase refers to the inauguration of the kingdom of God, but what does that have to do with our salvation? Paul, under the inspiration of the Holy Spirit, gives us more clarity here: Jesus was delivered over to death for our sins and raised to life "for our justification." Even as Jesus' death prevents our death, so his resurrection guarantees our resurrection.

What precisely does this final phrase mean? This is the only statement in the New Testament that links justification specifically with the resurrection. We're quite used to thinking of Jesus' death as being for our justification, and that is certainly true. But how was his resurrection for our justification?

Notice the two "for's" in verse 25: "for our sins" and "for our justification." The question we must answer is whether these two "for's" mean the same thing in both phrases. The answer is that they don't have to mean the same thing, and I think in this case the two "for's" actually mean something quite different. The first, I think, is clearly retrospective. It looks backward; it is causal. Jesus was delivered over to death "for our sins," that is, *because of* our sins and *in our place* as sinners. But would we not say, similarly, that Jesus was raised *because of* our justification? No, more likely Paul meant that Jesus was raised for our justification in the sense that his resurrection secured our justification. However exactly one understands that, suffice it to say that Paul's point here is that the resurrection is the completion of the crucifixion. By it Jesus fully and finally secured our justification.

Consider the alternative: what if Jesus had remained dead? What atonement, what justification, would there have been then? C. E. B. Cranfield writes, "What was necessitated by our sins was, in the first place, Christ's atoning death, and yet, had His death not been followed by His resurrection, it would not have been God's mighty deed for our justification."[5] Charles Hodge of Princeton put it this way: "Both, therefore, as the evidence of the acceptance of his satisfaction on our behalf, and as a necessary step to secure the application of the merits of his sacrifice, the resurrection of Christ was absolutely essential, even for our justification."[6] The resurrection was God's public vindication of Christ and his claims, his public acceptance of the sacrifice (see Rom. 1:4). Thus it is also the basis for our faith in Christ. As Paul said in 1 Corinthians 15, without the resurrection Christian faith is pitiable (15:19) and ineffective (15:17). It doesn't work.

Justification also involves relationship. So, of course, if we're going to be united with Christ, Christ must be raised from the dead. Justification through Christ is a judicial pardon for all our sins, but it's even more than that. It is a positive declaration that then restores us to fellowship with a holy God, and that positive declaration of righteousness comes on the basis of our union with the living Christ.

Jesus' crucifixion and resurrection together equal a whole, and Paul is here poetically representing their effects, none of which would have come about if either crucifixion or resurrection had not happened. Robert Haldane illustrated the relation:

> He was raised that He might enter the holy place not made with hands, and present His own blood, that we might be made righteous through His death for us. As the death of Christ, according to the determinate counsel of a holy and righteous God, was a demonstration of the guilt of His people, so His resurrection was their acquittal from every charge.[7]

Once the wrath of God against the sins of his people had been exhausted in the death of his forsaken Son, it was certain that Jesus would be

---

[5]C. E. B. Cranfield, *The Epistle to the Romans 1–8*, vol. 1 (Edinburgh: T&T Clark, 1977), 252.
[6]Charles Hodge, *Romans* (Edinburgh: Banner of Truth, repr. 1972), 129.
[7]Robert Haldane, *Romans* (Grand Rapids, MI: Kregel, repr. 1988), 183.

raised from the dead and would ascend to the right hand of his heavenly Father. To have remained in a state of death would have been to remain under God's penalty for our sins, and that would have left us unjustified. Spurgeon summarized it this way: "The dying Christ has purchased for us our justification, but the risen Christ will see that we get it. The risen Christ has come to bring it to us, and herein we rest."[8]

One final point: justification is not the same kind of *merely* objective act that propitiation is. Propitiation was an act wherein God the Son satisfied the wrath of God the Father. Christ's giving of himself satisfied the demands of the Father's justice against us. He did it alone; we played no part in it whatsoever.

Justification, however, includes us and our faith in a way propitiation did not. We must believe in order to be justified. That's what Paul's letter to the Romans is all about. Justification is something God does for us, and yet he does it through the instrumentality of our faith—not in any way *because of* our faith, but it is by faith that we take hold of and appropriate the gift of justification. The great application of this study, therefore, is that you believe. Believe that Jesus was so raised, and believe that he was raised so that you would be justified before God. Friend, if you would be saved, you must believe this message to be the truth, and you must *trust* God. Though your justification was purposed from the beginning of time, if you're one of the elect, and worked out only through Christ's dying and rising work, nevertheless you are only justified when you believe.

The nature of this saving, justifying faith is not merely a historical faith—"Oh yes, I think that happened." No, justifying faith is *trust* in Jesus Christ, the eternal Son of God, *reliance* on him as your only substitutionary Savior. And that kind of faith in Christ comes to us because of his resurrection. Paul says in Romans 10:9, "If you confess with your mouth, 'Jesus is Lord,' *and believe in your heart that God raised him from the dead,* you will be saved."

[8]Spurgeon, *Metropolitan Tabernacle Pulpit*, vol. 40, 189.

CHAPTER TEN

JUSTIFIED BY HIS BLOOD

Romans 5:8–10

MARK DEVER

In November 1993, about two thousand people (mainly women) gathered in Minneapolis for a theological conference. This one, however, had nothing to do with "Desiring God." The conference was called "Re-imagining God," and it was exactly what its name suggests. Lesbian feminist Virginia Mollenkott of the National Council of Churches suggested that it may be necessary for women to leave denominations in order to create a new holistic church. She also claimed that the idea of Jesus' atonement was "the ultimate in child abuse and a model of human child abuse" that depicts "God as an abusive parent." Aruna Gnanadson of the World Council of Churches, and Dolores Williams, then a professor at Union Theological Seminary in New York State, both agreed, condemning the idea of Christ's atonement as an abusive patriarchal system with the comment, "I don't think we need folks hanging on crosses, dripping blood, and weird stuff." Too many people today would agree with these women, that the story of the cross is simply "weird stuff." Yet, like it or not, there it stands at the very heart of Christianity. The cross is at the core of how we know what God is like.

Penal substitution is the idea that God forgives Christians the penalty due to us because of our sins, because Jesus took our place by living the life we should have lived and dying the death that we deserved because of our sins. One of the specific concerns that has been raised about this substitutionary understanding of the cross has been the simple irrelevance of the idea. Some scholars have suggested that such an idea of the atonement has no subjective, ethical impact on us because it is all about God satisfying God's wrath. What positive impact, the concerned ask, could there possibly be on us and our behavior? Critics ask, "What good is the cross to us right now? How does it affect our lives today?" Their conclusion is that it doesn't, so the cross, cut off from its effects, begins to look pointless and even ghoulish, as it clearly was presented at that 1993 feminist conference in Minneapolis.

Is the idea of penal substitution really empty in its ethical effects on people today, on our attitudes to each other, on how we treat other people? According to a substitutionary understanding of Christ's death, are there any benefits that come to believers in this life? Are there any effects on our morals or behaviors? To consider this and other questions, we turn now to Romans 5:8–10 (ESV):

> But God shows his love for us in that while we were still sinners, Christ died for us. Since, therefore, we have now been justified by his blood, much more shall we be saved by him from the wrath of God. For if while we were enemies we were reconciled to God by the death of his Son, much more, now that we are reconciled, shall we be saved by his life.

Let's remind ourselves of the context of these verses. In this letter Paul has in chapters 1 to 4 explained justification by faith alone in Christ alone. He blocks up the way of righteousness by works, concluding in 3:19–20 that by the way of works no one will be declared righteous. Do not even *try*, he says, to "religion" your way to heaven. Don't try to "good works" your way to heaven. It won't work. "But now," he says in 3:21, "a righteousness from God, apart from law, has been made known." That's the way of salvation. That's the way God has made available to us through faith in Jesus Christ and in his blood.

Lest anyone think this is a novelty, Paul in Romans 4 gives the example of Abraham, the father of the faithful. Even Abraham himself, he says, was justified not by works, but by faith, by believing what God said. So this is no innovation. Yes, it is new in that we now understand that God would do this in Jesus specifically, but this message of salvation, that God would account our faith in his promises as righteousness, is the very message that was revealed in Genesis in the life of Abraham. This is the mystery that is now fully revealed in Jesus Christ.

Now, in chapter 5, Paul begins to consider some of the benefits that come to us from God in this way. In a sense, Paul begins to explore exactly the question some modern theologians have raised as an objection. What good is this substitution? What good is a salvation we don't participate in but simply trust? What does it do? How does it affect us in our actions and attitudes toward others? Thus, Paul talks about the benefits that flow to us from the death of Christ and salvation by faith in this crucified and risen Christ—peace with God, joy in trials, and deep confidence in a restored loving relationship with God, both now and in the future.

Just before these verses, in Romans 5:2, Paul had said that we rejoice in the hope of the glory of God (also 5:5a). Then in verses 5 to 8, he backs this up by explaining the grounds for that confidence. We should notice four main points from this passage.

The Future Benefits of Christ's Substitution

The first main point to note is the future benefits of Christ's substitution. The second half of 5:9 reads, "How much more shall we be saved from God's wrath through him!" And 5:10 says, "How much more . . . shall we be saved through his life!"

The phrase "how much more," which Paul uses twice in these verses, is a common way of arguing. It's an argument from the greater to the lesser. That is, if God has already done the more difficult thing (Christ's death), how certain we can be that he will do the easier thing (save us from his wrath). Having saved us by Christ's death, *surely*, now that we are reconciled to him, he will treat us as friends and save us from wrath on that last day.

We really must pause to make sure that we've all noticed this little word at the end of verse 9, "wrath," and are thinking of it as we should. Some today deny that God is wrathful, saying that it's a terribly anthropomorphic way to speak about God. It is to speak about God as if he were a man, and thus it is dishonoring to God. Others say that God's wrath is just the impersonal working out of cause and effect in the universe. The universe is set up so that there will be bad effects from evil actions, but is that what wrath really means?

According to the Bible, God is clearly a God of wrath. Of course he is not *merely* a God of wrath, but he is a God of wrath. But God's wrath is not some embarrassing heavenly temper tantrum. No, God's wrath is always represented as right and correct and even good, because it is his uncompromising opposition to evil. Paul in this letter has already spoken repeatedly about how we have left ourselves open and liable to God's wrath because of our sins (e.g., 1:18; 2:5, 8; 3:5). We have sinned against a God who is uncompromisingly good. God's wrath is not the pique of a spurned lover. It is God's personal and powerful opposition to all who would do themselves or others harm. It is God's commitment to himself and to his own character, to oppose those who oppose him and his law. To oppose God's laws is to oppose God himself, for they are the expression of his character. How do we oppose him? By sinning. By spending this life, this *day*, on something other than what he made us to do.

But when will we experience this wrath? All of us are to expect that God will judge us, if he is truly good. Let me ask you, friend: what do you mean by saying that your God is good if he never judges evil? The Bible says that God will exact justice. He will judge. As Paul wrote to the Corinthians, "We must all appear before the judgment seat of Christ, that each one may receive what is due him for the things done while in the body, whether good or bad" (2 Cor. 5:10).

It is with this idea of final judgment that we come to understand the idea of a final salvation that Paul talks about here—a final judgment from which he says "we shall be saved." What does he mean by that? From what will we be saved? The answer, surprising as it might seem to some, is that we will be saved from God himself and from his right wrath. What we need to be saved from is a God who is committed to goodness and justice and righteousness and who will therefore oppose us because we have opposed him. This is why Paul wrote to the Thessalonian Christians about "Jesus, who rescues us from the coming wrath" (1 Thess. 1:10).

There's an interesting point to be learned here. If you're a Christian and someone asks you if you are "saved," you can in all honesty say no, at least in this future sense. It's not that you *won't* be saved—the whole reason Paul is writing this is so that we can have confidence that we will be when the time comes—but we haven't been saved yet in this final, future sense. The final judgment has not come. So while we are confident of our acquittal (it's been promised to us on the highest authority) we've not yet stood before the Judge. We're not dead yet. Scripture teaches about salvation in three tenses. We *have been* saved, it says many times, from the penalty of sin, and so we have that future acquittal assured to us. We *are being* saved right now from the power of sin in our lives, as we see it being broken. And then here in Romans 5 Paul talks about how we *will be* saved at the final judgment. The glory of all this is that if you're saved in any one of the senses, you're saved in all three. They go as a set. Indeed that's what Paul is arguing here. Having been reconciled, past and present, by the death of Christ, we can be sure that we will be saved on the last day.

Even so, we should not pretend that everything has already happened. To be sure, it's been made certain for us if we trust in God by faith in Christ, but the final judgment has not yet occurred in history. So Paul writes here about the confidence that we should have in our future salvation. What a glorious truth Paul is explaining here! Believers in Jesus Christ will *not* experience the wrath of God, but we shall be saved. This is the great assurance that Christians have. Richard Sibbes meditated on this as he considered the repentance, return, and forgiveness of Israel in Isaiah 15. As he exulted in this salvation, Sibbes pictured the scene:

> When our sins are set in order before us, the sins of our youth, middle and old age, our sins against conscience, against the law and gospel, against examples, vows, promises, resolutions, and admonitions of the Spirit and servants of God; when there shall be such a terrible accuser, and God shall perhaps let the wounds of conscience fly open and join against us; when wrath shall appear, be in some sort felt, and God presented to the soul as "a consuming fire," no comfort in heaven or earth appearing, hell beneath seeming ready to revenge against us the quarrel of God's covenant, Oh then for faith to look through all these clouds! to see mercy in wrath! . . . life in death! the sweetness of the promises! the virtue and merit of Christ's sufferings, death, resurrection, and intercession at the right hand! the sting of death removed, sin pardoned and done away, and glory at hand![1]

That is what we have to look forward to in Christ. We don't have to try to remove God's justice from him in order to hope that we might

---

[1]Richard Sibbes, "Returning Backslider," in *Works of Richard Sibbes*, vol. 2 (London: Nichols, 1862), 307–8.

be able to survive the final judgment. God himself has already acted for our salvation in Jesus Christ. He himself has made a way for us.

This benefit of a future salvation is said to come "through him," by which Paul means that Jesus is the means of our being saved on that last day, particularly because of his sacrificial death for us. As we discussed when we considered Romans 4, it is only by Christ and his resurrection life that we have confidence of Christ's continuing and effective intercession for us before the Father. As Matthew Henry said, "Christ dying . . . bequeathed us the legacy; but Christ living . . . pays it."[2] We walk now in that confident newness of life, as Paul is going to speak more about in Romans 6 (vv. 3–4, 8, 11).

My friend, if you are not a Christian, I wonder how this kind of confidence seems to you. When you think of the future, do you have this kind of confidence? What do you think happens after you die? How could you know? According to the Bible there *is* a God, and the Bible says that this God has revealed the truth about himself and about eternity to us. Not only so, but this God is *good*, and that's *bad* news for us because of our sins. You remember all those times you've done the right thing? Your good works are never going to outweigh your bad works. Salvation doesn't come that way. A good God will judge us for our sins. So what will you do, as you consider how to prepare for that day, whose date is unknown to you but whose coming is sure?

As Christians our hope for that day is in the risen Christ. Every true Christian has the same hope. We all end up in heaven only by virtue of God's Son. We have a unity that springs from our lines all ending up together in Christ. Thus, we are all moving toward that single hope, and as we do so, we become more and more united. Brothers and sisters, let's practice that unity here and now.

Have you ever noticed how even good things such as your work or even your family, are not ultimately satisfying? Have you ever wondered why that is? Did you ever think that those longings may be there to tell you about a future reality in Christ that *will* be ultimately fulfilling? O brothers and sisters, I pray that we may draw on this anticipation of a wonderful future to help us in trying days at work and to encourage us to fulfill our roles well in our families and with our friends. What a great hope and confidence and assurance

[2]Ibid., 398.

Jesus has given to us! May we therefore not be held hostage by any circumstance in this world. May we as a congregation be marked by a confident joy as we anticipate the coming good God has for us.

The Present Benefits of Christ's Substitution

The second main point to note is the present benefits of Christ's substitution. Throughout verses 8 to 10 are references to the present benefits that Christ's death on the cross secured for us:

- "Christ died for us" (v. 8).
- "Since we have now been justified by his blood" (v. 9).
- "We were reconciled to him through the death of his Son," and then again that phrase "having been reconciled . . ." (v. 10).

The whole Old Testament system of sacrifices was preparing God's people to understand the idea contained in this phrase in verse 8: "Christ died for us." All the supernatural phenomena that surrounded the death of Jesus Christ pointed to the unique status of Christ's death—he became sin for us, took our blame, bore God's wrath in our place. He did this *for us.*

Paul emphasizes this because this kind of love is unknown in human experience. In verses 6 and 7, he considers the differences between how human beings love each other and how God has loved us in Christ. Someone might perhaps die for a good person, Paul says, but Christ died for us while we were sinners and rebels against him. Consider again what Christ's death was. It was death by the barbaric cross, an execution of the utmost cruelty. It was an offensive, even obscene, death. Crucifixion was a widely employed form of torture and death around the world in ancient times, from India to the tribes of Western Europe and Numidian Africa. As we noted earlier, Rome used it only on the lowest of the low, those without rights or power—rebels and heinous criminals. It was the stuff of stories and tales, but the hero was never crucified. You wouldn't make up a story in which the hero was crucified. Yet Jesus was crucified.

Jesus Christ died this death for us, the ones who deserved to be so treated. He died as our substitute. This is substitutionary atonement—and it is for us. Jesus took the punishment we deserved. The horror of the cross only underscores to us what we deserved because of our sins. It wasn't arbitrary or by some sort of chance that *this* was the death that Jesus died. God in his provident sovereignty *chose* the worst sort of death in order to show to us the truth about our own spiritual state.

So, how is Christ's death effective for us today? Fact and faith must come together here. The historical event of the death of Jesus Christ for us and our reception of this fact by faith is how we come today to benefit from Christ's death. Faith is nothing without the cross. People often talk about faith as if there is some inherent power in it. "Just have faith," they say. But the reality is that faith is worthless apart from Christ and his death as the object of that faith. Faith can't be abstracted and separated from the cross. On the other hand, though, the cross should never be left as merely a symbol proclaiming God's love without my personal embrace of it by faith. Don't just think that because Christ died you'll be fine, and you needn't trouble yourself with religion. Christ's death on the cross calls us to trust him with our whole lives. Indeed, without such trust we will know no benefit through his death. Friends, Christ died so that you would come to see God's love for you and so that you would trust him. Trust him, therefore, with your whole life.

Paul goes on from this mention of Christ's death at the end of verse 8 to talk more specifically about what has come to us as a result of it. Verse 9 begins, "Since we have now been justified by his blood . . ." Christian brothers and sisters, we live in the present reality of justification. We have been justified; that is, we have been declared righteous by God, and our final acquittal before his judgment seat is assured. Sinners have escaped the judgment of God by God's own plan.

Some have said that justification has to do with our being made righteous by ourselves. But Paul's very point is that believers now are in a right relationship with God, and that we are so because of an amazing act of God in his love—Christ's death for us on the cross. Paul goes on to say that this justification happens by his blood; our being justified is only because of Jesus' death. Jesus was our substitute. We are justified, as Paul said in 3:25, only because we have faith in Jesus and in his blood. The crucifixion was at the center of Paul's gospel and his theology.

Not only does Christ's substitution secure hope, assurance, and justification for us, but it also secures reconciliation: "We were reconciled to him through the death of his Son" (v. 10). Look at Paul's words to the Corinthians:

> God was reconciling the world to himself in Christ, not counting men's sins against them. And he has committed to us the message of reconciliation. We are therefore Christ's ambassadors, as though God were making his appeal through us. We implore you on Christ's behalf: Be reconciled to God. (2 Cor. 5:19–20)

Christ's death thus calls us to be reconciled to God by trusting in God's promises in Christ. We cannot miss the centrality of the cross. As Paul says here, this reconciliation happens only "through the death of his Son."

We see something of what an amazing reconciliation this must have been by looking at the severity of Jesus' death. What a deep breach and wide gulf must have existed between us and God, because of our sins, to require a death like this in order to repair it. Crucifixion was a uniquely horrible and disgusting death, and yet Jesus Christ was willing to endure it in order to reconcile us to God. There we see the extent of our need and the extent of his provision.

By Christ's death, God sates his wrath and invites us to drown our enmity in his love. Reconciliation is presented here as a result of justification. These are two images for the same set of people. The offended judge (God) is the same as the estranged one (God), and the lawbreaker (man) is also God's enemy (man). So justification includes pardon and return, and reconciliation includes a spanning of a breach and a restoration of a relationship.

Non-Christian friends, that longing you have for a relationship that works is, at root, a longing for a relationship with God. He doesn't want you to be wrongly satisfied in your sin, dining in luxury while the Titanic sinks. God wants you to wake up to the spiritual peril you are in, and so in his kindness he leaves little messages around our lives of dissatisfaction, thoughts of "couldn't there be something more?" Freud and others in his field took those little signs as part of a universal human experience that somehow reflected some innate desire for more and better. But as Christians, we answer, "Well, yes, of course, but that desire is there for a reason!" Why do you assume those desires are present in so many people—even in all people? If there is no creator, then we have no real answer for that. But if there is a creator, we shouldn't be surprised that he would deliberately leave those desires there for us—his calling cards, as it were—to call us to turn and look to him.

God has loved us so in Christ. He has made us in his image to know him. But we also understand that we have sinned and broken our fellowship with God. Our first parents did so, and we have all ratified it in our own lives. None of us has objected. We also understand that God could be completely just and simply let us go in our sins. But in his amazing love, the eternal Son of God took on flesh, lived perfectly the life we should have lived, and died on the cross bearing the penalty not for his sins (because he didn't have any) but for the sins of all who would repent of our sins and turn to trust in him. We know that we can believe Jesus in this because God raised him from the dead. Our hope in Christ is confirmed by the fact that he was raised and then ascended into heaven. So we, as Christians, believe that we are now all commanded to repent of our sins, turn from them, and trust in him so that we will be justified, reconciled to God, and therefore certain of a future salvation. Non-Christian friends, all of that is there. Will you repent of your sins and trust in Christ? That can be there for you every bit as much as it's there for the Christians around you today.

Christian friends, are there any ethical implications of believing all this about the substitutionary atonement of Christ? Are you known as a peacemaker at work? Do you absorb wrongs done to you, or do you incite them and bring about more strife? In your marriage, do you hold grudges? In your family, how actively do you model reconciliation, bringing people together after a breach in relationship? Isn't this what the gospel is all about, our relating to God again in friendship and love? Our congregations are to be a living picture of reconciliation. We are a community for the guilty and alienated, pointing to forgiveness and restored relationships.

That reminds me of one more thing. Do you realize that Christians are unusual in speaking of a personal relationship with God? It's certainly not what Confucius or Buddha taught, and it sounds odd to Jews. I have often heard it mocked by Muslims. Friends, this isn't what other religions teach. Other religions don't even hold out a hope of a personal relationship with God. The most extraordinary thing about this Christian message is that God himself has come seeking us to be in personal relationship with him. Christians experience in our own lives a relationship with the one who made us, who knows why we've been made, and what we are ultimately here for. And that relationship—that reconciled relationship with God—is won for us by the death of Jesus on the cross in our place.

The Timing of Christ's Substitution

The third main point to note is the timing of Christ's substitution. Paul seems to underscore this point especially. In verse 8 he says that all this happened "while we were still sinners," or, as you could put it, "while we were totally messed up." Then again at the beginning of verse 10, "when we were [God's] enemies . . ."

This is the great story that Paul is pursuing. He shows in Romans 1 through 3 that we are all God's enemies. Then as he told the story of Abraham in chapter 4, he made clear that God justified the wicked who had faith in Jesus. God counted faith as righteousness. It wasn't righteousness in itself, but God counted it so. Some may decry such accounting as some kind of forensic fiction, but it is God himself in his Word who has said this is what he does. When he says there in 4:5 that God justifies the wicked, Paul is summarizing what he's been arguing up to that point in the whole of Romans.

Paul calls us all "sinners" here in verse 8. That's what the tax collector in Jesus' story in Luke 18:13 called himself. *Sinners* is a firm old word, describing us by what we do and what God thinks of it. Matthew Henry says, "Neither righteous nor good; not only such as were useless, but such as were guilty and obnoxious; not only such as there would be no loss of should they perish, but such whose destruction would greatly redound to the glory of God's justice, being malefactors and criminals that ought to die."[3]

Sinners.

In verse 10 Paul states it even more strongly: "For if, when we were [God's] enemies . . ." The Greek simply says "enemies," but it clearly implies that we are *God's* enemies. Earlier in the chapter Paul called us weak, and ungodly. In verse 8 he calls us sinners. But now, here, we're enemies. It's really an amazing and frightening thought when you stop to think about it—God's enemies. But that's what we were. (See Eph. 4:18; Phil. 3:18; Col. 1:21.) We opposed God—Father, Son, and Holy Spirit. We opposed God's people and his gospel. We were not

[3]Ibid., 397.

merely weak or erring, not merely ungodly or sinful, we were at war against God, his opponents. Therefore, we were justly the objects of divine wrath. This letter has been clear that we are by nature hostile toward God (cf. Rom. 7:8), and also that God, too, is hostile toward us—wrathful even, because of our sins against him. To quote Sibbes, "If we had all the creatures in the world to help us, what are they but vanity and nothing, if God be our enemy!"[4]

I've paused and thought about these two images—sinners and enemies—because of the link to the timing of Christ's substitution. Christ did not come and die as our substitute after a long series of humble entreaties from us and centuries of obedience on our part in an effort to make up for the sins of our first parents. Christ came and died *while we were still sinners* and *when we were God's enemies*. Can you imagine it? We here on earth have long and learned discussions among our most respected ethicists about whether we should torture our enemies, but God in heaven decides from eternity past to send his Son to die for his.

Now, why would Paul want to put everyone down like this? Is he denigrating us? Is he trying to discourage us? What's he doing? No, he's simply telling the truth. He is stressing this point in order to show that God's love for us is not based on anything in us—nothing we have done, nothing lovely in ourselves. It is all of God's grace. What God gives us is contrary to our merit. It's not what we deserve.

Non-Christian friends, I wonder what treatment you think you deserve at God's hand? What the Bible tells us is that if there will ever be salvation for you or me, it must be by God's grace. What we find when we turn to the Bible is that Jesus Christ is a gracious Lord. You can tell that even in the timing of his death for us. He didn't wait until we had cleaned ourselves up or until we worked to *deserve* his gift. He came when we were all sinners, all his enemies.

Christian brothers and sisters, if God has so treated his enemies, what does that tell us about how we should treat those who have wronged us? Think of those who have wronged you. As a Christian, what are your obligations toward them? If we're honest with ourselves, we think that when someone has wronged us, it pretty much clears us of any obligation toward them. We think, "Well, that's it. They've wronged me, so I now have carte blanche to treat them however I want to." Most of us probably couldn't even be said to really have any enemies. Maybe a rival here, or an annoyer there, a disappointer here, and someone unresponsive there, but not *enemies*. Yet see how God treated his enemies. How do we treat ours? Think of yourself at work. Think of someone in your office whom you find obnoxious, particularly irritating, someone who can really get under your skin. Perhaps worse, think of someone whom you feel has truly done you wrong. Do you feel the sharpness of your moral vision increasing, the acuity of your sense of right and wrong sharpening? That's because you're getting into a position where you feel you're right. Well, let that sense of your own righteousness pull you still higher. Look down on that one who is so wrong in the way they have treated you, and let your indignation rise. Now stop. Do you realize that you have been far more wrong in the way you have treated God?

Husbands, when was the last time you asked your wife to forgive you? Children, when was the last time you asked your parents to forgive you? All of us do things that are wrong. We sin, and therefore we must be those who ask for forgiveness, but we can only approach God for forgiveness through Jesus Christ, who has made a way for us—even for us sinners and enemies—to be justified and reconciled to God.

Brothers and sisters, we must let go of a mentality that thinks we've basically pleased God by our works this week. That's just not true, and it leads only to pride if we lie to ourselves and to despair if we tell the truth. If you would kill pride and arrogance and promote humility, then meditate on Christ's substitutionary death for you while you were still a sinner, while you were God's enemy. Get to know your own heart better, and you will become a better evangelist as well, because you will come to understand that which you have in common with every person you will ever talk to, and you will better understand how to introduce them to the one who died for people while they were still sinners and enemies of God.

The Point of Christ's Substitution

The fourth thing to note is the point of Christ's substitution. Did you notice the very first phrase in our passage? "But God demonstrates his own love for us in this." Christ's dying for us as a substitute when we were his enemies, thereby securing our justification, reconciliation, and final salvation forever, was all for one purpose—to manifest, to show, to set out, to prove, to confirm God's love for us.

By demonstrating his love in this way, God silenced the mouths of those who would deny his love toward us or diminish it in any way. Christ having died like this for us leaves no room to doubt God's love for us. Why would God so demonstrate his love? Because it is a most extraordinary idea. We might well be skeptical of the claim of it, if God hadn't done something to show it, to prove it. How could a holy God correctly love sinful men?

God is out to show, Paul says here, "his own love." Earlier we thought about these wonderful words: "For God so loved the world that he gave his one and only Son, that whoever believes in him shall not perish but have eternal life" (John 3:16). Consider also these words of Jesus: "Greater love has no one than this, that he lay down his life for his friends" (John 15:13). John wrote, "This is love: not that we loved God, but that he loved us and sent his Son as an atoning sacrifice for our sins" (1 John 4:10).

It's hard to speak about love in a Christian church. It's sort of the assumed thing. We all know we're supposed to be about love. After all, who's against love? We all know that love is presented as the supreme Christian virtue, but did you ever stop to consider *why* love is the supreme Christian virtue? It's because that's the way our God is. All that he has done in Christ, he has done to demonstrate his love. The greatness of love as a Christian virtue is rooted in God's nature of love, revealed supremely in Jesus' life, death, and resurrection.

God sent his Son when we were his enemies, to die as our substitute, in order to justify, reconcile, and save us forever. He was the sun ignored, the victor uncheered, the Creator unthanked, the truth disbelieved, the lord disobeyed, the counsel unheeded, the husband divorced, the family left, and the child slain, yet his love was such that he acted to forgive us in a way that protected both his holiness and his mercy at the same time. This is what it means to say that God is love.

My non-Christian friends, how do you react to news of such love? How do you get a demand for justice and love to work together? As Christians, we understand that this is the very heart of the gospel, mercy and justice working together as they do in Christ.

Notice here that not only is God love, but he will be *known* as being loving. If we are his children, we will love, too. What about those who are different from you—from a different nationality, race, or political view? Oh, friend, recognize those differences as the deliberate God-given opportunities for your love. The whole point of Christ's substitution for us was to display God's love.

So does believing in substitutionary atonement carry with it any ethical implications? How can you come to understand even the smallest part of who God is, and of who we are in Christ, and think that it doesn't? Of course God's loving us in this way has the most profound implications for how you and I live and treat others and for how we are called to act ethically. Perhaps most powerfully, it carries with it an assurance of God's love that transforms our lives, giving confidence and assurance and joy down to the very last day we draw breath.

My friend, your job is a chance for you to display this Godlike love in the way you conduct yourself. How can you ever be the loving person you're made to be unless you keep the big picture of what God is about in this world clearly in focus? In a fallen world, love requires a long perspective, and if you don't have that long perspective, you will not be loving. But if indeed you have that long perspective, if you see something of what God is doing, then you will be able to love as he calls you to do.

Have you found this in your marriage and in your home? All these things are to be the Christian's reminders and pointers to God's own love. They are small, but they indicate something much greater than themselves. Have you ever seen a photograph of the Grand Canyon? It's not nearly as grand as seeing the canyon for yourself, is it? But it's still much better than never having seen it at all. The photo begins to let you know that something more is out there. Look around you. Our churches are meant to show that something more is out there, something beyond what the world experiences in life. We—you and I in our lives and normal relations—are to be the pictures of God's cross-bearing love, even for his enemies, in Christ. How would we know of God's love if he had not shown us the real thing in Christ?

> Christ was all anguish that I might be all joy,
>   cast off that I might be brought in,
>   trodden down as an enemy
>   that I might be welcomed as a friend,

surrendered to hell's worst,
   that I might attain heaven's best,
stripped that I might be clothed,
wounded that I might be healed,
athirst that I might drink,
tormented that I might be comforted,
made a shame that I might inherit glory,
entered darkness that I might have eternal light.
My Saviour wept that all tears might be wiped from my eyes,
groaned that I might have endless song,
endured all pain that I might have unfading health,
bore a thorned crown that I might have a glory-diadem,
bowed his head that I might uplift mine,
experienced reproach that I might receive welcome,
closed his eyes in death that I might gaze on unclouded brightness,
expired that I might for ever live.

CHAPTER ELEVEN

CONDEMNED SIN

Romans 8:1–4

MARK DEVER

The world needs new control of nature and society and is told that the Bible is verbally inerrant. It needs a means of composing class strife, and is told to believe in the substitutionary atonement. . . . It needs faith in the divine presence in human affairs and is told it must accept the virgin birth of Jesus Christ.[1]

Those are just a few words from Shailer Mathews, dean of the divinity school at the University of Chicago in the last century, complaining about the way some Christians, in the face of real and pressing needs in the world, would champion what he thought were theological obscurities of no help to anyone. Why insist on such old ideas, he was saying, in the face of very real needs? Why insist on ideas that are so alien to the present world, ideas that don't mean anything to people today? Consider especially just one of them that he mentioned—substitutionary atonement. Why insist on something that seems so peripheral to life today and maybe even to the message of Scripture itself, at least some scholars suggest?

Many people might wonder why it is so important to have a book— or a series of sermons—making the same point over and over again, that Jesus died on the cross in the place of sinners, in their stead and for their sin. After all, doesn't the Bible use other images about the

---

[1]Quoted in Mark Noll, *A History of Christianity in the United States and Canada* (Grand Rapids, MI: Eerdmans, 1992), 375–76.

atonement—economic images of redemption, military images of victory, images of freedom and liberation? Some New Testament scholars today go even so far as to suggest that Christ being a bodily substitute on the cross and enduring God's wrath in our place is at best just a secondary teaching in the New Testament, if even that.

Looking through Scriptures, however, I think we have found that the concept of substitution was indeed central to what God has been doing with fallen humanity.

So we've seen even in the Old Testament. God was building the house of Israel as one magnificent preview and pointer to Jesus Christ. In the captivity of Israel in Egypt, we see a picture of our own bondage, our enslavement to sin writ large, and it is only God who could deliver us. In the exodus we saw a drama in which God acts to be our liberator. As part of that drama, we saw how there would be a lamb without blemish sacrificed for the people, while others—for whom the lamb was not sacrificed—were killed. We saw in Leviticus that there were other sacrifices set up, especially on the Day of Atonement, when one animal was sacrificed and another banished into the wilderness symbolically bearing the sins of the people. In Isaiah we saw the servant prophesied, called to suffer, and called to "bear the sin of many" (53:12).

These practices and prophecies were planted deeply in the people of Israel for centuries. They always displayed great truths about the holiness of God, about his kindness and his tender mercies, about the association of death with forgiveness. All this, the age-old tension between justice and mercy, was finally to be resolved at the cross. The substitutionary death of Jesus Christ for the sins of his people plucked the deepest chord that resounded with the ancient teachings, symbols, and images that God had implanted in Israel from the very beginning.

The teaching of Jesus Christ explained his own life and death in these substitutionary terms. He used images of a lamb, of bearing sins, of the Suffering Servant, of the high priest, of the temple and sacrifice. How are we to understand all these? We understand them by acknowledging that truth which is not itself an image but which is the thing itself, the thing imaged—the truth that Jesus died in our place. Jesus died as a substitute, taking on the death that we have deserved for our sins.

So then, substitution was not simply background for one image of the atonement. It is the central reality of the atonement, and, therefore, it is central to all Christian faith and life. In the last chapter we considered objections some have made against substitution, to the effect that there are no ethical implications that flow from it; that is, Jesus' death as a substitute for us doesn't make any difference in our lives. We have already seen that that's not the case. There are indeed implications for how we live that flow from this understanding of the cross. Now we come to a later section in Paul's letter to the Romans, one in which he makes this point even more explicit by talking about the newness of life we have in Christ. How interesting it is that when Paul thinks about our struggle with sin and how we are called to live by the Spirit, at the very center of his thinking is the death of Jesus Christ in our place for our sins.

> There is therefore now no condemnation for those who are in Christ Jesus. For the law of the Spirit of life has set you free in Christ Jesus from the law of sin and death. For God has done what the law, weakened by the flesh, could not do. By sending his own Son in the likeness of sinful flesh and for sin, he condemned sin in the flesh, in order that the righteous requirement of the law might be fulfilled in us, who walk not according to the flesh but according to the Spirit. (Rom. 8:1–4 ESV)

It's clear from verse 4 that God wants us, as his people, to have transformed lives. In fact, Paul has been talking about this since Romans 6. Having made clear our need for salvation, from 1:18 all the way through 3:20, and then making clear the way of salvation by faith in Christ, in chapters 3 to 5, Paul turns now in chapter 6 to speak of the new life we have if we are in Christ. Our identification with Christ now means that our old self, our flesh, was crucified with Christ so that sin is now no longer our master. We are, therefore, no longer slaves to sin but slaves to God. The law alone, Paul says, could never bring about this freedom; indeed, our own flesh rejects the law, so the law alone only seemed to exacerbate our desires to *dis*obey God. There is a struggle going on in this life, Paul says, because we are made in God's image and yet also under the curse. But now, by becoming a Christian, we've come into Christ, and in Christ we've been redeemed and released from bondage to the law, sin, and death, so that we now, Paul says in 7:6, "serve in the new way of the Spirit."

In these first few verses of Romans 8, we learn some important things about the transformation that has taken place in us as Christians.

Transformation Not Fundamentally by Understanding or Obedience

First, transformation doesn't come fundamentally by our understanding or obedience (8:3). In verse 2, Paul mentions our being in bondage to sin and death, and then at the beginning of verse 3 he says, "For what the law was powerless to do in that it was weakened by the sinful nature . . ." Paul's point is that the change we need, in our life and our status before God, will not come about through the law. The law was powerless, he says. It wasn't up to the job; it was impossible for the law to do it.

It was impossible, Paul says, because "it was weakened." It was as if the law were sick, its strength gone, its limitations exposed, helpless on account of our sinful nature or, literally, because of our flesh. That does not mean merely our physical bodies; it means the whole of our fallen human nature. It was because of our fallen human nature that the law was so powerless. Moses' Law, and the moral law of God that it expressed, cannot save. Paul says here that it was weakened in its effect because unregenerate people can't keep it. Sin and death result from fallen people's encounter with God's law, not salvation.

The upshot of this is that you can never save yourself by your actions.

Christianity does not give us a spiritual do-it-yourself kit. That's not what the Bible or the Christian gospel gives us.

My friend, if you're not a Christian, what would you say has been the best change you've experienced in your life—a new job, a new home, a new relationship, a new diet, or a new way to think? What's the best change you've ever experienced? My guess is that even with that change, you still find yourself disappointed in your expectations. Is that the case? Have you ever wondered *why* that's the case? What do you do with your knowledge of your moral failures? Christianity is not a spiritual resource center to help you make a perfect life for yourself here or build a paradise in this world. As Christians, we understand that Jesus Christ and his power are the only things that can finally change us, change our lives, and change this world.

One thing we Christians have in common, whether we're American or African, from Britain or the Caribbean, is our utter spiritual helplessness. No racial, political, or other demographic categories are more telling and revealing of our true identity than to say that we are sinners before our holy creator God. Thus, as Christians, we realize that our salvation must come from outside ourselves. It's not going to come from inside of us.

Even our work is not the thing that has ultimate value. Our career will not be what we should finally live for. We can't finally put our hopes in it. It will end before we do. We need to prepare ourselves for that day. We are more than our job. We are made in the image of God. For example, you can't save others, no matter how much you love them. Do you see your own limitations even in that? You can't save your own family members—not your parents, your siblings, even your children. You can't even save yourself. Have you realized this limitation? Do you realize, Christian brother or sister, that you haven't obeyed yourself into God's good graces? It doesn't work like that. You can't merely educate yourself into a better life. Education can achieve some limited goods, but it certainly hasn't been responsible for the transformation in our hearts that we have known if we're Christians.

This is so important for us to agree on that we even say it in our church's statement of faith: our salvation comes to us "not in consideration of any works of righteousness which we have done." Our acts, our knowledge, will never bring about the great change that everyone needs.

So that's the first point, and it is crucial that you understand it. If you try to mix any of the rest of what I'm going to say with the thought, "Well, you know, I really kind of saved myself," then you'll miss the point of this text. You won't see what Paul is talking about here. But if our actions don't cause the transformation that is Christian conversion, what does?

Transformation by God's Action

Second, transformation comes by God's action. The transformation of life that we experience as Christians comes as the result of God's action in our lives, and what a glorious work it is that God does! Let's notice three particulars about God's action in our lives from this text:

1) *Our penalty is paid, and we are justified*: "Therefore, there is now no condemnation for those who are in Christ Jesus" (8:1). Praise God for his kindness to us. In order to appreciate it, we need to remind ourselves that we've owed our whole lives to God, and yet we all, by nature and by choice, have spent our lives for ourselves. We have sinned against God, and because God is fair and just and good, he is committed to punish us for our sins, and this will mean our final condemnation. Jesus himself spoke about the wrath of God, even now, hanging over all those who reject him.

That's why this is such good news. *Now*, he says, we can know that there is no condemnation for those who are in Christ Jesus. The "now" is referencing the fact that the ages have changed with the coming of Christ and his death on the cross for us. The mystery hidden for ages past, as Paul says elsewhere, has been revealed here in Christ and in his death on the cross as a substitute for us. The charges against us have been dropped because Jesus Christ has been condemned for us, in our place. Our rap is paid. All of us who are in Christ know that our penalty has been expelled because it has been fully paid. Our penalty no longer haunts us because Christ has taken it and paid it fully.

Whose penalty did he pay? Jesus has justified all of those, Paul says, "who are in Christ Jesus." To be "in Christ Jesus" means to believe in him (Acts 19:4; Rom. 3:22, 26). As Paul wrote to the Galatians (2:16), we "know that a man is not justified by observing the law, but by faith in Jesus Christ" (cf. Gal. 3:22). To be in Christ is to share in the suffering, kingdom, and patient endurance that John said we have in Jesus (Rev. 1:9). Paul said in this letter to the Romans, "Count yourselves dead to sin but alive to God in Christ Jesus" (6:11). Being in Christ means belonging to all other Christians (Rom. 12:5). We glory in Christ, and we work together in him. We are sanctified in him and given grace in him. We live in him, and, if we are Christians, we will die in him (1 Cor. 15:18). All God's promises and all our hopes are rolled up together in Christ. We are indwelt by his Spirit, and we live for the praise of his name. This is something of what it means for us to be in Christ. Now, if you are one of those, then you can know that there is for you, now, no condemnation.

My non-Christian friends, what this means for you, if you are outside of Christ, is that you are laid open and liable to God's condemning you for your sins. In fact, even now, your sins call out to God to be just, to take vengeance against you for your sins. Perhaps that sounds extreme to you, but how bad do you think your sins need to be for God to condemn you for them? But God is a good God. He's not tied to the low standards of your sin or mine. He is perfectly just, perfectly righteous, and perfectly holy.

My Christian friends, Jesus Christ has been our ransom and our justifier. On the last day he will divide all humanity into only two groups. Jesus said in Matthew 25:33 that there will be sheep and there will be goats. To us it may seem important to be an old sheep, or a female sheep, or a married goat, or an empty-nester goat. But I promise you that on *that* day the only division that will matter is the division between the sheep and the goats, between those who are not condemned and those who are.

Brothers and sisters, rejoice in the fact that if you are in Christ, you now have no condemnation. Relish that fact. Rejoice at work, and rejoice at home. If you can learn to rejoice in that fact, it will do you more good than learning a hundred evangelistic gospel presentations. Learn to rejoice in the fact that God has brought you no condemnation in Christ. Praise God for the joy that gives us, for the truth of it, for the knowledge that our penalty has been paid in Christ, and that there is now no condemnation. Put your worries up against the magnitude of this certainty in Christ forever and rejoice knowing that your penalty is paid in Christ. There is now no condemnation for those who are in Christ Jesus.

2) *Our bondage is broken, and the spiritually bound are set free*: "because through Christ Jesus the law of the Spirit of life set me free from the law of sin and death" (8:2). The two laws mentioned here could be referring to God's law in its various forms—that is, God's teaching which brings life to some and death to others—or it could simply be an image Paul uses for a principle or way of life. Either way, the Spirit and sin both pull on us and in different directions. One pulls us to a self-centeredness, the other to a God-centeredness. But it is the Spirit's work that results in life. The Holy Spirit of God is the only one who can teach God's message to us so that we are freed. That's what Paul says has happened to Christians. We've been liberated from our bondage to sin and death.

If you are not a Christian, that may sound a little over-dramatic. You may think, "I have Christian friends who look a lot less liberated than I am." But we Christians understand that before we were

Christians, we were in bondage to sin, and we understand that that is your natural state, too. It's everyone's natural state, including our children's, our best friends', our worst enemies'. We all have this in common. I know this may seem incredible to you, but, really, that's not surprising. Our own sins are famously invisible to our gaze. They don't appear to us easily. We turn and try in vain to see things in our own moral shadows. We take them for granted; we are too accustomed to them. This is one reason the first weeks of marriage are often so interesting. When you put two sinners together, living together all the time, they see each other's problems in a way that no one else has ever been close enough to see before. All of a sudden someone else is seeing us as no one else ever has.

My non-Christian friend, do you realize your bondage to sin? Is this news to you? The reason you are alive is to know God as your Lord and heavenly Father. That's why you are made in his image. Your freedom will come not through your being driven to oppose any restraint on your actions, which is what our generation wrongly thinks freedom is, but rather in your being drawn to find the true purpose of your life—to know and adore and love God. And you are able to experience that only in Christ Jesus. That's the freedom the Bible talks about. I've often heard it said that anyone is free to use a piano as a vacuum cleaner, or a vacuum cleaner as a piano. You're free to do that if you want to talk about freedom in that sense, but the best freedom is understanding what that something's purpose is—how to use a piano as a piano and a vacuum cleaner as a vacuum cleaner. That's a homely illustration, I know, but it makes the point that true freedom is found in your true purpose as a human being.

Christian brothers and sisters, pray that you can see the truth about those you work with. Pray that God give you a love for them and opportunities to share this freeing truth with them. And remember to praise God for delivering you from the bondage of thinking wrongly about what it means to be a woman or a man, or wrongly about what it means to be a single person, or wrongly about what it means to be a son or a daughter. Hasn't God been good in delivering us from bondage to sin, from things that have kept us trapped? What kind of specific bondages to sin have you experienced? How has Christ freed you? When was the last time you shared that with one of your brothers or sisters in Christ to encourage them? When was the last time you recounted some specific goodness of God to you?

I recently watched a DVD dramatization of Alex Haley's famous book *Roots*. My sympathy for what African-Americans in our country have contributed and endured only increased by watching this movie series (though there was great controversy at the time that the series actually downplayed the viciousness and violence of life in the name of entertainment). Even so, as I watched it I had many thoughts, and one thing I was thinking about was the joy of freedom surely experienced by that first generation after slavery ended, the joy they must have known when they were released from bondage. I say this because the joy of freedom and the bond of former slaves illustrate what we Christians should know together in church. If we are Christians, then we are of those who know what it means to be in bondage to sin and death and then to be released by Jesus Christ. We are a meeting of former slaves, of those who were enslaved by sin and death and who have been brought together by the liberation of Jesus Christ. That brings us a bond and a joy that others can only imagine. We are those who have had our bondage to sin broken.

3) *Sin is condemned by God substituting his Son for sinners*: "For what the law was powerless to do in that it was weakened by the sinful nature, God did" (8:3). We must not miss the fact that the saving act here is again God's act, not our own. He has performed it, achieved it, done it. We should notice four things about God's action.

First, God ultimately condemns sin. We saw in the last chapter that Scripture describes God's saving action towards us in three tenses: God *saved* us from the penalty of sin, God *is saving* us from the power of sin, and God *will save* us from even the very presence of sin. So, salvation is presented as a past accomplished fact, as a present unfolding reality, and as a final, full, and future certainty. All of these are effected by God, and by God alone. What the law was not able to do, God did.

My non-Christian friend, what do you do when you are accused, and you know your accuser is right? What do you do when you're caught? That is your future, according to the Bible. You will, most certainly and most surely, be caught. We Christians are all those who've realized this about ourselves and have asked for God's mercy in Christ. What about you?

Oh, friends, Christ has been "caught" for us. He is our only hope. He is the only one who had clean hands, who had nothing to be "caught" for. But he was given up to death—for us. We Christians are those who, whether we're just married, poor, or doing well, whether we've spent years being educated, or not—we are those who have in common the same hope that God alone can save anyone.

You might be having a pretty rough week. Well, if you're a Christian, always remember there's more joy in Jesus than in the job. We have no promises in Scripture about the joy you will necessarily find in your job in a fallen world, but we do have promises about joy in Jesus. We should remember that. It's not that jobs aren't good gifts of God; they are. But they are not our ultimate hope, and as a part of this fallen world they *will* disappoint. But Jesus is faithful now, and will be seen by us to be so more and more as we go on with him. If you've found that to be true—that Jesus' faithfulness only increases in its evidence to us over the years—can you imagine how it will appear to us in heaven with all the scattered children of God?

Friends, how will you deal with sins honestly in your families and in your friendships apart from Christ? How will you have that wonderful combination of honesty and forgiveness, of reality and hope, of justice and mercy, apart from the graciousness that we see here of God in Christ? God has put himself inexplicably on our side, and isn't it wonderful to have God on our side? Praise God who is both good and kind to us, as he condemns sin for us. We could never have done that on our own, but that's what he has done for us.

Second, God condemned sin through the incarnation, by sending his Son in human likeness. Look again at verse 3: "For what the law was powerless to do in that it was weakened by the sinful nature, God did *by sending his own Son in the likeness of sinful man*," literally, of sinful flesh. All the sacrifices that God instructed his people in the Old Testament to present before him were not sufficient to condemn sin. In order to do this, God the Father had to send his Son, and his Son had to take on human flesh, blood, and bones. He had to identify with us, and thus he would be incarnate, "enfleshed." He would be like us in every way, except for our sin. The virgin-born Jesus had no sinful nature, nor did he commit any sin.

Sometimes people get confused and think that sin is essential for truly human nature. But it's not. Adam and Eve existed before sin, and if you're a Christian, you will exist *after* sin. Isn't that a wild and wonderful thought? You will outlast sin. There will be a *you*—but without sin. How wonderful is that to consider—a truly human and yet glorified you, a you as you were made to fully bear the image of God. Praise God for that!

So the eternal Son of God left his Father's throne to be born in a manger and to grow up as an obedient son to fallible earthly parents. He lived through his childhood , his adolescence, his twenties, and into his thirties, when, having instructed his disciples, he laid down his life for us on the cross, was raised bodily from the dead, ascended bodily to heaven, and will return bodily at the end of the age. He shared our nature so that he could bear our guilt. That's the Christian faith.

Non-Christian friend, this is our best understanding of Jesus of Nazareth, that he was fully and truly human and at the same time fully and truly God. What we reject is the idea that Jesus was merely a prophet or a good teacher. There is simply too much information embedded in the earliest records about Jesus, the New Testament, to leave anyone with the idea that he was simply a good teacher. He was either an egomaniac, an egotist of the first order, or he was who he said he was—the Son of God, come to be our savior.

Notice further that God didn't send the answer to our sin in some principle, some book dropped from heaven, or some life insight. You may remember Rhonda Byrne's book *The Secret,* which became a worldwide best-seller by telling people that they could get what they wanted just by wanting it. Just a few months later, the companion volume was released, *The Secret Gratitude Book,* which, selling for only twenty dollars, provided mostly blank pages on which you could "create physical manifestations of your gratitude," which means you could write down things you're thankful for. Now, friends, this is not the kind of thing God did to deal with our sin. We needed more than a trite principle and a blank book. Merely teaching us a new way to view life is wholly inadequate to the personal nature, the relational nature of sin, because sin is not against an abstract law but against a personal God. Every sin you have ever committed is a sin against God himself—his nature, his character, and what he made you to be like. So dealing with it will take a lot more than just thinking differently.

Therefore, God dealt with sin personally by sending his Son—fully God, fully man—to restore our relationship with God. Have you shared this great news with your friends at work? Is your life with your friends and family marked by this kind of Christlike, self-giving love? If not, and you have this good news but don't share it with them, what does it mean to say that you love them? Do you have the

humility that Paul illustrates by pointing to the incarnation? Do you
begin to see how lavishly God has loved us by sending us his Son? I
love this statement by Jonathan Edwards about the purpose of the
church and what it has to do with God's sending his Son:

> The creation of the world seems to have been especially for this end, that
> the eternal Son of God might obtain a spouse, towards whom he might
> fully exercise the infinite benevolence of his nature, and to whom he might,
> as it were, open and pour forth all that immense fountain of condescen-
> sion, love and grace that was in his heart, and that in this way God might
> be glorified.[2]

Third, the purpose of the incarnation was to deal with our sin:
"For what the law was powerless to do in that it was weakened by
the sinful nature, God did by sending his own Son in the likeness of
sinful man *to be a sin offering*" (v. 3). Those last words are literally,
"and for sin," meaning that God sent his Son in order to deal with
our sin. The NIV translates the phrase more specifically as "to be a
sin offering" because this was the Greek phrase used in the Septuagint
to translate the Hebrew idea of "a sin offering." The NIV is simply
giving us the meaning of the idiom.

So the Son was incarnate in order to deal with our sin by a sacrifice.
This means that God's purpose in the incarnation included *us* and
had our sin particularly in view.

My non-Christian friend, are you understanding Christianity better
as we walk through this? Jesus Christ didn't come merely to give *The
Secret*–like tips on life, on how to improve your circumstances or how
to make you a more efficient vessel or tool for achieving your own
ends. He came to change your ends. He came to change what you're
about. He came to change your purpose in life. You may have all the
accoutrements of a good and moral person. You may be sweeter and
kinder and more truthful than I am or another Christian is, but what
is the end to which you are sweet and kind and truthful? *That* is the
heart of what Jesus Christ came to change. He came to teach us that
we don't live for ourselves supremely but for the God who made us.
That is where we find our purpose. Jesus came to reorient your life
from being centered on yourself to being centered on him.

---

[2]Jonathan Edwards, "The Church's Marriage to Her Sons, and to Her God," in *The Works of
Jonathan Edwards*, vol. 25 (New Haven, CT: Yale University Press, 2006), 187.

Jesus Christ came to save us. He came to save us from ourselves and from our own self-made disaster of a life. Most fundamentally, he came to save us from himself, from God's sure wrath against us for our sins—sins that hurt us and others, sins that divide and destroy, sins that dishonor the God who made us.

We Christians know a continuing war against sin, don't we? Christ dealt with the penalty of sin, so its over-mastering power is broken. Yet there is a continuing struggle in our lives, and there will be that struggle until we finally are made fully like him when we are in his presence in glory. We now struggle with sin, in the office, in the store, on the computer, in our words, in our attitudes and thoughts and tastes and opinions, and in our actions.

Sometimes we get the mistaken idea that maturity in the Christian life is growing to an understanding of grace so that our sins don't matter or, the opposite error, thinking we grow to a state of perfection in this life where we never intentionally sin. Both of these errors are dangerous, and you should watch out for them.

Have you established relationships with other Christians that help you war against sin? That's one reason that you should join a good church. If you're a Christian who is not a member of a local congregation of Bible-believing Christians, let me urge you to do so. God established churches to this end. We covenant together in order to deal with our sins, in order to help each other get rid of all bitterness, rage and anger, brawling and slander, and every form of malice. We work to encourage each other, to be kind and compassionate to one another, forgiving each other just as in Christ God forgave us. That's what Paul said in Ephesians 4, and that's what we try to live out together in our church here, as we deal with sin.

Fourth, sin was finally condemned by Christ's substitutionary death. He condemned sin in his body. Look once more at verse 3: "For what the law was powerless to do in that it was weakened by the sinful nature, God did by sending his own Son in the likeness of sinful man to be a sin offering. *And so he condemned sin in sinful man.*"

That last phrase, "in sinful man," is one of the NIV's poorer translations, and it obscures Paul's point. In fact, if you have an NIV just cross that out. Translated literally, it's just "in the flesh." To understand that as meaning "in sinful man" is going to mislead you, I fear. I think what Paul means here is that God condemned sin in the flesh *of Jesus Christ.* That's how God has condemned sin—in the flesh of Jesus Christ.

It's in this sentence that we see most clearly how it is that God has dealt with our sin through Jesus Christ. Here most clearly we see that Jesus came to do more than be an example or to teach. God actually condemned sin in the flesh of Jesus. God didn't just overlook sins. He's a good and just God, and his sentence of condemnation on our sins was executed on the cross of Christ. It has been discharged.

Non-Christian friend, this is what we Christians understand to be the basis of our hope that there is now no condemnation for us. So we also call on you to realize that God made you to know him. You've sinned against him, and yet he sent Christ to live a perfect life and to die on the cross in the place of all of those who would repent of their sins and trust in him. In fact, he calls you to do that now. Repent of your sins. Let go of them. What have they ever brought you? And take hold of Jesus Christ. Cast your life on him.

Christ is our substitute. He is the substitute for all his people, regardless of age or gender or nationality. Thus, our commonality in Christ is sufficient for our fellowship together. As Christians, we should be marked by fully giving ourselves for God's purposes in our families, in our jobs, in our communities.

I wonder, then, if we live as those whom the Holy Spirit has freed from the bondage of sin. Here's a lengthy quotation from the late second century:

> The difference between Christians and the rest of mankind is not a matter of nationality, or language, or customs. Christians do not live apart in separate cities of their own, speak any special dialect, nor practise any eccentric way of life. The doctrine they profess is not the invention of busy human minds and brains, nor are they, like some, adherents of this or that school of human thought. They pass their lives in whatever township—Greek or foreign—each man's lot has determined; and conform to ordinary local usage in their clothing, diet, and other habits. Nevertheless, the organization of their community does exhibit some features that are remarkable, and even surprising. For instance, though they are residents at home in their own countries, their behavior there is more like that of transients; they take their full part as citizens, but they also submit to anything and everything as if they were aliens. For them, any foreign country is a motherland, and any motherland is a foreign country. Like other men, they marry and beget children, though they do not expose their infants.

No infanticide, no abortion among the Christian. Any Christian is free to share his neighbor's table, but never his marriage-bed. Though destiny has placed them here in the flesh, they do not live after the flesh; their days are passed on the earth, but their citizenship is above in the heavens. They obey the prescribed laws, but in their own private lives they transcend the laws. They show love to all men—and all men persecute them. They are misunderstood and condemned; yet by suffering death they are quickened into life. They are poor, yet making many rich; lacking all things, yet having all things in abundance. They are dishonoured, yet made glorious in their very dishonour; slandered, yet vindicated. They repay calumny with blessings, and abuse with courtesy. For the good they do, they suffer stripes as evil-doers; and under the strokes they rejoice like men given new life. Jews assail them as heretics, and Greeks harass them with persecutions; and yet of all their ill-wishers there is not one who can produce good grounds for his hostility.[3]

Please don't think that I'm suggesting by this that Christians don't sin. We do. But if sin has been condemned, our penalty paid, and our bondage broken, we do live a new life. We live a life that looks different. I like the way William Arnot put it: "The difference between an unconverted and a converted man is not that the one has sins and the other has none; but that the one takes part with his cherished sins against a dreaded God, and the other takes part with a reconciled God against his hated sins."[4]

Whose side will you take?

Those who have been set free by the Spirit live by the Spirit.

[3] Epistle to Diognetus," in *Early Christian Writings*, rev. ed., ed. Andrew Louth, trans. Maxwell Stamforth (London: Penguin, 1987), 144.
[4] William Arnot, *Laws from Heaven for Life on Earth* (London: Nelson and Sons, 1884), 311.

CHAPTER TWELVE

BECOMING A CURSE FOR US

Galatians 3:10–13

MICHAEL LAWRENCE

You have surely heard of the Forbes 400, the richest people in America. It used to be that the people at the top of the list had inherited their wealth. The last time that happened, though, was well over a decade ago. These days, to be among the richest of the rich, you have to be a self-made billionaire. It's new money, not old, that sits atop the Forbes 400. This fits in well with the way we like to think of ourselves. Americans have perfected the myth of the rugged individualist, the self-made person. From the Marlboro Man to most of our modern presidential candidates, to the folks at the top of the Forbes 400, the image of the self-made individual predominates. A moment's honest self-reflection, though, shows that it really is only a myth. John Donne was right: "No man is an island, entire unto himself."

Maybe you're naturally intelligent, but I bet that didn't stop you from getting a good degree to prove it to employers. Maybe you were born beautiful, but I guarantee that as you age, you'll be tempted to enhance that fading beauty. Maybe you were born rich, but then that makes my point, doesn't it? Or maybe you're like most of us, who weren't born rich, beautiful, or extraordinarily smart and so have had to work hard, build networks, gain skills, establish reputations— in short, try to gain any advantage you can to make it in life. No, contrary to myth, we're all relying on something outside ourselves to help us get through life.

The real question, it seems to me, isn't whether we're relying on something outside ourselves, but whether that which we're relying on is sufficient for the task. This is where Christianity has something unique to say. I don't know of a thoughtful Christian who wouldn't agree that money, good looks, and a great education are helpful in getting on with life in this world. But the question Christianity asks is: Are those things sufficient for getting on with God?

The fact is that God doesn't care how smart you are, how beautiful you are, how successful you are. By definition, he's smarter, prettier, and more successful than you, so you're not going to impress him that way. Intuitively, I think, most of us recognize that if there is a God, he's concerned with how good we are. So what are you relying on to commend yourself to God? Is it your good deeds? Is it your religious practices? Is it a sense that you're at least as good as the guy next door, and maybe even a little better, since you went to church this week and he did not?

Now, for some people—you may be one of them—this idea that we need to commend ourselves to God is the real problem with Christianity. It seems to imply that God is angry and needs to be appeased, that he's picky and has to be satisfied. Surely a loving God wouldn't attach conditions to his acceptance of us. And surely a loving God wouldn't demand the death of Jesus in order to accept us, which is what Christians have historically taught and believed.

For many who aren't Christians, this line of thinking means that the only way to understand the cross is as a tragedy, a shame: he was a good man, and it shouldn't have happened. This same line of thinking has led many theologically liberal theologians to explain the cross as more than tragedy but less than a penal substitution, Christ suffering the punishment that we deserved on our behalf. For them, the cross is a profound display of God's love, but it is emphatically not his active judgment of sin in the flesh of Jesus Christ. For these theologians, Christ did not suffer God's active wrath against sin for us but simply shared the human experience of suffering the natural consequences of sin with us.

Inevitably, this brings us back to the uniquely Christian question: What can I rely on to commend me to God, and how can I be sure it's up to the task? If Jesus simply shared in experiencing the consequences of sin with us rather than suffering God's wrath for us, then we are left with two equally bad options: either Jesus suffered for his own sin and so is no help to any of us, or an innocent Jesus suffered unjustly and uselessly. I say "uselessly" because we need more than sympathy; we need a reliable means of escape from God's curse.

The question of what we can rely on to escape God's curse is the point of Galatians 3:10–13:

> For all who rely on works of the law are under a curse; for it is written, "Cursed be everyone who does not abide by all things written in the Book of the Law, and do them." Now it is evident that no one is justified before God by the law, for "The righteous shall live by faith." But the law is not of faith, rather "The one who does them shall live by them." Christ redeemed us from the curse of the law by becoming a curse for us—for it is written, "Cursed is everyone who is hanged on a tree" (ESV).

Paul is supremely concerned in this passage with what we are relying upon to commend ourselves to God. He's writing to a group of churches in the region of Galatia, which is in modern Central Turkey. These churches had been started by Paul as they heard the message of the gospel and put their trust in Christ and his death to bring them into a right relationship with God. Galatians is one of the very first and therefore one of the oldest books in the New Testament. Paul is writing to them because, since his last visit, false teachers, claiming to be Jewish Christians like Paul, had arrived, and they'd been teaching that in order to be right with God, it is not enough to rely on Christ. These teachers taught that you also had to rely on the Law of Moses. In effect, you had to become a Jew before you could become a Christian.

Paul is deeply concerned to correct this error. He begins his letter, therefore, by establishing his authority as an apostle, particularly making the point that authority is not attached to his person but rather to the gospel he preached. He demonstrates that point through an encounter he had with Peter. Peter, also an apostle, had begun to practice differently from what the gospel demands, and Paul confronted him for it. He dared to confront a fellow apostle, because there's nothing special about being an apostle if that apostle has abandoned the gospel that made him an apostle in the first place. After recounting that story, Paul goes on to illustrate what he means by "the gospel"—that salvation is by faith in Christ and not by the law—and he does so by pointing to the example of Abraham. This is where our passage lies in Paul's argument, quite literally at the very crux of his argument. According to Paul, to rely on anything other than Christ is to be under God's curse. But to rely on Christ is to be delivered from God's curse because of what Christ accomplished on the cross. Let's consider Paul's argument by looking at three contrasts he makes.

Principles of Life

First, consider the contrast between two different principles of life: the principle of law and the principle of faith. In verse 10 Paul speaks of a group of people who "rely on observing the law." These are people whose lives are characterized by law keeping. This is not the first time Paul has mentioned this way of living. In 2:16 he states three times that justification before God does not come from this law-keeping way of life, and in 3:2 and 3:5 he asks the Galatians if their experience of the power of the Spirit of God came because of their law-keeping way of life, the implied answer being no.

But in verse 10 Paul speaks of a particular group of people who are characterized by this life principle. In the context of the letter as a whole, it's clear that he's referring to those false teachers who were saying that to be accepted by God, one must first become a Jew and then continue to keep the demands of the Mosaic Law. We're not entirely sure which aspects of the law they focused on, but it seems to have been especially those parts that set the Jews off as distinct from the Gentiles—circumcision and dietary laws, for instance.

These people, Paul says, are living lives characterized by the principle of law. And what is that principle? Paul lays it out in verse 12: "But the law is not of faith, rather 'The one who does them shall live by them'" (ESV). Paul is quoting here from Leviticus 18:5, in which God says, "Keep my decrees and laws, for the man who obeys them will live by them." That is to say, the man who obeys his law will be rewarded with life. Thus, the law lays out a very straightforward proposition: if you keep the law, you live; if you don't, you die. It's pretty simple. There's no charity involved, no special cases.

Paul makes a very similar point in Romans 4:4: "Now when a man works, his wages are not credited to him as a gift, but as an obligation." According to the principle of law, everyone gets exactly what he's earned, exactly what he deserves. It's a quid pro quo system. And according to the law principle, spiritual life that is characterized by being accepted and approved of by God is gained through faithful observance of the law. If you were to ask one of these people what they were relying on to commend themselves to God, they would point to their works of the law and say, "That's why God will accept me. I've been good. I've kept the law."

Now while Paul is talking about a group of people that history has come to call Judaizers—Jewish Christians who thought one had to become a Jew first in order to be accepted by God—it's clear that this principle has a wider following among humanity, even today. Isn't this what's behind the general notion that so long as our good deeds outweigh our bad, God is going to accept us? And isn't this why the public is convinced that Hitler and a few others will be in hell, but they're not sure about anyone else? Contrary to what you might think, that's not the principle of license at work. That's the principle of law, albeit with a fairly generous standard.

I wonder if you can see this principle at work in the way you evaluate your own life. If you're not a Christian, are you hoping that God will accept you because your good deeds outweigh your bad? Do you take some quiet satisfaction that your life is not in as much disarray as your neighbors' or your officemates'? I'm constantly amazed at how much the media tells us about the goings-on of relatively minor starlets and celebrities. I wonder, "Why do they think we're so interested in what's going on in the lives of these people?" Well, because we buy the magazines. They wouldn't do it if we weren't reading it, right? But why would anybody care about the latest throes and woes of Britney, or whoever the other starlets are out there? Well maybe we all read this stuff because, if nothing else, it convinces us, "My life is better than hers. It could be a lot worse. I must not be that bad."

Or perhaps you take encouragement from the fact that you've been "raised right." As a Southerner, that's the way I was raised. If you're a Southerner, you'll recognize the phrase. You were "raised right." You've got good manners and good taste; you are politically astute and careful; you think globally and act locally; you reduce, reuse, and recycle. Or maybe you feel good about yourself because you could be out there making lots of money in the private sector, but instead you're giving some time to public service. Or maybe you've left public service and now you're making lots of money (or preparing to), but you take confidence from the fact that you know you're not as greedy as the partner down the hall. Friends, the standards vary, but the standards are immaterial. The point is that all of this operates according to the law principle: as long as I keep to the standard, God will accept me.

At this point I have to ask you: If you're not a Christian and you're working at one of these standards, or maybe one I didn't mention, what happens when you fail to keep even your own standard? Would God have the right to judge you then, or do you get to change the law?

Those of us who are Christians would do well to consider where this principle of law keeping is at work in our own lives. Christian, how can you tell if this principle has found a home in your heart? I'll tell you one way: when you give the people around you exactly what they deserve, and when you're offended when you don't get what you think you deserve. Of course, what "they" almost always deserve is punishment, because they're lawbreakers, and what you generally deserve, but don't get, is credit. That's how you know. I don't know what it's like with you, but I've noticed that this principle really flares up when I'm at home. The rest of the time I mainly just see it when I'm at work. It seems to follow me around. I wonder what's following you around. I wonder if this principle is evident in your life. If you haven't seen it, maybe you should ask the people around you.

In contrast to this, Paul points to a different principle, the principle of faith. He refers to it there in verse 11: "Now it is evident that no one is justified before God by the law, for 'The righteous shall live by faith'" (ESV).

Here is a different path to receiving the reward of life, of being commended to God, and it's not by being good. It's from faith. Back in verse 6 Paul explained what he means by living by faith, using the example of Abraham: "Just as Abraham 'believed God, and it was counted to him as righteousness'" (ESV). In Genesis 15 we read of how Abraham began to wonder if God would really keep his promise to make him into a great nation. After all, he was an old man married to an old woman, and they had no children, much less grandchildren. God took Abraham outside and had him look at the night sky. "Count the stars—if indeed you can count them. So shall your offspring be." Genesis 15:6 tells us that Abraham believed God—he trusted God's promise—and God credited that faith as righteousness. God approved of Abraham and counted that faith. Here's how Paul talks about it in Romans 4:5: "However, to the man who does not work but trusts God who justifies the wicked, his faith is credited as righteousness."

The principle of faith is not about quid pro quo. It's not about getting what we deserve. It's not about earning anything. In fact, the way of living by faith rather than works is not really about us at all. The principle of faith that Paul contrasts with the principle of law is all about God and his trustworthy promises. A life of faith in God does not come and demand, "All right, God, give me what I deserve; I earned it." No, the life of faith stands before God in utter humility and receives as a gift what it does not deserve and cannot earn—the promise of life, the promise of God's blessing and approval, the promise of a right relationship with God, the promise of the Spirit of God dwelling in us. We don't deserve this, because, as we've already seen, all of us are lawbreakers. But faith receives it as a gift, not as a wage.

To most people, this may be the most offensive thing about Christianity. I understand there are a lot of things about Christianity that are difficult for modern sensibilities, but this must rank right up there at the top. Perhaps nothing cuts against the grain like this—getting something we didn't work for and that we therefore don't deserve. It may be Christian, but it's not American. As Americans, disparity that is earned is fine with us; it's undeserved disparity that gets at our pride. After all, it's not rich people who offend us; it's trust-fund babies who didn't work a day to get their privileges. It's also what bothers us about the implication of Roger Clemens in the baseball steroid scandal. Nobody would care if some no-name journeyman player used steroids. But if you get to the top of the game, earn millions, and set records, if you are a cultural icon, you better have earned your way there. Otherwise, why can't I be there? The law principle is offended by the faith principle—they are at war with each other, and nowhere more than on the question of who gets into heaven.

So let me ask you, if you're not a Christian, what are you relying on to commend yourself to God? Are you sure it's not just your pride?

Christian, I wonder how your faith is doing. Do you wish for stronger faith, for more faith? I want you to notice that here in Galatians, as far as Paul is concerned, the important thing isn't the quantity or quality of your faith. It's the *object* of your faith that counts. Abraham believed strongly in God. He didn't have faith in faith. He heard God's words of promise, and he believed them because God said them. He trusted the character and the power of the one who spoke those words. Do you want to strengthen your faith? Do you want more faith? The answer isn't to focus on your faith. The answer is to set your mind on God in Christ. Meditate on his character, consider his words, reflect on his faithfulness, goodness, and mercy to you in Christ, and see what happens to your faith.

The End Result

Second, we need next to consider the end result to which each of these principles of life leads. According to Paul, the difference is the contrast between being cursed by God and being justified by God. Look again at verse 10: "For all who rely on works of the law are under a curse; for it is written, 'Cursed be everyone who does not abide by all things written in the Book of the Law, and do them'" (ESV).

Paul could not be clearer about the result of relying on the law to commend ourselves to God. All who do so are under the curse of God. To prove his point, Paul quotes from Deuteronomy 27. He quotes specifically from the last verse, but I think he has in mind the whole chapter. In that passage, God instructs Israel to divide into two groups once they have crossed the River Jordan and entered the Promised Land. One group is to stand on one mountain on one side of the valley and declare God's blessings if they keep the law. The other group is to stand on the other side of the valley, on a different mountain, and declare God's curse if they disobey his law. The final statement in that declaration is the one Paul quotes here. The point is obvious: if we're going to find life by the law, then we're going to have to keep the whole law—every last bit of it. Perfectly. There's no sliding scale. We don't get to pick and choose. According to Scripture, when we fail to keep the law, we don't at that point get to adjust the standards. As James says: "Whoever keeps the whole law and yet stumbles at just one point is guilty of breaking all of it. . . . [He has] become a lawbreaker" (James 2:10–12). Such people, Paul says, are cursed by God.

What does it mean to be under God's curse? It's not some sort of magical spell, as if God was some celestial wizard. To be under God's curse is a judicial statement. It is to be disapproved of by God, condemned by him and subject to his judicial wrath. And that's not just the fate of Jews who break the Mosaic Law; this sentence applies to all of us.

In using the language of God's curse, Paul is not only referring to the language of Deuteronomy, but he's reaching back past the events at Mount Sinai, all the way to the beginning of the human race in the garden of Eden. There, Adam and Eve stood at the head of the human race, representing us all. They were given a very straightforward law. If they obeyed, they and all their posterity would be established in life forever. But if they disobeyed, they would die in judgment for their sin. Adam and Eve chose to disobey, so they suffered the curse of God. This was no passive working out of consequences. Rather, God in his judgment of Adam and Eve changed the very order of nature. On that day they were exiled from his presence, at war with each other and the world around them, which was now opposed to them, plunged into a state of judgment, suddenly subject to physical death, and liable to the eternal wrath of God.

They plunged us into that state with them. We are each one of us, by nature, lawbreakers. If you don't believe me, consider for a moment this past week. Is there even one day to which you can point that you went to bed without a single cause for regret—not one unkind remark, not one good deed left undone, all your work done to the best of your ability, all your words both perfectly true and perfectly motivated by love? And all this *not* for your praise and glory, but for the praise and glory of the one who made you? Look, I'm sure you're a pretty good person compared to me. But I'm not the standard. God is. And as Jesus said, "Be perfect, therefore, as your heavenly Father is perfect" (Matt. 5:48). We are all lawbreakers.

The irony of it all is not only that we are all lawbreakers, but that we are by nature people who think we can commend ourselves to God by keeping the law. There's only one explanation for that kind of thinking in the face of all the evidence to the contrary—our pride. Sinners like you and me love the law, especially if we can shape the law into something that we think we can keep, because then we can commend ourselves to God based on our merit. We don't have to humble ourselves to receive something from him that we don't deserve. Instead, we can stand on our own merits. Though God's law is all about displaying the exacting standards of his perfect righteousness, my desire to commend myself to God based on my law keeping is all about displaying me and my worth and my glory. This is why the world is full of pious, religious, law-keeping sinners, and why Jesus saved his harshest comments for hypocrites. The very thing meant to drive us to the grace of God is what we twist into the proof that grace is the last thing we need.

What will it take for you to have an accurate view of your life? What will it take for you to abandon your pride and consider the truth that you, like me, are a lawbreaker and therefore under God's curse?

In contrast to the curse of God for our vain attempts at law keeping, Paul is at pains to point out that the result of faith is to be justified before God, to have his approval and not his curse. This is the point of verse 11, which quotes from Habakkuk 2 and builds on Paul's earlier treatment of Abraham. In Habakkuk 2, Israel faces the prospect of invasion and devastation. But in the midst of that prophecy, Habakkuk declares that "the righteous will live by his faith" (v. 4). His point was that God's promises, not the Israelites' circumstances, would be the basis of their relationship with him. Paul then picks up that verse as a summary of Abraham's experience and the experience of all who are declared righteous, that is, justified, before God. God's approval does not come through the law and our keeping it. God's approval comes as we trust in him to freely give us what we cannot earn for ourselves.

Christian, are there ways in which you are tempted to stop living by faith and return to the law? Are there ways in which you need to hear Paul's piercing question to the Galatians: "After beginning with the Spirit, are you now trying to attain your goal by human effort?" (3:3). There's a lot of talk in conservative churches about what theologians call "the third use of the law." It basically says that now that we're justified by faith, not law, the law shows us how we should live, what it looks like to follow God. In one sense, that's right, because the law shows us God's holy character. But in another sense, and I fear in the sense that we often use it, that's wrong, if we take it to mean that the Christian life is anything other than the life of faith. Christian, we're not justified by faith and then sanctified by law; we're not saved by faith but then grown by law. No, from first to last the Christian life is the life of faith. It is a life that depends upon the grace of God for everything—from our justification to our present obedience in sanctification, from our new life in our calling and regeneration in Christ to our growth into maturity. The law may give us the pattern, but it cannot provide the power, and it never supplies the motive. Faith looks to Christ—there is the power for a life that pleases God, and there is the motive for a life lived unto God.

Do you want to see greater holiness in yourself, in your family, in your friends? Do you want to see greater holiness characterized in the life of your church? Then do not point to the law. Point to Christ. For it is Christ who is the power of God and the wisdom of God, and it is in Christ that we have been given everything we need to live a life unto God. That's why as a church we want to be careful to always rightly prioritize the preaching of Christ, the preaching of this gospel of grace. It is this gospel that transforms the lives of sinners, and it is this gospel that impacts the society around us as sinners saved by grace and transformed by grace to go out and live inexplicably different lives than the world around us.

Why, then, did God give the law, if it wasn't so that we could keep it and earn his approval, and if it wasn't so that by it we could be sanctified? Look at Galatians 3:21–24:

> Is the law then contrary to the promises of God? Certainly not! For if a law had been given that could give life, then righteousness would indeed be by the law. But the Scripture imprisoned everything under sin, so that the promise by faith in Jesus Christ might be given to those who believe. Now before faith came, we were held captive under the law, imprisoned until the coming faith would be revealed. [24] So then, the law was our guardian until Christ came, in order that we might be justified by faith. (ESV)

The point of the law is not that we would twist it and lessen it and explain it away into something we can keep. The point of the law is to teach us that we cannot keep it and to drive us to faith in Christ. The point of the law is to cause us to despair of ourselves, and so turn outside of ourselves, to find in God through Christ all that we need. So, you see, if law keeping exalts us and our glory, faith in Christ exalts God and brings him glory, showing him to be the powerful and trustworthy and gracious God that he is, because it trusts in his promises, not in our efforts.

What has he promised? He's promised that everyone who believes in Christ will not die but have everlasting life (John 3:16). He's promised that all who confess with their mouth that "Jesus is Lord" and believe in their hearts that God raised him from the dead will be saved from the curse (Rom. 10:9). He's promised that all who call on the name of the Lord, repenting of their sins and trusting in him, will never be put to shame (Rom. 10:11). He's declared that he is the resurrection and the life, and that whoever believes in him will live, even though he dies, and whoever lives and believes in him will never die (John

11:25–26). He's promised that whoever comes to him, he will never drive away (John 6:37).

Do these promises sound too good to be true? If I were making them, they would be. But, friend, consider that every one of those promises are not my words but God's. The fact is that Christianity does ask you to take a step of faith, but it is not a blind leap; it is not an irrational choice. Rather, as Paul reminds us, our faith is to be like Abraham's, who was "fully persuaded that God had power to do what he had promised" (Rom. 4:21).

Look, if there really is no God, then Jesus was not God incarnate, and after he was crucified, he did not get up from the dead—his bones are still rotting in the ground somewhere near Jerusalem. But those bones were never produced, not even in those early days when it would have been comparatively easy to discover their whereabouts, therefore disproving the whole thing. Why is that? The Bible declares that it's because Jesus *is* God incarnate, and God is exactly the kind of being who can raise people from the dead so that there are no bones to be found. He's exactly the kind of person, therefore, who can keep promises that sound too good to be true, promises that we could never dream of making, let alone keeping. After all, we can't even keep the law. But the law is just a display of God's beauty. God is exactly the kind of person who can keep the promises that I declare to you. Friend, what are you relying on? What are you believing in? Are you believing in yourself, when you can't even keep the promises that you make to yourself? Will you believe in God?

The Contrast

Finally, we should notice the contrast between the accursed and Christ. Look once more at verse 13: "Christ redeemed us from the curse of the law by becoming a curse for us—for it is written, 'Cursed is everyone who is hanged on a tree'" (ESV). Just how is it that God can remove the curse from lawbreakers like us who have earned his judgment? How is it that he can reward our faith in Christ with justification and give us life? The answer is found at the cross. Paul declares that on the cross Jesus Christ became a curse for us. He wasn't just caught up in the common experience of suffering that is the lot of this world under God's judgment. Paul's discussion of the curse in verse 10 makes clear what he means. On the cross, Jesus Christ took on himself the guilt of lawbreakers like us. On the cross, he endured the penalty of a lawbreaker. He bore God's wrath and condemnation; he was cut off from God and experienced in his flesh the judicial sentence that we deserved.

The contrast is striking. We deserve the curse. He did not. We could not escape the curse on our own. He took it on voluntarily. We are born into the curse and daily confirm the rightness of it. He had to become a curse, for it had no natural hold on him. But the most important contrast is that we could never satisfy the curse. We, in fact, can never be punished as much as our sins deserve. But he not only satisfied the curse; he exhausted it. Because he was delivered over to the curse of death, we are delivered from the curse of the law. Through his death, we receive life. Because of his condemnation by God, we are justified before God. He died for us as our substitute and exhausted the penalty that should have been ours.

Christian, this is what Christ did for you. He didn't experience this to sympathize with your plight. He did it to redeem you from your plight, so that in him you might receive the promise of the Spirit (v. 14). Why does Paul move from the cross to the promise of the Spirit? And what does this Spirit do in you? Does he lead you back to a fearful law keeping, lest God be angry at you again? No. The Spirit of God leads you to call out, "Abba, Father," and to live in the freedom of the sons and daughters of God—children who delight in their Father's will because they delight in their Father's love (Gal. 4:6ff.).

Friends, this confident delight that says, "I don't need to commend myself to God anymore, because Jesus Christ has done it for me"—this confidence does not come through law keeping. It comes only through faith in Christ, as we repent of our sins and our vain efforts to commend ourselves and instead trust in Christ's perfect commendation of us through his death and resurrection for us. So I ask you again: What are you relying on to commend yourself to God?

Rely on Christ and his death for you. Nothing else will do, and nothing else is needed.

CHAPTER THIRTEEN

BORE OUR SINS IN HIS BODY ON THE TREE

1 Peter 2:21–25

MARK DEVER

"Violent, irrational, intolerant, allied to racism and tribalism and big-otry, invested in ignorance and hostile to free inquiry, contemptuous of women and coercive toward children: organized religion ought to have a great deal on its conscience." That's Christopher Hitchens, from his book entitled *God Is Not Great: How Religion Poisons Everything.*[1]

Another author, A. C. Grayling, also published an aggressively athe-istic book, modestly titled *Against All Gods.*[2] In it, Grayling defines faith as "a commitment to belief contrary to evidence and reason."[3] So it's no surprise that he says that, in his opinion, "the phrase 'religious think tank' has a certain comic quality to it."[4] Grayling charges that "most wars and conflicts in the world's history owe themselves directly or indirectly to religion. By their fruits, we are told, we shall know them. A simple test of the relative merits of science and religion is to compare lighting your house at night by prayer or electricity."[5]

Hitchens's and Grayling's books are part of a wave of new public insults to Christianity. From Richard Dawkins's *The God Delusion* to Sam Harris's *Letter to a Christian Nation,* the bookstores are full

---

[1]Christopher Hitchens, *God Is Not Great: How Religion Poisons Everything* (Boston: Twelve, 2007), 56.
[2]A. C. Grayling, *Against All Gods: Six Polemics on Religion and an Essay on Kindness* (London: Oberon, 2007).
[3]Ibid., 15.
[4]Ibid., 35.
[5]Ibid., 50–51.

of irreligion. There's even a new intriguingly *religious* atheist book on the shelves, Andre Comte-Sponville's *The Little Book of Atheist Spirituality*.[6]

These books are selling, too. Indeed if you simply type "God" into Amazon's search engine, the first two books that come up are Christopher Hitchens's *God Is Not Great* and Richard Dawkins's *The God Delusion*. How is that possible? It's because they're selling. In fact, there have been so many atheistic books published lately that it's now being called a movement named "the New Atheism." I have to tell you, as a former agnostic I feel the weight of some of these criticisms of religion.

This is all hardly *new*, however. Atheism? Yes. New? Not at all. Over two hundred years ago, Thomas Paine was making similar assaults on Christianity:

> Whence arose all the horrid assassinations of whole nations of men, women, and infants, with which the Bible is filled; and the bloody persecutions, and tortures unto death, and religious wars, that since that time have laid Europe in blood and ashes; whence arose they, but from this impious thing called religion, and this monstrous belief that God has spoken to man?[7]

Christian, you and I may believe that our message is universally true, but we must know it is certainly *not* universally accepted. It never has been. The theme of the suffering of the godly in this fallen world is found throughout the Bible. The psalmist refers to the many troubles that the righteous have (e.g., Ps. 34:19). Joseph is thrown in the pit, and Jeremiah in the well. Christ himself suffered (e.g., Luke 24:26). Jesus said to his first disciples, "If the world hates you, keep in mind that it hated me first. If you belonged to the world, it would love you as its own. As it is, you do not belong to the world, but I have chosen you out of the world. This is why the world hates you. . . . If they persecuted me, they will persecute you also" (John 15:18–20), and, "In this world you will have trouble" (John 16:33).

Paul taught the early Christians, "We must go through many hardships to enter the kingdom of God" (Acts 14:22). He wrote to the

---

[6] Andre Comte-Sponville, *The Little Book of Atheist Spirituality* (New York: Viking, 2008).
[7] Thomas Paine, "The Rights of Man" (1791), cited in James A. Haught, *2000 Years of Disbelief: Famous People with the Courage to Doubt* (Amherst, NY: Prometheus, 1996), 87.

Philippians that he desired to share in Christ's sufferings, and to Timothy he wrote that "everyone who wants to live a godly life in Christ Jesus will be persecuted" (2 Tim. 3:12). The writer to the Hebrews encouraged the early Christians when they were facing insult and opposition, and reminded them that Jesus "endured the cross, scorning its shame, and sat down at the right hand of the throne of God. Consider him who endured such opposition from sinful men, so that you will not grow weary and lose heart. In your struggle against sin, you have not yet resisted to the point of shedding your blood" (Heb. 12:2–4; cf. James 1:2–4).

Peter also talked about this in his first letter, especially in 1 Peter 2:21–25:

> To this you were called, because Christ suffered for you, leaving you an example, that you should follow in his steps. "He committed no sin, and no deceit was found in his mouth." When they hurled their insults at him, he did not retaliate; when he suffered, he made no threats. Instead, he entrusted himself to him who judges justly. He himself bore our sins in his body on the tree, so that we might die to sins and live for righteousness; by his wounds you have been healed. For you were like sheep going astray, but now you have returned to the Shepherd and Overseer of your souls.

To understand this passage, we must again look at its context. Peter refers to our being called to "this" in verse 21. What is the *this* to which he refers? It's defined in verse 19: "It is commendable if a man bears up under the pain of unjust suffering because he is conscious of God. But how is it to your credit if you receive a beating for doing wrong and endure it? But if you suffer for doing good and you endure it, *this* is commendable before God."

Peter is talking about enduring, and continuing to do good, even in the face of insults, trials, and mockery for being a Christian. Really, this is what this whole letter is all about. When you look back through it, you begin to see more clearly the situation Peter was addressing, the situation these early Christians were facing. He is addressing what we might call the lesser persecutions—insults, false accusations, personal rejection. There's no evidence that people were being killed for being Christians at this time and in the place to which this letter was written (Asia Minor, which is modern-day Turkey). But they were certainly facing suffering, especially false accusations and insults. That's what Peter writes to them about. In 1:6–7, Peter writes:

> In this you greatly rejoice, though now for a little while you may have had to suffer grief in all kinds of trials. These have come so that your faith—of greater worth than gold, which perishes even though refined by fire—may be proved genuine and may result in praise, glory and honor when Jesus Christ is revealed.

And in 2:4:

> As you come to him, the living Stone—rejected by men but chosen by God and precious to him . . .

And in 2:11–12:

> Dear friends, I urge you, as aliens and strangers in the world, to abstain from sinful desires, which war against your soul. Live such good lives among the pagans that, though they accuse you of doing wrong, they may see your good deeds and glorify God on the day he visits us.

Then, after our passage in 2:25–31, Peter continues in 3:9–17:

> Do not repay evil with evil or insult with insult, but with blessing, because to this you were called. . . . It is better, if it is God's will, to suffer for doing good than for doing evil.

Then in 4:12–19:

> Dear friends, do not be surprised at the painful trial you are suffering, as though something strange were happening to you. But rejoice that you participate in the sufferings of Christ, so that you may be overjoyed when his glory is revealed. If you are insulted because of the name of Christ, you are blessed, for the Spirit of glory and of God rests on you. If you suffer, it should not be as a murderer or thief or any other kind of criminal, or even as a meddler. However, if you suffer as a Christian, do not be ashamed, but praise God that you bear that name. . . . So then, those who suffer according to God's will should commit themselves to their faithful Creator and continue to do good.

And in 5:6–10:

> Humble yourselves, therefore, under God's mighty hand, that he may lift you up in due time. Cast all your anxiety on him because he cares for you. Be self-controlled and alert. Your enemy the devil prowls around like a roaring lion looking for someone to devour. Resist him, standing firm in the faith, because you know that your brothers throughout the world are undergoing the same kind of sufferings. And the God of all grace, who called you to his eternal glory in Christ, after you have suffered a little while, will himself restore you and make you strong, firm and steadfast.

The theme is clear: do good in spite of persecution. The problem these Christians were facing was this: as Christians, how do we deal with evil? And more specifically, how do we deal with our own sinful, self-serving desires, especially the desire for retribution, when we're wronged? How do we deal with suffering for doing good, especially insult, rejection, and false accusations?

The answer we find in our passage is that at the center of our call to live for righteousness is the call to emulate Christ's life of *entrusting* rather than *retaliation*. Here we again see ethical implications of Jesus' death as our substitute, his laying down his life for the benefit of others. Peter presents Jesus as the answer to these Christians' problem. What we learn is that in Jesus' life and death, while he was certainly doing something *unique*, he was also doing something that was to be *exemplary* for his followers.

Christ's Unique Life: Dying on the Cross as Our Substitute

We have to begin this by considering that Christ was a *unique person*. Jesus Christ was sinless. That's what we see here in verse 22: "He committed no sin, and no deceit was found in his mouth." Peter here refers to Isaiah's statement about the servant in Isaiah 53:9: "nor was any deceit in his mouth."

That is an extraordinary statement, when you think about it—that Jesus committed no sin. Yet, Judas, after betraying Jesus, declared that he had betrayed an innocent man (Matt. 27:4). Pilate, too, declared him innocent (John 18:38), and Jesus himself said, "I always do what pleases him [God]" (John 8:29). Then he challenges the crowd: "Can any of you prove me guilty of sin?" (John 8:46). John said of Jesus that "in him is no sin" (1 John 3:5). Paul referred to Jesus as "him who had no sin" (2 Cor. 5:21). And the writer to the Hebrews said about Jesus that "we do not have a high priest who is unable to sympathize with our weaknesses, but we have one who has been tempted in every way, just as we are—yet was without sin" (Heb. 4:15).

So Peter is adding his testimony of Jesus' unique sinlessness to that of many other New Testament writers, and Peter knew Jesus as well as anybody. Jesus is not like Moses or Gandhi or Lincoln or Socrates in this. We usually admire a frank admission of guilt; that helps us trust a person. And when we don't have that frank admission of guilt, we tend not to trust the person. Moreover, we know from experience with others that such a frank admission is usually true, and frankly we know that from ourselves, if we're honest. But Jesus is not like that. Christ did not present himself like that.

Some people mistakenly think that "to err is human, to forgive is divine." They're right on the forgiveness part, but the idea behind that phrase, "to err is human," is that sin is essential to being truly human because we're limited, and therefore we must sin. The Bible nowhere teaches that. In fact, Scripture teaches that the first people, Adam and Eve, were made without sin. It also teaches us that Christians will eventually live without sin, as glorified people, forever with God. Friend, if you are a Christian, you will live longer than your sin. You will live to know a time when you will experience humanity that is not perverted by sin. So when you read this about Christ, you should in no way think that this diminishes his humanity. Jesus Christ was fully human. You could argue in one sense that he was even *more* fully human because he was without sin.

If you're not very familiar with Christianity, I want to make sure I explain this correctly for you. The Bible teaches that everyone in this world sins and keeps on sinning. That's the Christian understanding of the moral evil in this world. That's why we are not surprised by it. When a tragedy happens to our nation, such as 9/11, Christians are not surprised. We are certainly saddened, but we're not surprised, because, frankly, we read this in Scripture and we read this in our own hearts. We understand something of the sinfulness of humanity.

This is where I've had interesting conversations with atheist friends. Atheists like Hitchens and Dawkins may, if they're honest, admit the strange pervasiveness of moral evil, but they have no real explanation for it. It's like a coin flipped six billion times always coming up tails. I think something's going on there. Indeed, as a Christian, I'm not surprised by it. You see, the Bible's explanation is that we are all, to use theological language, fallen. We are fallen away from God because of the sin of the first man, Adam. From the beginning, God declared the first man to be in a special, representative relationship with us. He would decide for us all. And since his fateful decision, we have all been not unhappy conscripts saying, "Oh, I don't really want to sin but Adam is making me sin," but rather happy rebels against God.

Jesus Christ, however, is different in this sense. Though fully human, he was also fully God. Untainted by original sin, he never sinned against his heavenly Father.

Friends, we do not have a sinless church, but we do have a sinless Savior. We love and serve and know one who is completely good and moral and virtuous and right and noble and kind and merciful and holy and compassionate and delightful and powerful and able and knowledgeable and reliable and trustworthy and fair and glorious, and he is the one around whom we are all united—our unique, sinless Savior, the God-man Jesus Christ.

Because Jesus Christ was so unique in his person, he was able to accomplish a *unique work:* Jesus suffered as a substitute for his people. You see that there in the second part of verse 21: "because Christ suffered for you." That's spelled out even a little more fully in verse 24, where we read that "he himself bore our sins in his body on the tree."

Some time ago a prominent public official announced his resignation from office, and he began his statement by saying, "In the past few days, I've begun to atone for my private failings." We all know what he meant. He was trying to make it up to his wife, trying to regain her trust and love, though he had so grievously and publicly abused it—and her.

Of course, strictly speaking, this official can't atone for his sins. He can't go back and undo those actions. Even if he could, he can't go back and undo the decisions that led to the actions, let alone the desires that led to the decisions that led to the actions. He's already done them, and no amount of other good he may do subsequently, even if it were to "morally outweigh" his transgressions in your mind or mine, would ever expunge them. They've been done. He sinned against his wife, the other woman (or women), his children, the women's families and future spouses, the people who elected him, and his friends. That's just on the human side, too, for we haven't even mentioned the fact that his sin was fundamentally against God. God is the one who gave him life and will judge him. God is the one who invented people and sexuality and marriage and parenthood and authority, and all of these in themselves reflect God in his goodness and holiness and creativity. All this and more he sinned against. He sinned against God personally, in a way that God detests.

And it isn't just *this* sin. All the sins that this person committed have treason and betrayal and ingratitude and rebellion and rejection of people, and supremely of God himself, tied up in them. But here's the most important point: it's not just *his* sins that are like that, or just sexual sins. All our sins are like that. Friends, this is the nature of sin—to be against God personally and directly—and this is why none of us can ever atone for our own sins. It is beyond our ability.

Peter here reminds these troubled early Christians of the one who was uniquely able to atone for our sins, and *did*. Throughout this passage, Isaiah 53 stands in the background—that beautiful song of the Suffering Servant. Do you remember those verses? "Surely he took up our infirmities and carried our sorrows, yet we considered him stricken by God, smitten by him, and afflicted. . . . We all, like sheep, have gone astray, each of us has turned to his own way; and the LORD has laid on him the iniquity of us all. . . . He poured out his life unto death, and was numbered with the transgressors. For he bore the sin of many" (vv. 4, 6, 12). Atoning is not your job or mine; it's the job of our perfect Savior, the Suffering Servant, Jesus Christ.

The very fact that Peter used the word he did for "tree" here in verse 24, instead of using a word that we would take and think of using as cross, probably means that he is recalling to his readers' minds the statement in the Law (Deut. 21:23) that "anyone who is hung on a tree is under God's curse." That means that anyone who falls under that capital punishment for their serious sin is under God's curse. That's why so many Jews were so confident that Jesus could never be the Messiah—he was so clearly cursed of God according to the law. But that's staring right at it and missing it. This was exactly the heart of the good news. Christ became accursed for us. He who had no sin was made sin for us, so that we might become the righteousness of God. He bore the curse we have earned.

Friends, this is the basic message of Christianity. This is the good news that we have: we have lived in such a way, all of us, that we deserve God's curse, and God would be entirely just to let us be forever under his curse. But in his amazing love, the eternal Son of God came and took on flesh and lived a sinless life, the life that you and I should have lived. And he died the death that we deserve, taking on the punishment for our sins because of God's love for us. God raised him from the dead to show that he accepted this sacrifice, and he calls us now to repent of our sins and to trust in Christ. So we will be given a new life, forgiveness, and fellowship restored with our heavenly Father forever. This is the *substitution* that we've been talking about throughout this study. Do you see something of God's grace to us in this? Of his kindness? Of how marvelous he is being toward us? Praise God for this unique work that Jesus Christ did for us!

This unique work, done by a unique person, had a *unique result*— it worked. The death of the sinless Son of God actually atoned for our sins. This is good news. This is somebody calling you when you are financially distressed and telling you that someone just paid your mortgage. This is finding out that something you assumed could never happen, happened. This is *that* kind of news. The death of the sinless Son of God actually worked. It atoned for sins. His death brought us healing. That's what Peter says in the last part of verse 24, "By his wounds you have been healed." This, too, echoes Isaiah 53. Not only have we been healed, but we will now be kept safe: "For you were like sheep going astray, but now you have returned to the Shepherd and Overseer of your souls" (v. 25). Again, we think of that portion of Isaiah 53: "We all, like sheep, have gone astray, each of us has turned to his own way; and the LORD has laid on him the iniquity of us all."

Peter, you see, is recounting their conversion. The word "returned" there in verse 25 can be translated "turned," or "converted." That's what they've done; that's what has happened to them. They have turned away from the sin that once dominated their lives, and that turning *away* from sin can only happen by turning *to* God.

Verses 24 and 25 make up a wonderfully comprehensive presentation. It presents our problem: we were straying from God; we went away from him. And it presents the solution: we were healed by Christ's wounds. Thus, the relationship that was broken has been restored. We have been returned, converted, made safe, and saved.

So often we are resistant to that kind of solution. I know; I was an agnostic. I would constantly make up rationales for how I was living and why. We as human beings love *excuses* for our actions more than *changing* them, don't we? We're like this fellow I recently read of who argued at his trial:

My car's speedometer wasn't working; if it were, then the cop's radar surely wasn't; but in any case, I was driving at the average pace of traffic; I certainly wasn't speeding; but if I were, I do sincerely apologize; you can understand, I was rushing to a funeral.[8]

My friend, God sees the excuse before you even have time to make it up—and he sees right through it. He knows the truth. Aren't you sick of being alienated from God, estranged from him?

If you're not a Christian, consider this—have you sinned against God? As a professional religious person, my advice to you is this: pray to God and simply ask him to show you the truth about yourself. But let's say you are convinced that you *have* sinned against God. I have many friends who aren't Christians who do believe in God and do think they've sinned against him. My question to you is, what will you do with your sins? Friend, you need a Savior, and that's who Jesus Christ is. There's no government solution for this problem. There is nothing we can promise or fund. For our sins, we need the only savior there is—the sinless Christ who died as a substitute for all those who would ever repent of their sins and trust in him.

In our congregation, it is the elders who are the special representatives of our Shepherd and Guardian. So in chapter 5 Peter exhorts the elders, "Be shepherds." It's the same word he's just used of the Lord Jesus a bit earlier. "Be shepherds of God's flock that is under your care, serving as overseers" (5:2). In the ministry of the elders in our church, our congregation sees a picture of God's own radical service to us. I confess it's a dim picture, but it is nonetheless really a picture of God's radical service to us in Jesus Christ.

This is one point Satan has attacked ever since the fall, denying that authority and love can go together: "You can't tell me you love me and tell me no at the same time!" That's the essence of our sin and our rebellion. In all the structures of authority we are involved in, whether in society or in our work or at home, we are involved in picturing the way God has called us to relate to him. In the church, the elders have that kind of authority, and they are to use it with wisdom and love for the benefit of those over whom they have authority. It is a terrible blasphemy against God to abuse authority for selfish ends. Authority is a very tender point in our lives, and it is meant to teach us to trust.

[8]Garin Hovannisian, "An Unbeliever's Prayer," *Weekly Standard*, March 17, 2008.

Our sinful natures, though, don't want to believe that's ever the case, so we rebel against it. That's why we must pray especially for those in authority, that we not abuse that authority God gives us.

Finally, thank God, my Christian brother and sister, that God has healed us and that he has paid *such a high price* to heal us. How he must love us! If he has healed us, he has healed us like this: he has turned us, converted us from our rebellion against him, to loving regard for him and his authority in our lives. Friends, if God has so loved us, we can be confident of his kindness and compassion as a shepherd and overseer. Christ has uniquely loved us. The unique Christ has loved us uniquely with these unique results.

Christ's Exemplary Life: Living through Suffering as Our Example

Jesus intended his life to be exemplary. We see this in the last part of verse 21, where Peter says that Jesus was "leaving you an example." The word for "example" here conjures up the image of a pattern that taught children how to write correctly, tracing the shape of letters over models or examples. That's what Jesus' life is for the Christian. It's a life that we are to follow in order that we might learn how to live a truly, fully human life.

How are Jesus' sufferings an example, as it says in verse 21? Haven't we just said that his sufferings were unique? Well yes, they were unique in their effect, but they were also a model, an example to us. Perhaps that's why Peter doesn't say "death" here in verse 21, but "suffering"—he means to include all that led up to his death, because Jesus' followers would face that same kind of opposition.

You may be surprised to hear such talk of Jesus as our example. There is, in fact, what is sometimes called another whole theory of the atonement named the "moral example" theory, which says that Jesus' death was really only effective if it leads to our imitating Jesus in his self-sacrificial love.

But the moral example theory of the atonement is, by itself, incomplete and even false. In order for Christ to be a good example, his death must accomplish something. Otherwise it's no more than an example of a pointless death. Indeed, the cross can only be a good example, a moral example, when we believe his death is substitutionary. It has accomplished something. So when we accept Christ's death as one that he himself uniquely did not deserve because he hadn't sinned, but one which he himself uniquely accepted for us, *then* he's an example of someone whose self-sacrificing love we can follow. Does the New Testament speak of Christ's death using other language than substitution? Certainly. Does any of the other language that the New Testament uses for the death of Christ make sense *apart from* Christ dying as our substitute? Certainly not.

Here we are called to follow Christ's example in being willing to suffer for doing good. Peter writes in verse 21, "To this you were called." It is part of your vocation as a Christian to suffer for doing good. Don't be surprised by it. That's what Peter is saying at the end of verse 21, "that you should follow in his steps." Jesus suffered for doing good, and so will you, Peter says. This is not advanced Christianity where we're getting into the radiant glow of martyrs. No, this is Christianity 101. This is you and me claiming to follow Jesus and knowing we will therefore suffer for doing good. "Do not be surprised," Peter says a little bit later, "at the painful trial you are suffering, as though something strange were happening to you" (1 Pet. 4:12). Suffering for doing good is not strange to Christians. It may again sadden us. It may cause a worldly fear in us. But it's not strange, and it's not unexpected. It's not a signpost that we're going the wrong way; it's a signpost that we're actually going the right way, and that we're actually following Jesus.

It's interesting when you consider who is saying this. Do you remember when Peter first confessed Jesus as the Messiah? Jesus said he was going to suffer, and Peter rebuked him for it. He wouldn't hear of it; he didn't think it was appropriate. Then Peter was the one who refused to even acknowledge knowing Christ on the night of his arrest, presumably lest he himself suffer. This is the one who is saying this—Peter, who knew the depths of cowardice, who knew what it meant to fear man more than God. Yet now he is Peter, the one who has come to learn what it means to fear God more than man.

Along with this image of the child tracing out the shapes in that word "example," we also have this phrase "follow in his steps," which would have evoked images of disciples walking along behind the rabbi, walking in his way, and sharing his destination, his end. That's what Peter presents here as a Christian's way of life. He can remember how he hadn't done that and how he now must do that if he would call himself a Christian.

Jesus Christ is the example for *all* Christians. The important fact about his disciples is not that they're old, or that they're from Iran, or that they have German heritage, or that they're female, or engaged, or young parents. It's not their ethnicity, their gender, or their age. It's that they are following Jesus. I pray that God will help you to follow Christ wherever he leads you—through a difficult work situation, a challenging family, a changing church. We are to follow him, and as we do we display his glory, especially as he leads us through hard times.

Peter tells us that Christ modeled the typical Christian response to suffering. He did this negatively and positively.

Negatively, Jesus' example teaches us that when suffering comes that we don't deserve, there is to be no retaliation. Peter says in verse 23, "When they hurled their insults at him, he did not retaliate; when he suffered, he made no threats." Again, Isaiah 53 is in the background (v. 7): "He was oppressed and afflicted, yet he did not open his mouth; he was led like a lamb to the slaughter, and as a sheep before her shearers is silent, so he did not open his mouth."

My Christian brothers and sisters, does talk about suffering for being a Christian, even being insulted for being a Christian, seem remote to you? Is this teaching for people overseas who are working in "closed" countries? Friends, the Bible is *full* of people who have been persecuted for doing what is right, and they don't always respond correctly. So even Moses, when he was provoked to anger, reviled (Num. 20:3). But not Jesus. Have you considered his example of silent endurance? When Jesus is tried before the chief priests and Pilate, it is so striking how he who would be so able to retaliate did not. Before the high priest "Jesus remained silent and gave no answer" (Mark 14:61; cf. Matt. 26:63). "They spit in his face and struck him with their fists. Others slapped him and said, 'Prophesy to us, Christ. Who hit you?'" (Matt. 26:67–68). "When he was accused by the chief priests and the elders, he gave no answer. Then Pilate asked him, 'Don't you hear the testimony they are bringing against you?' But Jesus made no reply, not even to a single charge—to the great amazement of the governor" (Matt. 27:12–14). The abuse continued, and so did his silence (Matt. 27:28–31, 39–44; Luke 22:63–65; 23:9–11; John 19:9–10). Even in the most severe suffering, Christ did not retaliate.

Peter tells the Christians here in 1 Peter 2:24 that Christ died on the cross so that we would die to sins, and not least among those sins would be the sin of retaliation. As Paul teaches in Romans 6, we have died to the dominating power of sin. We do not have to respond to evil with evil.

Friend, if you're not a Christian, how do you deal with this? I understand how I as a Christian can deal with injustices that are done toward me, but how do you deal with bitterness toward somebody? With those memories—whether years old or only hours old—how do you deal with that confident knowledge that you have been wronged? What do you do with that sense of having been wronged?

My Christian friends, I don't want us to misunderstand these instructions. There's nothing wrong with being a policeman or a judge, because we're not acting in a personal capacity. It's not wrong to press charges against a criminal, especially for the good order and safety of society. But you as a Christian must not personally retaliate; and more than that, you must forgive. In your job, in your family, even at church—a wonderful place for conflict—you must follow the example of Christ and *not retaliate*. We have wronged Jesus, and yet he has not retaliated against us. This is the example we are to follow.

How can we possibly obey this? Is the Christian way to ignore justice in the name of forgiveness? No. We are called not to ignore justice but rather to realize that we're not competent to administer it. It is not personally within our ability to administer the justice that is needed. This is why the Lord of old said to Israel, "It is mine to avenge; I will repay" (Deut. 32:35). This is the passage Paul quotes when he tells the Roman Christians, "Do not take revenge, my friends, but leave room for God's wrath" (Rom. 12:19; cf. Col. 3:25; 2 Thess. 1:5–6; James 5:7–8). So we Christians do not retaliate, and we do not take revenge, not because we're necessarily pacifists or morally indifferent but because we're following the way of Christ.

Positively, Jesus taught us to trust God. Look again at 1 Peter 2:23: "Instead, he entrusted himself to him who judges justly." The "himself" here is not in the original, but I think it is implied. Certainly in going to the cross Jesus was entrusting himself to God. We see this in the garden of Gethsemane. But also, and in a different sense Jesus entrusted those injuring him, the whole situation, and even the outcome to God. My friend, who else would you trust? Who is better for you to trust than this God?

Christ's meekness here didn't come from self-doubt or uncertainty. It came from his strong confidence in his heavenly Father's purposes and powers. So the answer to being unjustly treated isn't the self-centered answer of expressing our anger or the equally self-centered answer of stoically suppressing our anger. The answer we Christians should give to being unjustly treated is to deeply trust God. He is good, and he is utterly worthy of our most complete trust. He sees and knows everything. No person, no plan, no combination of circumstances that in your mind would be ideal are as worthy of trust as is this God. He is worthy of your trust during any trial or suffering or persecution you are currently considering, better than your own wit can figure out.

We can trust God to judge sin and evil. God's judgment for every sin ever committed falls either on the sinner eternally or on Christ on the cross. He will issue his sovereign verdict. And it will prevail.

I love the picture of the aged apostle John when he's persecuted by the Roman Empire. He's an old man put on this stony island of Patmos in the middle of the Aegean Sea, away from the flock that he had shepherded for so long. And what does he do? Does he capitulate in anxiety? No, God inspires the book of Revelation, and that aged apostle roars at the Roman Empire. He puts the Roman Empire on notice that it will be judged by the sovereign God who is good. John's confidence was not in how he could figure out a way to get off the island of Patmos. He was confident that at the center and end of history is God's throne.

Brothers and sisters, you need to know this personally. I can tell you that in the most difficult things I have been called to deal with in my own life, the way I have dealt with them is by just going right to the throne and saying, "You know, it ends up really, really good," and then just backing up from there. I might not see how we get there from my place in a situation that causes such pain, but I know without a shadow of a doubt that it does end up there. So I'm just going to import my joy from there. I am confident in what it's going to be like for all eternity in Christ, so I'm just going to borrow a little of that for today and use it to help me walk through whatever this day holds.

This is the only way we can obey the command in verse 24 to "live for righteousness"—by trusting God. This is why we can share the gospel with people who are hostile to it and even plan to give our lives away in ways this world will neither appreciate nor even understand.

My non-Christian friend, this is how we Christians can exercise mercy and patience, even if we are the victims of extreme injustice.

I've seen this in stunning ways, for example in the black African community in South Africa, as Christians show amazing forgiveness toward the very Afrikaans and White Anglo Christians that oppress them, sometimes even quoting the Bible to them. Is there forgiveness because they're indifferent to justice? No! It's because they humbly know that they cannot finally mete out all the justice that is needed. That is the business of God. *Our* business is to follow the way of Christ. This is how we as Christians can experience injustice and yet show mercy and patience without being indifferent. We are confident that God will ultimately sort it out. But, again, if you're not a Christian, I wonder: how do *you* show mercy and patience without indulging in a kind of indifference to injustice? I don't have an answer for you; it's just a question I'm asking.

Brothers and sisters, follow the example of Christ. Trust God. Don't retaliate. Jesus is an example for us in this. We are his people, and therefore we should look like him.

I love what John Bunyan, himself imprisoned for twelve years for his faithful following of Christ, said about the persecutions we face as Christians: "Persecution of the godly was of God never intended for their destruction, but for their glory, and to make them shine the more when they are beyond this valley of the shadow of death."[9]

Do you see how confidence in this leads us as Christians to live different lives? I also love the example of Adoniram Judson, who wrote to his beloved's father, asking his blessing on their marriage. This is from his letter to John Hasseltine, his beloved Nancy's father:

> I have now to ask, whether you can consent to part with your daughter early next spring, to see her no more in this world; whether you can consent to her departure, and her subjection to the hardships and sufferings of a missionary life; whether you can consent to her exposure to the dangers of the ocean; to the fatal influence of the southern climate of India; to every kind of want and distress; to degradation, insult, persecution, and perhaps a violent death. Can you consent to all this, for the sake of him who left his heavenly home, and died for her and for you; for the sake of perishing, immortal souls; for the sake of Zion, and the glory of God? Can you consent to all this, in hope of soon meeting your daughter in the world of glory, with the crown of righteousness, brightened with the acclamations

---

[9]John Bunyan, cited in Marcus Loane, *Makers of Puritan History* (Grand Rapids, MI: Eerdmans, 1961), 157.

of praise which shall redound to her Saviour from heathens saved, through her means, from eternal woe and despair?[10]

"Degradation, insult, persecution, and perhaps a violent death"—was Judson being melodramatic? No, that's in fact what some people we know and love have experienced even in these last few months.

Peter himself faced this. Tradition tells us that Peter finally suffered and died for his faith in Christ. But don't misunderstand. It was nothing heroic Peter did that caused God to accept him. We so often look for our own attempts at heroic, God-obliging obediences, but imagine how such attempts at self-justification must look from God's perspective. Can you imagine your five-year-old son coming up to you with a list of reasons why you should feed and clothe him? We love our children because they're children, and because they're *ours.* So it's just as ridiculous for us to come to God with a list of our obediences, our good actions—even our martyrdom—as the basis for why he should love and care for us. God loves us because we are in Christ, not because of anything we do. There is no love of God to be earned by us. Christ has done that for us. "By his wounds you have been healed."

Do you see the ancient images coming to their fulfillment here—the Servant Suffering for us, the goat forsaken for us, the lamb slain for us? When we had alienated ourselves from God, he brought us back by his own life of perfect trust in God and his submitting himself to death, even death on a cross, to bear our sins away.

---

[10]Courtney Anderson, *To the Golden Shore* (New York: Little, Brown, 1956), 83.

CHAPTER FOURTEEN

CHRIST DIED FOR SINS

1 Peter 3:18

MICHAEL LAWRENCE

There is a relentlessness to the story of Jesus' crucifixion. Again and again there were opportunities for the whole terrible scene to screech to a halt. Pilate could have stood up to the Jews and to the crowd; he could have insisted that he would not put an innocent man to death. But, then, Pilate had never been known for political backbone. He certainly wasn't going to show it now. The soldiers could have disobeyed what was clearly an unjust, immoral, and illegal order. But, then, who are soldiers to get involved in political affairs? They were just doing what they were told. The disciples could have tried to stage a rescue, but they were afraid for their own lives and kept a safe distance from the whole sorry affair. Judas could have realized the folly of betraying the Son of God before it was too late.

One missed opportunity after another, to bring the whole thing to an end and keep this monstrous evil from happening. But the most troubling missed opportunities are not the ones that Pilate or the disciples passed by, but the opportunities that first the Father and then the Son had to put an end to this madness, opportunities presented and then passed by. In the garden, Jesus asks God to spare him this hideous fate that is coming. None of the Gospels records the Father's reply to Jesus' agonized request. All we hear is the silence of heaven. And then there's Jesus himself, who, despite his pleas, seems strangely complicit in the whole affair. The Jews mocked him as he hung there dying: "Come down from the cross and save yourself if you can" (See Matt. 27:40–42). They're convinced, of course, that he can't. After all, that's why he was there; he was a fraud. Yet what the Bible's text drives us to acknowledge is not that he *can't* but that he *won't*. From his first prayer in the garden to his last cry on the cross, it is clear that Jesus understood not just that he might but that he must die.

Why? Why this relentless movement to the cross? Why this unimaginable suffering? Why did Jesus have to die? Here is the answer that Peter, one of Jesus' disciples and closest friends, gave to this question. He said, "For Christ died for sins once for all, the righteous for the unrighteous, to bring you to God. He was put to death in the body but made alive by the Spirit" (1 Pet. 3:18).

Why did Jesus die? He died for sins, Peter says. Peter doesn't mean that Jesus died because sinful people sinned against him, though that's certainly true. No, as Peter is at pains to point out, Jesus was judicially executed, physically put to death as a penalty and payment for sins. In fact, the phrase he uses here, "for sins," is the same phrase the Old Testament used to speak of the sacrifice for sin required in God's law in the Old Testament.

I think this is a difficult concept for us to understand—that someone would have to die on account of sins. For one thing, there's not much we're willing to call "sin" anymore these days. Polls show a large majority of Americans still think adultery and racism are sins, but there isn't much else agreed upon by the majority. Those same polls show that premarital sex, getting drunk, or using drugs don't even rate.[1]

Then there's the question of the punishment sin deserves. If you're unlucky enough to get caught at one of those things still agreed upon by society as sin, not much seems to happen. If you're in elected office, you might have to resign. If you're already famous for some other reason, it just adds to your celebrity. But for the rest of us? As one sociologist recently observed, "People don't burn in hell, they burn in the court of public opinion."[2] I might add, "or not."

But that's not what Peter is talking about, and it's not what was happening on the cross. When Peter says that Jesus died for sins, the law he had in mind was not Roman law, and the judge passing sentence

[1]Kathy Lynn Grossman, "Has the 'Notion of Sin' Been Lost?" *USA Today*, March 19, 2008.
[2]Barry Kosmin, quoted in ibid.

was not Pilate. Peter was thinking of God. The God who created us is also our lord and our judge, and from the beginning he has made known to his creatures his will for them. This means that sin is not merely breaking a law. It is a personal affront against a holy God. It's a rejection, not merely of a rule but of a person—the ruler, God.

How does a just and loving God punish sins that are committed against him, as all sins are, sins that are an affront to his character and his person? This is a heinous offense. On the day God placed Adam in the garden of Eden, he said, "You must not eat from the tree of the knowledge of good and evil, for when you eat of it you will surely die" (Gen. 2:17). Death is the only suitable punishment for sin, not just the end of physical life but also an eternal spiritual death in which the rebellious soul experiences the just wrath of God in conscious torment, forever suffering the penalty for sin. Sin is an offense against an infinite God and earns for itself an infinite penalty. Just how long does it take for a finite creature to satisfy, or pay off, an infinite debt to justice?

The Old Testament is full of images and warnings of this judgment. But as terrible as the images from the Old Testament are, they pale in comparison to what we see here. That terrible day in Jerusalem, an innocent man was flogged until he was unrecognizable, stripped of every last vestige of clothing, beaten and mocked, and then in public shame nailed hand and foot to a wooden cross. While all this was happening to his body, something else, something even more painful, was happening to his soul. On the cross, Jesus Christ suffered the wrath of God and was cut off from his Father's love, a love that he had known without interruption for all eternity. He was abandoned by God, not just to the abuse of men, but abandoned by God to the fury of God. Like the sacrificial sin offering of a lamb in the temple, Jesus endured a personal holocaust on the cross. But these were not the flames of burning wood he knew on his flesh. These were the flames of hell itself. For what are the flames of hell, other than the consuming fire of the wrath of God, poured out on sin? This is the wrath that was poured out on Jesus' soul.

Friends, do you want to know what hell looks like? Do you want to know what sin really deserves? Then look at Christ on the cross. For there we see judgment day breaking into history. There we see what it means to pay the penalty, to suffer the sentence of death for breaking God's law. Peter wants us to understand that Jesus Christ died for sins, because that is what sins deserve.

But why should Jesus die for sins? He didn't have any of his own. As Peter points out, Jesus was righteous. He was in a right relationship with God, not a broken one like we have. He deserved to be with God, not cut off from him. He deserved his blessing, not his wrath. So why did the righteous Jesus have to die? Peter tells us: he died for the sins of the unrighteous. That is to say, he died as a substitute for people like you and me.

The idea of a substitute for sinners is at the very center of the story of the Bible. In fact, it's hard to think of a major event or institution in the Old Testament that isn't teaching us about our need for someone to take our place, to stand in our stead, to do what we cannot do. We see it in the seemingly endless sacrifices offered in the temple as day after day, week after week, month after month, year after year, century after century, countless animals are offered as sacrificial substitutes for the people's sin. We see it other places as well. Joseph is sold into slavery, as good as dead, but that "sacrifice" of one son results in the unexpected deliverance of the entire family. Abraham is about to sacrifice his one and only son, Isaac, but God stops him and provides a ram as a substitute instead. The Passover lamb is killed so that the firstborn of Israel are not. It may even be that the very first substitute in the narrative of Scripture was the animal God killed in order to clothe Adam and Eve the day they fell into sin.

In the Old Testament, though, the substitute doesn't merely pay the penalty we deserve. The representative substitute also delivers us from our enemies, sometimes at the cost of his own life. So David, representing the armies of Israel, defeats Goliath and delivers Israel. Abraham goes out alone and rescues Lot from the Canaanite kings; Moses alone leads God's people out of slavery. And Samson alone gives his life to destroy the Philistines and free his nation from bondage.

Friends, that terrible day in Jerusalem, Peter may not have understood what he was witnessing as he watched Jesus die on that cross. But he came to understand what we desperately need to know—that on the cross Jesus died as the representative substitute for sinners, unrighteous people like you and me. Everything that came before, from the examples of Isaac and Joseph and David, to the yearly Passover and the daily sin offering—all of that was meant to prepare us to recognize the one and only true and sufficient substitute when it was finally offered, the sacrifice of Jesus Christ. This is why Peter says he died once for all.

Here at last was a sacrifice that would not need to be repeated. Here at last was a substitute whose death actually accomplished something so that no other sacrifice and substitute would ever be necessary. An animal cannot take responsibility for your sin. The Israelites understood that; so should we. No, only a human being can take responsibility for a human problem. But what person can substitute for you and your sin problem? No matter who you point to, no matter how good or how worthy he is, there is no one in all of history who does not have his own sin problem to deal with—no one except Jesus, the righteous one. Here at last, then, is the true Son, who perfectly obeys his Father. Here is the second Adam, who, unlike the first Adam, says no to Satan's temptations, not just once but for his entire life right up to the very end. Because he is righteous, Jesus alone can also be the true Passover Lamb, whose death saves us from death. Here is the true, the final, and the all-sufficient sacrifice for sin. Jesus not only endures God's just wrath on the cross, but he exhausts and satisfies it, draining it down to the bitter dregs, so that there is none left. In satisfying God's wrath, Jesus also shows us that here at last is the true king and judge who conquers the enemy of his people—not flesh and blood, but sin and death—and delivers us from the power of both.

Jesus died once and for all for the unrighteous. But did Jesus die for you? It depends. Do you know yourself to be unrighteous? That's not language we use these days, but the concept isn't difficult to understand. If you're honest with yourself, would you have to admit that your life is fundamentally self-oriented? Are you at the center of your universe, with God, if he's there at all, in a safe and distant orbit around you? Do you understand that your life is lawless, ungodly, and disobedient, not because it's blatantly immoral, but because it ultimately disregards God and his rightful supremacy in your life? Do you understand that all this has earned for you God's just and eternal opposition? Friend, if this is what you understand yourself to be, then you need to know that you have a substitute and a savior in Jesus Christ. He calls you who recognize your sin and who have come to detest it to put your faith in the sufficiency of his death for you; he calls you to turn away from your self-worship and self-sufficiency and instead to trust in him, to depend on him and on his substitutionary death as the only thing you'll ever need to deliver you from sin and the death it deserves and put you right with God. Today is the day to give up your pretensions to being good enough for God, to humble yourself, turn away from your self-centeredness, and confess that Christ died for the unrighteous—that Christ died for *you*.

It's extraordinary to think that Christ would do such a thing. You and I can almost imagine dying for someone. We can almost imagine giving our lives for the sake of someone who was really good, really worthy. We can imagine dying for someone who had an unimpeachable claim on the love and affections of our hearts, like a spouse or a child. But that's not what Christ did. Christ died for the unrighteous, for people who hated his Father, reviled his Father's law, and ridiculed God's Son. Though he himself is God in the flesh, he died for creatures who, in their arrogance, believed themselves to be God's equal or better. Why would he do such a thing? Again, Peter tells us: Jesus died for sins. He died for the unrighteous in order to bring us to God.

This is such a radical statement—"to bring you to God." Indeed it's so foreign to our way of thinking that we tend to completely miss the point. We hear a religious platitude. We think, "Isn't that nice. We get to be with God. I wonder what heaven will be like. I hope my friends will be there. I wonder what we'll do. I hope I don't get bored." In thinking about it that way, we fail to recognize that we are not the point of what Peter is saying in this verse. There is an uncompromising God-centeredness to this statement that should take our breath away if we understand it correctly.

From the fall in Genesis 3 until the crucifixion of Christ, the whole story of the Bible is about the separation that exists between God and man because of our sin. Part of that story is our attempts to run from God, hide from him, avoid him, and instead pursue our own agendas, our own man-made gods to worship. But that is only part of the story of our separation from God. The other part of that story, and, in fact, the larger part, is the story of God's exclusion of us from his presence. Adam and Eve didn't voluntarily leave the garden of Eden. They were expelled. The curtain that separated the Most Holy Place from the rest of the tabernacle where the priests served and the series of courtyards and walls of the tabernacle that kept the people at an even greater distance weren't Moses' idea. They were God's. It was God who said to Moses, "You cannot see my face, for no one may see me and live" (Ex. 33:20). It was God, not David, who struck down Uzzah for daring to cross that divide and touch the ark of the covenant. And it was God who sent the nation into exile, expelling them from his Promised Land.

Again and again it is God who separates and excludes. It's not just that we aren't interested in him, though that's true. As sinners, we're not. More importantly, he has barred the door. After God expelled Adam and Eve from the garden, he placed cherubim and a flaming sword at the entrance. Whether they wanted to or not, Adam and Eve could not bring themselves back to God. To attempt to enter the garden was to face the sword of God's wrath. The same is true for every one of us. No, if we are to get back to God, we'll need someone to open the way, someone to bring us back safely.

Friends, God's word assures us that on the cross, Jesus Christ, the righteous one, faced that flaming sword for us. He walked alone into the presence of God with our sin placed on him, and there he suffered the punishment that the sword of God's wrath brings. But consider what—no, consider *who*—is on the other side of the sword. Jesus didn't die just to free us from sin and then leave us to our own lives. He didn't die just to give us hope and meaning wherever we might find it. No, he walked through that flaming sword to bring us to the point of this verse, to bring us to *God* as testimonies to his amazing love and unimaginable grace. God would give his own Son to bring us to him.

God is the ultimate focus of Christ's death on the cross. Yes, Jesus died for sins and for the unrighteous, but ultimately Jesus died for God and his glory. For when Christ brings us to God, he brings us into a right relationship with God. It's as if the universe is set back where it should be—a relationship in which he is the center and we orbit around him in a safe proximity and nearness, a relationship in which his glory is the point and we find our joy and meaning in being a display of *his* worth rather than our own.

The reason Jesus can bring us to God like this is that though he was put to death in the body, as Peter points out, he was made alive by the Spirit. Jesus did not stay dead. Having satisfied the sword of God's wrath, he got up from the dead. And having opened the way, he kept walking into the garden, into the presence of God, but no longer alone. He faced the flaming sword alone, but now that he has satisfied it he is alone no more. Now he walks with a crowd, a multitude that cannot be numbered, men and women from every tribe, tongue, people, and nation, purchased for God and given to him as a tribute to the praise of his glorious grace.

When Peter wrote these words, he was writing to Christians who were suffering for their faith in Christ, oftentimes in small ways, but nevertheless real. Earlier in this letter, he exhorted them to persevere in suffering, because they were following Christ's example (2:21). Here in this verse he's doing something different. He's reminding them that Christ's suffering was unique, that it atoned for sin and redeemed sinners. He's reminding them that Christ's suffering has been vindicated. It has come to an end. He is raised from the dead and is seated at the right hand of God. These aren't examples for us to follow; they're truths to bank our lives upon.

Christian, your sins have been paid for, your substitute was sufficient, and you have been brought to God. Christ is done with your sin—and so are you. The trials of this life are small in comparison to the future Christ has secured for you. So do not grow fond of this world's love, and do not faint under this world's scorn. Christ died for sins, for sinners, for God, so that you may live for God and with God, now and forevermore.

SUBJECT INDEX

SCRIPTURE INDEX

9Marks

Building Healthy Churches

9Marks exists to equip church leaders with a biblical vision and practical resources for displaying God's glory to the nations through healthy churches.

To that end, we want to see churches characterized by these nine marks of health:

1   Expositional Preaching
2   Biblical Theology
3   A Biblical Understanding of the Gospel
4   A Biblical Understanding of Conversion
5   A Biblical Understanding of Evangelism
6   Biblical Church Membership
7   Biblical Church Discipline
8   Biblical Discipleship
9   Biblical Church Leadership

Find all our Crossway titles
and other resources at
www.9Marks.org